CRAZY MAN CRAZY

Teds v Punks and other Gang Wars 1976–1982

NOEL SMITH

This updated edition published in the United Kingdom in 2016 by
Rocket 88, an imprint of Essential Works Limited.

First published in the United Kingdom in 2008 by
Apex Publishing Ltd as Warrior Kings

Cover image Virginia Turbett/Redferns

ISBN, PAPERBACK: 9781910978030

ISBN, HARDBACK: 9781910978047

10 9 8 7 6 5 4 3 2 1

rocket88books.com

CONTENTS

Acknowledgements   vii

Introduction   I

Part One: The Teddy Boys   3

                The Long Hot One   5

                The Wind of Change   13

                The Johnny Kidd Memorial Night   28

                All the Fun of the Fair   40

                Making A Name for Ourselves   47

                Summer Comes to an End   57

Part Two: The Rebel Teds   65

                Return of the Rocker   67

                Rise of the Rebel Teds   75

                The Party Lights   82

                Getting My Colours   90

                Kicking off at The George   98

                The Wildkatz at The Chick-A-Boom   106

                Doing the Clapham Common Punks   115

                We Fought the Law … and the Law Won   124

                Jailhouse Rockers   132

Part Three: The Rockabilly Rebels   141

                Enter Popeye   143

                Bopping with the Crawley Cats   149

                Influences   155

                The Balham Baldies   162

A Visit to Mad Harry 167

Taking Our Turf 173

Meeting Psycho Joe 179

My Baby Done Gone 188

Revenge Served Hot 195

Double Trouble 202

Part Four: The Hillbillies and Psychobillies 211

Hillbilly Heaven 213

Murder at The Balham Hotel 219

True Love Ways 229

Attack of the Killer Smoothies 235

The Beat Slows Down 241

Lean Times 248

Storming The Castle 255

You Can't Win 'Em All 261

The Night of the Long Knives 267

Aftermath 273

1st Edition Afterword: The Living End 277

2nd Edition Afterword: The Final Chapter 283

Where Are They Now? 287

Acknowledgements

This book has been a labour of love for me and I would like to thank my agent, Mal Peachey, of Essential Works for the chance to get it out there. Big thanks to my family and my extended rockin' family for all their support and help. And to everyone who was rockin' in the golden era. If your name isn't in this book, then it's only due to the constraints of space and not because you've been forgotten.

I'd like to thank everyone who helped with photos and research. And to Big Beat Kris, Runaround Stu of The Wild Wax Roadshow, and my old pal Adrian Street, who ain't no square! Thanks to Adrian Street senior – one of the original Teds – for allowing me to use his photo. Also big thanks to my fellow dee-jays and stalwarts of the South London rockin' scene: Tommy Hogan, Gary The Phantom and Rockhouse Mark, Swanee, and Cockney Rebel.

Also a big shout to some good friends: Mick and Carol, Richard and Kate Thompson, Paul 'Bopper' Baldwin and his lovely wife Tina, Nige Grant, Fulham Phil, Billy Coomber, Snapper, Pete Hutchinson, Rocker Bill, Milkman Rick, Steve Chadwick, Rockin' Em and his lovely wife Dawn, Lena Phee, Jackie Toppin, Anne Crowley, Pete 'Lofty' Edwards, Steve Roommate, Johnny 'Blue Suede Dreams' Earl, Teddy Boy Paul and the lovely Anja, Bob Butfoy, Gerry Suggers, Tawnee Morgan, Flat Top Mark, Alan Wilson, Peter Taylor and Denise Byrne, Tony 'Red Leicester' Woodbridge, Dave 'Silver Bear' Pearson, Lyn 'Honeybee' Williams, Dave Fleming, Neil Williams, Tina Green, Linda Fountain Boyle, Rockabilly Gerry and his rockin' family, Steve Scollan and Sacha-Marie, Terry Smith, Linda Smith, Jimmy and Penny Harris, Dave Fitzgerald and Shirley, Lez and Megan Bruton, and Micky White.

Most of all – a salute to everyone who lived it, friends and enemies alike. And if you don't remember it the way I do, then write your own book!

As Elvis once said – 'rock'n'roll music … if you like it, you just can't help but move to it!' I think he was on to something there!

Introduction

Isn't it funny how a smell, a sound, a casually-spoken name or the snatch of a half-forgotten tune can bring back the past in such vivid detail that you almost think you are back there for a second? This seems to happen more and more to me as I approach middle age. I get to wondering how my life might have turned out had I taken different roads at different times and what I would change if I were able to go back. But that is a pointless exercise because I cannot change any of it, none of us can, it's there and will remain so. I can only be what I am, and that is what my past has made of me. And though a lot of it was bad, some of it wasn't.

In the winter of 2003 I completed the story of my life as a career criminal and exposed my failings for all to see. The book, *A Few Kind Words and a Loaded Gun*, sold fairly well all around the world and received some rave reviews, even entering the *Times* Literary Best-sellers Top 30, opening a career for me as something other than a professional criminal. In the book I touched on my teenage years as a Teddy boy/rockabilly and mentioned something of the gang culture that existed in the 1970s and early 1980s among South London teenagers. But I only scratched the surface.

According to popular misconception, the last years of the 1970s belonged to the punk rockers. Whenever I read about that time now, it always seems to be from the perspective of ex-punks and it seems strangely ironic that so many of that snarling, grunting, spitting sub-culture have become such articulate members of society. There has been plenty written over the last four decades about the punk movement – books, articles, even songs – but for a lot of kids the late '70s/early '80s were about other things. Sure, the punks were there, but so were the Teds, skinheads, mods, rockabillies, psychobillies, soul boys, new romantics, rockers, disco freaks and the smoothies; it wasn't all safety pins, gob and bin liners.

Just lately I've been thinking a lot about those years and a story of that time that needs to be told before it's lost forever. The time I am writing of will seem long ago and far away to some people, particularly the generations that have come after mine, but to me it seems like only yesterday. We all like to think that our own era was the golden one and no other time can quite match up to it and, in a way, we are right. Memory, like time, is relative. And I am writing this story from memory.

Once, long ago and not so far away, some members of my generation fought a little-known and mostly forgotten war. We fought on the streets of London and other major cities the length and breadth of Britain, in the pubs, clubs and council estates, down in the tube stations and up on the parks and playgrounds. We fought over differences of music, fashion, haircuts, for gang loyalty and acceptance, and some of us just for the hell of it. Our war was often bloody but rarely fatal and sometimes attracted the spotlight of the national media, though not often. In the end there was no official truce or surrender and just like other old soldiers we began to fade away.

But once, we were warrior kings … And this is how I remember it …

Noel 'Razor' Smith
Ex-Balham Wildkatz '76–'82

Part One

The Teddy Boys

Teddy Boy, ted i boi – an unruly adolescent, orig. in the 1950s, affecting a dandyish style of dress reminiscent of Edward VII's time. Teddy Girl – the Teddy boy's female companion and counterpart in conduct.

The Long Hot One
(Where it all began)

To my generation, the summer of 1976 is known as 'The Long Hot One'. Because it was long and hot, obviously. On 26 June 1976 the temperature in London reached 95°F (35°C), the highest temperature recorded in the capital since records began. It was a summer so hot that the tarmac on the roads melted from the heat and became as pliable as soft toffee. You could literally leave footprints in the road and daytime temperatures reached a consistent 89°F on 17 consecutive days. Records were set for both beer and ice-cream sales and for the number of spectators who fainted during the tennis at Wimbledon. It was so hot that at the Henley Royal Regatta that gentlemen were allowed to remove their blazers in the Stewards' Enclosure for the first and only time. On 1 July the Government rushed through new drought laws to curb the use of water for hosepipes and garden sprinklers, and there was countrywide panic-buying of vegetables as it was feared that crops were being affected by heat and lack of rainfall. But the fierce heat was tempered by cool, misty mornings when the air, even in the concrete canyons of the inner city, seemed as clear and fresh as the water in an Arctic stream. For the young, it was a summer that seemed as though it would never end, and it became a summer of change and revolution. For those of us who were coming of age there was an almost indefinable air of expectation floating in the sun-dappled shadows of the streets and council estates of south London.

To me, at age 15, it felt like that silent and breath-catching moment you reach on a fairground roller-coaster as the train clanks to a standstill at the top of the precipice. Looking down that steep and narrow track you cannot help but feel a mixture of gut-clenching fear and giddy excitement at what is to come. And that was exactly how I felt in the early part of the summer of 1976.

Musically that year started with a big surprise as an obscure rockabilly singer, Hank Mizell, crept his way into the national charts with a 1957 stomper called 'Jungle Rock', reaching number 3 in March. 'Jungle Rock' was played on *Top of the Pops* but Hank didn't appear as he was probably too busy driving the Hickery Hollow bus in Pisstown, Alabama, but Pan's People did a reasonable rendering of rocking in a jungle. Maybe it was due to 'Jungle Rock', or maybe not, but there seemed to be a definite 1950s vibe to things that year. The television adverts I remember were for *Elvis 40 Greatest*, a double LP of hits from 'Heartbreak Hotel' to 'Don't Cry Daddy'. Another LP getting plenty of ad-time was called *20 Heart Breakers*, featuring hits from Roy Orbison and Johnny Tillotson, and there was also a cartoon bear wearing wrap-around shades and sporting a Tony Curtis hairstyle advertising a sugar-laden soft drink called Cresta – 'It's frothy, man!' Then there was the Pepsi-Cola ad with the rocker and the nerd – 'Hey Eddie, how come you're such a big hit with the girls?' – where 'Eddie', looking like he'd just stepped out of 1959, proceeded to bop and sing about the chick-pulling qualities of Pepsi-Cola. It was as though, to use a more modern phrase, the 1950s were the new black.

In the charts, rock'n'roll-style artists were making a living parodying the music and fashions of the 1950s but keeping everything 1970s enough to satisfy their core audience. Alvin Stardust, in black leather and with the biggest quiff-cum-afro you've ever seen, had loosely based himself on '50s rocker Gene Vincent. Stardust had already had a genuine rock'n'roll career in the late '50s and early '60s as Shane Fenton. With his band, The Fentones, he had recorded some pretty good records and notched up a couple of minor British hits with 'Moody Guy' and 'Cindy's Birthday'. In 1979 Stardust would return to his Fenton roots when he became a regular on the revamped 1950s television show *Oh Boy!* singing rock'n'roll hits alongside Shakin' Stevens and Joe Brown. Showaddywaddy, on the other hand, were an eight-piece 'rock'n'roll revival' band who dressed in colourful drape suits and recreated minor pop hits of the rock'n'roll era, having many top-ten hits in the 1970s, including a number one with a song called 'Under the Moon of Love'. They were absolutely detested by the real Teddy boys and classed as piss-takers. At some Teddy boy clubs, it was rumoured, Showaddywaddy records were ritually burned in front of cheering crowds. The reason for the Teds' hatred of Showaddywaddy had a lot to do with the band's image. The drape suits that they wore were like grotesque parodies of the real thing, with slit-backed jackets and – oh my God! – flared trousers. The Teddy boys were sticklers for tradition and considered their own style of dress to be the epitome of sartorial elegance. Showaddywaddy didn't even bother getting the haircuts right either and long hair was anathema to the Teds. This pirating of the Teddy boy clothing was to lead to violence in the summer of 1977 when punk rockers began to wear brothel creepers and drape jackets with pins and badges all over them. It's worth mentioning that the Hell's Angels have a similar outlook when it comes to their identity, and anyone who dares to wear their colours and insignia without being a member is in for a good kicking.

It wouldn't be until later in the year that England would see its first showing of *Happy Days*, an American sitcom set in the 1950s and featuring the archetypal '50s bad boy, The Fonz, but you could still catch both *American Graffiti* and *That'll Be the Day* in the cinema and buy the soundtracks, which featured all rock'n'roll. There seemed to be a strong flavour of the 1950s even in the warm air that was coming down off the Sahara Desert and causing the heat-wave of 1976. The musical charts were ripe for change in some way. Apart from 'Jungle Rock', which appeared to be an anomaly, most popular music was aimed either at prog-rock fans or teeny-boppers. At the point in June when London had its hottest day, the number one record on Capital Radio's Top 20 was a former television advertising jingle called

'Jeans On' by David Dundas, a piece of musical dross that seemed typical of the rubbish that 'the man' was trying to palm off on us. Teenagers were bored with the here and now, and those who weren't looking back to the past for something different, were on the verge of something that would take the world by the scruff of its boring and staid neck and give it a good shake. Punk rock was taking its first infant steps in a boutique on the King's Road and in the sub-urbs of South London. By November 1976 it was picking up a fast jog, and by December it was running flat out, stopping only to hurl a few expletives at the nation from a television studio in West London.

On the dusty, sunbaked streets of London that summer, the Teddy boys were marching and attracting publicity and support for their cause. In June '76 a protest rally was held in Hyde Park, attended by 3,000 Teddy boys, rockers and other assorted rock'n'roll fans, who were demanding that BBC Radio play more 1950s rock'n'roll. After the rally, featuring music from live bands and speeches from prom-inent fans, a protest march, complete with banners, took place. The March of the Rockers, as it became known, ended outside the BBC's headquarters at White City. In the face of such a public display the BBC had to take notice and one year later created a one-hour slot on BBC Radio 1 every Saturday evening called *It's Rock'n'Roll,* hosted by one of the Teds' favourite dee-jays, Stuart Coleman. The Teddy boys were on their way back and determined not to be taken lightly.

When I wasn't on the run from the police or Stanford House Juvenile Remand Home, for committing various petty thefts and hot-wiring motorbikes, I was living with my parents, brother and sister, in a third-floor council flat in the London borough of Lambeth. The Sinclair Estate could be described as almost up market so far as council estates go, with hardly any graffiti or broken windows, though the kids would piss in the lifts. Built after the Second World War on the site of a couple of rows of houses that had been bombed by the Luftwaffe and situated in a triangle of land between the junction of King's Avenue and Thornton Road, the estate consisted of three yellow-brick blocks of three storeys each. The three blocks were named Sinclair House, Ingle House and McGregor House. We lived at number 16 Sinclair and were surrounded by some nice residential streets that a modern estate agent might describe as 'desirable residences'. The estate, though small and fairly clean, particularly when compared with the dark and grimy New Park Road Estate less than half a mile away, still seemed out of place in the middle of the beautiful pre-war houses with their huge front and back gardens.

There were many young families living on the Sinclair Estate and they had a lot of kids, maybe 40 in all three blocks, and we did a lot of kid stuff such as scrumping in the fruit-laden gardens of the local dwellings, and hedge-hopping, which involved throwing ourselves onto the otherwise immaculate topiary of our well-off neighbours. We also did the usual 'knock-down ginger', knocking loudly on the doors of the houses and running away. For the fortunates in their private houses it must have seemed as though an invading army of barbarians had decided to settle in their midst and build mud huts. It's no wonder the locals tended to look down their noses at us. To the west of Sinclair Estate, beyond the boundary of King's Avenue, lay Brixton Hill which led down into Brixton proper. To the east, over Thornton Road, was Balham, which Peter Sellers once whimsically described as 'the gateway to the south'. North, straight down King's Avenue, led to Clapham, and south, up Thornton Avenue, was Streatham Hill. Geographically, the estate was bang in the centre of all four districts and a kind of no-man's land. One side of the estate had an SW12 postcode and the other side was SW2, but if anyone asked me what area I lived in I always answered 'Balham' because our flat was closest to the east side of the estate. It would have been easy to grow up confused and with a siege mentality on Sinclair Estate, and a few of us did.

By the summer of '76 about half the kids on the estate were teen-agers of varying degrees and a pretty tight-knit group. There was no real animosity between us, though most of us boys had fought each other over the years. Our fights had always been with fists only, and the usual stuff you get between young boys. I had a bit of a reputation as a puncher and I had fought both the Finn brothers, Joey and Derek, the O'Donahues, Terry and Gary, Tony Bender and Billy Murray on several occasions as we had been growing up. It didn't really matter whether you won or lost these fist fights as we were all friends anyway. We saved our real venom for outsiders. Nobody had to tell us that kids from other estates were our ene-mies, we just knew it instinctively – probably some kind of tribal instinct. Sinclair Estate was our 'turf' and we had the same wagon-circling mentality found in most kids on council estates. We knew that if we went onto some other gang's turf we would get a kicking and they would get the same if they came on Sinclair. That was just the way it was and I don't really know why. Collectively the kids on my estate were known as the Sinclair Mob, just as we knew other kids by the names of their estates. There were the New Park Road Gang, the Poynders Gardens Crew, the Tilson House Job and var-ious others spread amongst the surrounding areas. Ever since we were nippers we had been issuing and accepting challenges to fight the kids from other estates. We didn't really class ourselves as gangs but more as defenders – cowboys protecting the homestead from marauding Indians.

In our pre-teen years inter-estate battles were normally fought with fists and boots. There might be an exchange of words or blows between a couple of kids from different estates on some neu-tral ground, such as on Tooting Bec Common where we all went to play football or in Agnes Riley park. Then that could result in the kids from one estate marching on the opposing estate and having a punch-up en masse. The trick was to keep the invading group off your own turf and fight them on the boundaries of the estate. If they could 'run' you, that is make your whole mob leg it in fear, or get right onto your turf, then you might as well give up because word would soon get round and kids from other estates would start taking liberties with you. It was all about testing each other's strength and courage. From fists and boots we advanced to throwing clods of earth at each other. Then it was stones and sometimes blood was drawn. At the age of 13 or 14 we started using sticks and throwing bottles, and the next step was air guns. Carrying an air gun seemed a pretty huge and dangerous step to us in those more innocent times. Little did we know that 20 years later kids of our age and in the same location would be carrying, and sometimes using, real firearms on each other. The favoured air pistol amongst the warring tribes of the 1970s council estates was the Diana SP50. Shaped a little like a Browning automatic, the SP50 could fire a .22 lead slug over a distance of about 15 feet and give your target a good sharp sting. However, at any distance over six feet they were about as accurate as Billy Liar's CV. The Gat-Gun, a .177, was also popular but looked too much like a spud-gun to be taken seriously and was only really carried by the younger kids. But the real daddy of all air guns was the Crossman pump-action repeater, an American-made machine-gun-looking fucker that could fire 25 .177 slugs in quick succession. My pal, Mickey Allen, had a Crossman and became an invaluable asset in our battles as he could pepper the enemy very quickly and over a greater distance than a pistol. We all bought our air guns at a strange little shop in Tooting Bec called The Treasure Chest. It sold everything, from second-hand stereos to commando daggers and had a wide range of imitation guns and air guns. By rights you had to be over 14 to purchase an air gun, but at £8 a pop the owner of the shop didn't bother asking for any ID as he was making more sales than a nappy salesman at an incontinence rally. I had a Diana SP50 and I coveted Mickey's Crossman, like we all did, but it cost around £55. I managed to buy a second-hand .22 rifle with a telescopic sight. It was no good for estate wars as it was too unwieldy and slow to load as a single-shot, but I would sometimes climb up on the roof of Sinclair House and take potshots at people passing by outside the estate or sunbathing in the surrounding gardens. It wasn't very powerful over any distance but it would sting.

Air guns began to drop out of vogue after there was a lot of publicity in the *South London Press* over a kid who lost his eye in a gang shoot-out. The police began to get very proactive in stopping and searching kids for air guns and the juvenile courts started handing out probation and big fines. I got nicked for aiming an air pistol at a police car that had been passing the estate and ended up in Stanford House, a juvenile remand home in Shepherd's Bush, for a couple of weeks. So air guns faded out, but they were soon replaced by knives of all shapes and sizes.

A lot of the kids I knew carried knives. Knives were mainly for show, but if you asked why they were being carried the answer would be, 'For protection'. In the 1990s there was a lot of uproar and media attention over the carrying of knives by kids but it was nothing new. In South London in the 1970s you could probably have built a battleship out of the number of knives being carried had you melted all the metal down. There were a lot of stabbings and slashings, particularly around the Brixton area, that went unreported to police and hospitals. One little firm out of the Stockwell Park and Angel Town estates had the MO of stabbing rivals in the buttocks. A wound of this kind would be painful but it wouldn't kill you and it would be embarrassing to report for a teenage boy. I was stabbed in the buttocks by a gang who surrounded me outside a pub called The Crown & Sceptre at the top of Brixton Hill. I treated the wound with Dettol and found it painful to sit down for a couple of weeks but I would never think of reporting it to the authorities, it just wasn't the done thing.

The first knife I remember buying was a Commando dagger, which were very popular at that time. The Commando dagger was based on the knife carried by British commandos during the Second World War and it had no other purpose than to kill your enemy. The handle was made out of heavy iron with a huge nut screwed onto a bolt as the pommel. Leaving aside the blade, if you wanted to do some damage you only had to clump someone on the head with the handle. But the blade was also awesome and designed for killing – eight inches long and tapering to a very sharp and narrow point, it was also double-edged which meant you could slash as well as stab. The deluxe model had a black blade so you could kill your enemies in the dark without giving them the warning of that telltale glint of metal. Just as a later generation of adolescents would be attracted to the Rambo knife, the Commando dagger was our fascination. I carried a Commando dagger for a while, usually down the waistband of my jeans, but the only thing I ever used it for was throwing into trees on the estate when we had knife-throwing contests. I was more a fisticuffs man than a tool-merchant at this time and the thought of plunging a piece of metal into someone's body scared and sickened me, but, by the end of the summer, my attitude began to change. I had ambitions to become a Teddy boy.

The Wind of Change

I had always liked the music and style of the 1950s; to me there was nothing cooler. I loved watching old black and white Elvis films and wished I could have lived in those days and worn those clothes and hairstyles. But I was a teenager in the wrong time. Instead of sleek greased-back haircuts, snappy pegged suits and bopping at the hop I was living in the age of shaggy perms, clunky platform shoes and The Glitter Band. I felt cheated. The music was crap, the clothes were crap and, at my age, I couldn't have afforded a shaggy perm even if I had been so inclined. To me the 1950s represented some golden age when everything had been clean and well defined. Maybe the slightly seedy unisex feel of the 1970s disgusted the Catholic in me. I didn't want to look like a girl or be able to wear the same clothes as my sister. I wanted short hair and a man's attire but I wasn't yet mature enough to assert myself in this direction, so I spent the early '70s with hair down to my shoulders and ever-widening flares.

Then one day, in May 1976, I suddenly realised that how I looked was entirely my own choice. If I wanted to sport a 1950s haircut then, by God, I would and no one could stop me. Along with my two mates, Paul and Tony, I went down to Mick the barber's, in Balham, and ordered a James Dean. *Rebel Without a Cause*, Dean's classic 1955 film of teenage angst, had recently been shown on the telly and I became an instant fan. Paul, Tony and I walked into that barber's shop looking like roadies for Status Quo and walked out again an hour later feeling the wind on our ears for the first time in many years. At first we looked strange to each other, and probably everyone else, but the look increased in its appeal to us very quickly. I realised that there was no point doing half a job; if I had the haircut then I wanted the clothes as well. Paul and Tony were not so sure about going the whole hog; they had the haircuts more for a laugh and were now happy to leave it at that. I had no intention of walking around with a 1950s head on a 1970s body though, and as I was flush with a few stolen pounds I dragged them down to Solbros on Balham High Street. The one claim to fame of Solbros of Balham is that it got a mention by Del Boy in one of the early episodes of the BBC comedy series *Only Fools and Horses*, which is not really surprising as the series' writer, John Sullivan, grew up in Balham and probably shopped there. Solbros was a small, narrow shop a couple of doors away from the 100 Club near Balham tube station.

There was a boot and shoe display rack outside on the pavement during opening hours containing examples of what I would call tough classic footwear. There were Doc Martens, boots and shoes, Commando boots with steel toecaps and screw-on soles, leather brogues and oxfords, desert boots and penny loafers. The shoe rack alone looked capable of kicking to death half the people on the High Street. The clothes in the window displays looked as though they had been thrown there by an epileptic blind man during a fit, and the theme, if there was one, seemed to be chaos. Inside, the shop was crowded, not with people but with racks of clothes, and as gloomy as a Black Sabbath album track. The owner (for I assume it was he) sat on a stool at the back of the shop and peered at me through world-weary eyes. 'Help you?' he asked, making it sound as though it were the last thing he wanted to do. 'Yeah,' I said. 'Got any drainpipe jeans?' He pointed to a rack in front of me on which hung around 50 pairs of jeans. There was a piece of card taped to the top of the rack which whispered, 'Jeans – £1.50p per pair – Bargain!!!' I guessed that when the card had originally been written it had been screaming its message but many years had passed since then.

I left Solbros 30 minutes later and around £27 lighter. I had bought a pair of drainpipe jeans, a red Harrington jacket, a pack of three plain white cap sleeved T-shirts and a pair of 12-hole Commando boots with steel toecaps. The outfit, especially the red Harrington, was almost identical to what James Dean had worn in *Rebel Without a Cause*. The only difference was that Dean had worn motorcycle boots but they didn't sell them at Solbros. When I put my new clobber on I immediately felt right and comfortable. At last, after feeling like a miserable misfit for as long as I could remember, I really felt like myself. It is strange how clothes can do that but I have felt the same all through my life: if I don't feel comfortable in my clothes I don't feel comfortable at all. Clothes can be a massive part of identity, and are important to a kid. There's nothing worse than wearing something that makes you stand out from the crowd or feel uncomfortable when you have no choice in the matter. Standing out from the crowd should be a kid's own choice. I came from a poor family where there was a struggle to put food on the table let alone provide new clothes. Twice a year we were treated to a brand new pair of plimsolls and a pair of jeans from Tesco Home & Wear. There used to be a little song about Tesco jeans when I was a kid. It went – 'Tesco bombers, big and strong, 1/6 – and you can't go wrong, wear them night and wear them day, guaranteed not to wear away.' The '1/6' referred to how cheap they were: about 70p in today's money. I sometimes got a bit of stick from other kids for how I dressed and I would usually end up rolling around the ground with them over it. I had never been what you might call 'in fashion' but I had managed to blend in eventually. So in 1976, when I came out of the fashion closet as a James Dean clone, it was like being released from prison.

The kids on my estate were shocked by my transformation and I got a lot of attention, particularly from the girls, I noted. We used to stand in the porch area of Ingle House in the evenings, smoking Park Drive and drinking cider, and all the girls wanted to run their fingers through my newly shorn hair. It was great being different, though there was a lot of piss-taking from the lads. 'Hey, Elvis, where's your guitar?' and 'Well-a-wop-bop-a-loo-bop!' were shouted at frequent intervals in my direction. Peter Mayne had a habit of doing a very poor parody of the bop, which was a 1950s dance, but it just looked ridiculous with his 24-inch flares and stack-heeled shoes. I handled all the piss-taking by raising an eyebrow and saying nothing. I thought this made me seem cool and enigmatic. After about a week I was no longer so much of a novelty and the piss-taking became sporadic.

Now that I felt comfortable with my new image I decided it was time to come out of the musical closet as well. I was pretty tired of having to pretend that I liked Rod Stewart and Elton John just to fit in when, in reality, I thought they were a pair of tossers and their music had about as much soul as a couple of diesel chainsaws. I had a little Grundig tape player, the oblong portable one with a leather-look carrying strap, and I bought a couple of rock'n'roll compilation tapes to play on it. That evening I took my tape player down to the porch and treated the gang to a bit of real music. They laughed at 'Rave On' by Buddy Holly & The Crickets, howled at 'Be-Bop-A-Lula' by Gene Vincent & The Blue Caps, and positively doubled over when they heard 'Sea Cruise' by Frankie Ford. I didn't give a shit; I liked it and no one else had a tape deck so it was listen or fuck off. Though I didn't realise it at the time, there were converts in that giggling gaggle of teens, and they would soon make themselves known. A few days after I had played my rock'n'roll tapes Peter Mayne turned up with a duck's arse (DA) haircut and wearing what looked like a de-mob suit. He shrugged off all the catcalls and whistles that greeted his arrival at the porch and nodded at my tape deck. 'Stick that Buddy Holly one on, 'Rave On' is it?' I was delighted. In the next month or so half the kids on the porch had made the change. There were more quiffs and ponytails than in an episode of *Happy Days*. Obviously the retro style was not to everyone's taste and some of the kids stuck with their long hair, flares and belted Starsky cardigans, and a rift began to develop. It was subtle at first, the retro kids grouping together almost unconsciously and the '70s kids doing the same. But in a short time it became more tribal and insults and banter were being traded back and forth between the two groups. We were still the Sinclair Mob, but now we were two separate groups instead of one. And soon our loyalty to the estate and the status quo was to be tested.

Dave Wall lived on an estate further down King's Avenue from Sinclair. He was a tall kid, around six foot, and was always the main target of the Sinclair Mob during our estate wars because of his size. We instinctively knew that we could demoralise enemy troops by bringing down the bigger kids. Once their figurehead or hardest fighter hit the deck the rest of the kids would scatter and the battle would be over. I had spent years lobbing mud bombs and stones and shooting air guns at Dave Wall, but I doubt if I had ever spoken more than two words to him. Then, in the early summer of '76, I saw Dave Wall getting off a 137 bus opposite Sinclair Estate and he was wearing a light grey two-piece Italian box-suit and a pair of black oxfords. His hair was James Dean short and Elvis slick and he looked as if he'd just stepped off the cover of *Now Dig This*. I had been sitting on the low wall that surrounded the estate with Tony Brooker, Peter Mayne and John Carey and when Dave spotted us he started walking quickly down King's Avenue towards his own estate. I was intrigued. I called across the street, 'Hey, Dave.' He looked over but didn't stop walking. 'Where'd you get the whistle?' I shouted. Dave slowed and then stopped and turned to face us. 'What?' he shouted over. 'The whistle and flute, the suit?' I called. 'It's fucking pukka. Where'd you get it?' Dave shrugged self-consciously. I waved him over. 'Here, mate. Gi's a butchers.' He hesitated on his side of the road for a moment and then walked over to our side. It turned out that Dave had come second in a talent contest at a holiday camp during the Easter holiday. He had sung 'Old Shep', the same song that Elvis had sung on his talent contest debut in 1945 as a ten-year-old, and he had sung it in the Elvis style. Dave was, it turned out, a good singer and could do a very passable impression of Elvis, which he quickly realised was great for attracting female attention. So, figuring he might be able to double his chances with the girls, when he came back from his holiday he decided to try to look like Elvis as well as sounding like him. He had bought the suit for £2 at an Oxfam charity shop in Streatham and had it cleaned and pressed, got his hair cut at Mick's of Balham and bought a pair of tough black Oxford brogues from Solbros and he was away. I had to admit I loved the suit and I saw the possibilities of being equally as stylish at little expense. We stood there talking to our old enemy about clothes, haircuts and music, all old rivalry and animosity forgotten. At that exact moment, although nothing was said or even intimated by any of us, a peace between the estates was settled and a new era of inter-estate free association was ushered in. The children's war was over and the next time we would go into battle would be as young men but for equally passionate and stupid reasons.

Dave turned out to be a nice kid and he also had a collection of original rock'n'roll 45s that were new to us. With music, as with fashion, we were still finding our way. My own knowledge of 1950s rock'n'roll was limited to two compilation tapes of hits and a few 45s and LPs in my parents' record collection. I knew a lot of Elvis stuff and a bit of Buddy Holly, Jerry Lee Lewis and Little Richard, but it was through Dave's collection, which he had inherited from an uncle, that I discovered such delights as 'Jitterbop Baby' by Hal Harris and 'White Lightning' by George 'Thumper' Jones. The more I heard of rock'n'roll the more I liked it.

That evening Dave walked across the stretch of tarmac and pavement that had always separated us and joined us on the porch. The '70s kids were shocked and outraged. This was unheard of, a kid from another estate walking on our turf and not getting his head kicked in! But he was welcomed by the retro crew as a friend and ally. The message, had anyone chosen to analyse it, was clear – our loyalties had shifted from tribe to subculture. The '70s kids left the porch in protest and hung out on the opposite side of the estate in a porch in McGregor House and they remained there until well into the summer. I felt the loss, though only momentarily, and a tinge of sadness at the split, but I was also excited by the newness of everything and the anticipation of more to come. The next day Dave took us to the Oxfam shop in Streatham and I picked out my very first suit. It was a black lightweight Pierre Cardin single-breasted box, with straight trousers. The name 'Pierre Cardin' meant nothing to us in those days and I had chosen the suit only because it was in a 1950s style and it fitted me. I paid £1.75 for the suit and 90p to get it dry-cleaned, but the first time I put it on, with a white shirt, black skinny tie and a pair of my dad's old black army shoes, I felt like a million pounds on the hoof. Dave Wall became a regular in the porch from then on. Dave was the first kid from another estate to make the crossover but pretty soon others followed. On his own estate Dave had been the only retro kid but we also welcomed his younger brother, Bernie. Bernie was a 'hairy', meaning he had plenty of hair and was inclined towards heavy rock music, but as he shared a bedroom with his brother he couldn't help but be exposed to a bit of rock'n'roll and, though he didn't wear the '50s clothes, we classed him as an honorary retro. Bernie became a good link between us and the '70s kids over on the McGregor porch and did a lot to ease our partial reunification later in the summer. He would hang with us, usually getting the piss ripped out of him for the length of his hair, and then approach the '70s kids. At first he faced a bit of hostility for being an outsider and for hanging with the retros, but Bernie had a great personality and a calmness and logic that denied his 14 years, and he was soon able to move between the two groups as he pleased. The barriers were truly crumbling. Soon we had kids from as far away as Acre Lane coming to hang on our estate. It was all word of mouth: someone knew someone who knew someone who was into the 1950s.

'Big Nose' Eamon turned up on a pushbike with a tape deck hanging from the handlebars playing rock'n'roll but he looked weird. He was a white kid, who lived in Brixton and had an afro hairdo and a Bob Marley T-shirt. It was only the fact that when he pulled up the music blaring from his tape deck was 'Rockin' Pneumonia' by Huey 'Piano' Smith that he didn't get a kicking straight away. Eamon confessed to liking a bit of reggae but liking rock'n'roll more. He was a funny kid and had us all in stitches with his stories and impressions so we let him stay but gave him a bit of sartorial advice. The next time Eamon showed up he had lost the afro and Bob Marley T-shirt and was looking more like a '50s hoodlum on a pushbike. Unfortunately for him, the huge afro had kind of taken the dairy off his nose and without it his hooter was pronounced enough to make him the first among us with a nickname – 'Big Nose' Eamon.

We also picked up a couple of converts from the New Park Road Estate, which was a hotbed of soul boys. Lee and John Carey had recently got into rock'n'roll and, because he was 17 and already working in a factory, Lee was going up the West End and over to Camden Town to buy the clothes and records. Lee had a good record collection, including a couple of HMV 78s of early Elvis hits, which we envied, and a mint copy of the Eddie Cochran *10th Anniversary* album with all the hits like 'Summertime Blues' and '20 Flight Rock'. John was more a fair-weather retro but he hated soul boys and that's why he preferred our company to that of the kids on his own estate.

It wasn't only the 1950s that were coming into vogue amongst the dissatisfied teens during that summer. We heard about kids on other estates who were harking back to the late '60s and early '70s by adopting the skinhead fashion and music. It was as though the youth had reached a stage where they were becoming sick and tired of what was deemed 'popular' music and fashions and were looking for something that was different and new, to them at least. Up on the New Park Road Estate at Brixton Hill the kids had formed a gang who were all into soul music and fashions. They were a multiracial gang and called themselves The New Park Dreads. The NP Dreads were a pretty scary bunch even amongst their peers; mostly good individual fist-fighters, they were one of the first gangs in the area to use knives.

The nucleus of the NP Dreads was a group of brothers of Irish extraction called the O'Carrolls, who were led by Biffo O'Carroll.

He got the nickname of 'Biffo' not from looking like a cuddly cartoon bear but because he had a penchant for 'biffing' other kids in the face. The brothers' closest pal was a black amateur boxer, well known for his violent temper, named Clive. I had had the occasional run-in with the O'Carrolls and Clive, and on one occasion I was knocked unconscious by Clive in a straightener, after I had made the mistake of passing their estate on my own in broad daylight. The NP Dreads had become soul boys, first adopting the plastic sandals and cheesecloth shirt look before moving up in the sartorial stakes to Farah slacks, silk shirts and fake crocodile-skin slip-on shoes. They began to frequent a notoriously down-market club at Streatham Common called The Bali Hai and became involved in a lot of knife fights which were frequent there. The kind of music they were into ranged from early 1960s soul to modern 1970s funk. James Brown was a big favourite on the soul boy scene.

A skinhead gang who were also coming to prominence at this time came from Balham and were known as the Zennor Road Mob. The Zennor Road Mob were mainly young football hooligans who followed Chelsea FC and had got caught up in the far right's recruiting drive at football grounds. They adopted the skinhead look of shaved heads, rolled-up jeans, Crombie overcoats and Doc Marten boots, but, surprisingly enough given their right-wing pretensions, they listened to reggae and ska music from the early 1960s. So, to the east of Sinclair Estate were a soul boy gang and to the west were a skinhead gang. We were stuck in the middle and were fast attracting a 1950s crowd. We were not what could be classed as Teddy boys, although we were into the same music and period of time. We were what the real Teddy boys of the day would disparagingly refer to as 'plastics'. A 'plastic' was someone who was not fully committed enough to shell out for a tailor-made drape suit and all the accoutrements of the Teddy boy lifestyle. We were amateurs, but more than that, although we didn't know it until later, we were originators of what would evolve into the rockabilly movement. We were not rich, though some of us, myself included, were nicking a bit of cash, being petty thieves and robbers, and we were not old enough to work legally, so getting together £80 for a bespoke drape suit was beyond us. And, until we had the right clothes, we would not be accepted by the Teddy boy hierarchy. We were aspirants, but until we owned at least one drape suit we would be outsiders on the rock'n'roll scene.

Teddy boys had been the flag bearers for rock'n'roll since the 1950s and their position at the top of that food chain seemed unassailable. The Teddy boy was an English working-class phenomenon that grew out of the austerity of post-war Britain. Evolving from the spiv and the cosh-boy, the original Teddy boys were, on the whole, nothing more than flashily-dressed petty criminals. Their name comes from their adoption of the Edwardian style of dress as their own: long velvet-trimmed jackets, brocade waistcoats with watch chains and thick-soled suede shoes, known as 'brothel creepers'. In the early 1950s they started sporting quiff hairstyles with the backs combed into a DA, in the style of the popular Hollywood film star Tony Curtis. Some cultivated mutton-chop sideburns as a further nod to the Edwardian era. The Teddy boy first came to the public's notice in 1954 when it was reported that they had slashed cinema seats with flick knives and cut-throat razors during the showing of the 1955 teen flick *Blackboard Jungle* at a cinema in the Elephant and Castle in South London. The music played over the opening credits of the film was by an obscure American band called Bill Haley and The Comets, the song being 'Rock Around the Clock'. It went on to clock up sales of 20 million copies, entering the British Top Ten on no fewer than three occasions over the next 25 years. After the incident with the cinema seats, which was copied by Teddy boys up and down the country wherever the film opened, Teddy boys became inextricably linked in the minds of the press and public with two things – violence and rock'n'roll music. When I first heard the story about the cinema seat slashings I couldn't understand why they had done it, and it wasn't until I spoke to one of the Teddy boys who had actually been there on that night at the Elephant and Castle that I realised the power of rock'n'roll music. Far from just slashing the cinema seats as an act of malicious damage, it was actually a protest. The film itself was supposed to have been pretty mediocre, but the infectious sound of Haley and The Comets made the Teds want to dance. Don't forget that this was a time when Vera Lynn still topped the British music charts and 'How Much Is That Doggy in the Window?' by Lita Roza was as exciting as it got.

People often cite Elvis's 'Heartbreak Hotel', in 1956, as being the pivotal moment of musical awakening for British teens, but fair do's, go and have a listen to the stuttering electric guitar and slapped bass of 'Rock Around the Clock' and imagine the excitement that must have engendered amongst the bored and surly teenagers of South London on some wet foggy evening in 1955. Anyway, the management of the cinema ordered the Teds to cease dancing and sit down and they responded by slashing and ripping out the seats so that there was nothing to sit down on. The police were called in and a riot ensued, ensuring that the notoriety of the Teddy boy would last into history.

The Teds did plenty to live up to their violent reputation throughout the 1950s and it seemed as though a week didn't pass without a report of a knifing or razor slashing committed by some young tearaway with a Tony Curtis haircut. Looking through old newspaper reports now, it's shocking to realise how much publicity the original Teddy boy movement got. In 1956 the *Daily Sketch* and *Daily Record* devoted their front page headlines to the 'Teddy boy Menace', with reports that 400 Teds had rioted at The Prince of Wales cinema in Harrow Road, London, during a showing of a film featuring the song 'Rock Around the Clock', and said that police were standing by for riots in other London cinemas. The *Daily Sketch* featured a picture of broken cinema seats with the line: 'Rock'n'roll Fever Did This!' The fact was that, since their emergence in 1954, any mention of Teddy boys was bound to sell newspapers. The Teds were already interesting because of the fact that they were the first recognisable teen subculture in the UK and because their style of dress seemed exotic in post-war Britain, so the press made them more so by demonizing them. Any outrageous or criminal act by any young person could be attributed to the evils of the Teddy boy cult. They were different and therefore legitimate targets to the press. Reading the newspapers of the time you could be forgiven for assuming that there had been a Ted bogeyman lurking behind every hedge and privet just waiting to cosh some innocent passer-by and then jive on the body. As early as 1954 the *South London Advertiser* led with 'Girls Blamed for "Edwardian" Gang Fights' and spoke of the 'growing menace of violent Teddy boy gangs' in South London. And it wasn't just the London papers. Later the same year the *Brighton and Hove Herald* had 'Youths Slashed by Teddy boy Thugs' and the *Oxford Mail* front-page headline was 'Armed "Teddy boys" Hold Up Americans', though the story was not as dramatic as the headline promised and actually concerned a wallet being stolen from a parked car owned by an American tourist. The *Evening Express* screamed 'Teddy boys Hold Up Postmistress With Gun' while the *Sunday Dispatch* kept it simple with 'War on Teddy boys' and the story below the headline opened by stating that, 'In some places groups of Vigilantes have been formed to combat the thugs in Edwardian dress who, often armed with bicycle-chains, knuckledusters and razors, have terrorized peace-loving citizens in recent months.'

Public and press hysteria over the violent Teddy boy reached its peak after the Notting Hill race riots of 1958, when it was reported that the disturbances had been kicked off by gangs of Teddy boys attacking Jamaican immigrants. By the early 1960s some of the

Teddy boys had evolved into rockers: leather jacket-wearing, motor-bike-riding ton-up boys who were battling it out with the group who should have been their natural successors, the dapper mods. Mods and rockers turned several seaside towns into battlegrounds every bank holiday, terrifying holidaymakers and day trippers and hor-rifying small-town magistrates into making speeches about 'petty little Sawdust Caesars' and dishing out large chunks of porridge to all and sundry.

By around 1962 the Teddy boy had slipped into the background and become no more than a story that parents used to scare their children into compliance. Those who had been Teddy boys had either long outgrown it all and hung up their drape suits, or not. For some strange, unknown reason there were a small bunch of hard-core Teddy boys who had been there when it all began and were still there in 1976 and beyond. When you consider that most of these men and, in some cases, women were in their late thirties by 1976, you have to consider their sanity – or at least their inability to let go and move on. Throughout the '60s and '70s these original Teds had married, had kids, held down jobs and walked the streets in their drape suits and brothel creepers. They had their own clubs, usually tucked away in the backrooms of pubs, their own customs and language and it seemed as if they all knew each other. How they had survived, like the Mohicans never did, is a mystery and I can only put it down to an absolute fanatical love for the music and lifestyle. And, perhaps, a belief that someday they would be back on top again – and, in this, they weren't wrong, though it would be short lived and not at all what they were hoping for. The original Teds became the keepers of the rock'n'roll flame. At regular inter-vals they would gather at their clubs and pubs to worship their gods, both dead and living.

The mid-1970s were tough times for the Teds, though. By 1974 Bill Haley and The Comets were reduced to appearing as a novelty turn on a north of England TV show called *The Wheel-Tappers and Shunters Social Club*. Elvis was still the king but was tarnished and contaminated by the modern world. Buddy Holly and Eddie Cochran were still fresh-faced young men staring out of laminated LP cover photos, and who though dead many long years since, always delivered the musical goods. Chuck Berry, Little Richard and Jerry Lee Lewis were still touring as parodies of what they had once been (think Chuck Berry's 1972 hit 'My Ding-A-Ling') but, to the Teds, they were better than nothing. The Teds wore the same clothes they had worn in the '50s, listened to the same music, had the same hairstyles and passed it all on to their children. They didn't want anything to change, would brook no interference in their creed and would scathingly castigate anyone who advocated such things. Everything had to be right. If a DJ were to play the 1960 version of 'Rock Around the Clock' instead of the 1954 version he would be met with silence and frowns from his audience – if he was lucky. Wearing an off-the-peg drape suit in public was considered a matter of deep shame and humiliation for the wearer and all those who had not managed to avert their eyes before catching sight of it. Such a blasphemy could result in excommunication for the wearer. Not wearing a black armband on the anniversary of any rock'n'roll god's death was like a Christian pissing on a splinter of the true cross. Each death anniversary was marked with a 'do', where the dead artist's records would be played all night. On one such night, in 1974, at a Teddy boy pub in Old Street called The Black Bull, a Buddy Holly Memorial Night got out of hand and turned into a mini-riot as 120 pissed-up Teds vented their anger and misery at Buddy's untimely death. It was no joke – being a Teddy boy was serious stuff.

So while we retros had aspirations towards Ted-dom, it was unlikely we would ever be able to integrate fully into the Ted scene. As far as the Teds were concerned they were pretty much a closed shop unless you were an original or the child of an original. The

Teds already had their king, an original from North London known as Sunglasses Ron, 'The King of the Teds'. They also had their high priests, who had carried the banner through the lean times, and all they needed were grunts and foot soldiers. But our ignorance of this at the time amounted to a healthy bliss. We carried on discovering more rock'n'roll music and gaining recruits and thinking we had a good chance at the Teddy boy thing. So, as what was to become the long hot summer of 1976 commenced, we were surrounded by enemies in the form of other teen subcultures and were still pretty alienated from the core of our own chosen subculture. I also had other problems in the fact that I was already a petty criminal with a police record for theft, burglary, assault, criminal damage and offensive weapons. I had already been sentenced to three months in a detention centre for the theft of a motorcycle and had spent periods remanded in custody at Stanford House juvenile remand home. I wasn't the only one in our crowd who had a criminal record, either. Both Peter and Harry Mayne had been in juvenile jail, Peter having already served a borstal sentence by the summer of '76, and Tony Brooker had a long record, too. We were an average group of inner-city council estate kids, some of us good, some of us bad, a couple of us definitely mad, but our love of rock'n'roll was our bond. And it would keep us together, through some very violent times, for the next six years.

The Johnny Kidd Memorial Night

The Edwardian Club was a large function room situated up a wide flight of stairs at the rear of a pub called The Loughborough Hotel, at Loughborough Junction in Brixton. With its large stage and horseshoe-shaped bar it could comfortably hold around 150 people, but on Friday nights it sometimes packed in more like 250. On summer nights it got so crowded that condensation would roll down the walls like mini-rivers and pool under the tables. The Edwardian was a Teddy boy club and the creation of one of South London's most well-known original Teds, Tommy Hogan. Tommy had been a Ted since 1953 and had been at the Trocadero cinema at the Elephant & Castle on that fateful evening in 1954 when the Teds made their name in an orgy of seat-slashing and riot. Tommy was married to an original Teddy Girl named Lynne and they had five kids, all brought up to worship and respect the golden age and its idols. The oldest son, Tony, known as Bopper, was a year younger than me and well known on the Teddy boy scene. Then there was Tommy Jnr, Tina, Mandy and Jimmy, who was no more than a toddler at this time. The family were rock'n'roll through and through.

At The Edwardian Club Tommy Snr was the DJ, Lynne took the money on the door and Bopper showed his dancing talent on the dance floor. Other people helped out as well, but it was basically a family business. Tommy's sound system was called 'Edwardian Dreams' and if there was a rock'n'roll record that he didn't have then it was one that had never been recorded. The bands who were booked were mainly the Ted bands of the day, solid four-piece rockers who could recreate the records with little deviation. The Teds didn't hold with deviations in their music, and trying to play 'Tutti Frutti', for example, as a mid-tempo country tune would get them bottled off the stage. On Friday nights the club was packed and rocking and the place to be if you were a hip young retro, or an ageing Teddy boy. It was my first real outing to a rock'n'roll club, or any club come to that, and I was as excited as a long-tailed cat in a room full of rocking chairs. I had greased the back and sides of my hair and teased the front forward into a reasonable quiff in front of the mirror at home. My James Dean cut was growing out and starting to look like Elvis circa '56, especially with the amount of Brylcreem I had slapped on it. I dressed in my black suit with a plain white, small-collared shirt and a dark blue slim-jim tie, which I had purchased for 10p at the St Bede's jumble sale, and my dad's black army shoes polished like mirrors. I finished the job with a more than liberal splash of Brut aftershave lotion. I was ready to rock at the Johnny Kidd Memorial Night.

Johnny Kidd, or plain old Frederick Heath as he had been christened, had been the lead singer with British rock'n'roll band Johnny Kidd and The Pirates. The band had had a number one hit in 1960 with a song called 'Shakin' All Over' and had a few more top 20 entries before the lead singer was killed in a car crash in 1966. Johnny Kidd held a special place in the hearts and memories of the original Teds because he had been one of the few homegrown exponents of rock'n'roll music who had not 'sold out' to 'the establishment'.

The first of the British rock'n'rollers had been Tommy Steele who, as early as 1956, had made a clutch of recordings that could easily stand comparison with the American imports. 'Rock With the Caveman', 'Elevator Rock', 'Build Up' and 'Singing the Blues', to name but a few, were real British rock'n'roll recordings and were guaranteed to get the Teddy boys bopping and jiving. But by 1957 Tommy Steele had ruined his rebel reputation by becoming an all-round family entertainer, going on to star in many films and variety performances and recording such songs as the *Children's Hour* favourite 'Little White Bull'. The Teds had a wild and dangerous reputation to uphold and Tommy Steele's comedy caperings and nicey-nice recordings just did not fit in. By the mid-1950s the Teds wouldn't even spit on Tommy Steele.

Next to take the crown as the king of British rock'n'roll was a hip young dude named Cliff Richard. With his band, The Shadows (originally called The Drifters), he burst onto the scene in early 1959 with a menacing record called 'Move It', and became the Teds' new favourite. In the early days of his career Cliff made some fantastically wild rock'n'roll recordings, some of which were still filling the dance floors of Teddy boy clubs 20 years later. 'High Class Baby', 'My Feet Hit the Ground', 'Livin', Lovin' Doll', 'Mean Streak' and 'Apron Strings' proved that Cliff and The Shadows were worthy of the Teddy boys' acclamation. But then, like a repeat of the Tommy Steele experience, Cliff too became an all-round entertainer, abandoning the guitar-jangling, foot-stomping brand of Teddy boy rock'n'roll for more middle-of-the-road recordings like 'Loving Doll' and 'Summer Holiday'. The Teds hung their heads in sorrow.

Billy Fury was the next strong contender for the British rock'n'roll crown. He had the looks and the attitude and his first album, the mainly self-penned ten-inch, *The Sound of Fury*, contained some outstanding rock'n'roll that was bordering on a rockabilly sound. Billy Fury could easily have taken the crown had he not been so predisposed towards ballad singing. As far as the Teds were concerned, ballads were okay for a slow dance with your bird at the end of the evening, but you couldn't bop or jive to them. Two Billy Fury recordings that did make the grade and live into the 1970s were 'Turn My Back on You' and 'Gonna Type A Letter', a pair of blistering boppers that were de rigueur at any Teds' do.

The rest of the British rock'n'roll contingent, such as Marty Wilde, Vince Eager, Duffy Power et al. were considered to be too 'soft' for the hardcore tastes of the real Teds. But Johnny Kidd was different gravy. Johnny Kidd and The Pirates were all breathless menacing vocals and nerve-jangling guitar riffs over explosive drum sounds. You could bop to Johnny Kidd records and still look as hard as nails. For a lot of Teds Johnny Kidd was the true king of British rock'n'roll and as such he deserved to be honoured. Hence the memorial night at The Edwardian Club.

Personally I could take or leave Johnny Kidd. I thought his music was okay but I was no big fan. Of all the British rock'n'rollers Billy Fury was my favourite, ballads and all. But the Johnny Kidd night was to be my debut on the rock'n'roll club scene, so I was listening to his 20 *Greatest Hits* LP on my Dansette as I was getting ready. I ran the steel comb through my hair for the final time and winked at my reflection in the bathroom mirror. I looked cool.

The intense heat of the day was gone but it had left the evening comfortably warm as I headed down the three flights of stairs from our flat to meet up with the lads on the porch of Ingle House. The Edwardian Club had an 18-and over rule, but though none of us was over 17 we knew we would have no trouble getting in. Bopper had promised to take care of it and his dad was running the club. There was me, Big Nose Eamon, Dave Wall, Peter Mayne and Lee and John Carey, all dressed in our '50s finery, combing our already immaculate hair every five minutes and smoking like James Dean, with the fag permanently hanging from the corner of the mouth. It was around 7 p.m. but it wouldn't even start to get dark until after 9, and there was a good and excited feeling among us as we gathered around the porch chatting and practising our dance moves. Someone passed around a bottle of cider mixed with cheap gin and I took a good drink from it. The '70s kids were hanging around the opposite porch and they started shouting over to us and a bit of banter developed. They now had a cassette player over there and the sound of Abba or The Brotherhood of Man drifted on the summer air. I dogged out my butt and slapped my hands together. 'Fuck this shit! That music is giving me the creeps. Let's split.' Peter drained the cider bottle and launched it into the bin chute and we moved out as a group.

Getting down to Loughborough Junction involved a bit of a journey for us. We caught the 137 bus just outside the estate, getting off at Streatham Hill station, and then caught a 159 bus down to The White Horse pub on Brixton Road. Then it was a walk down to the junction. Big Nose Eamon kept us amused on the journey with his outrageous patter. As the 159 pulled up outside the bowling alley on Streatham High Street we spotted three skinheads. They were around our age and wearing the uniform of half-mast jeans, braces and boots and were standing in a group smoking. We were upstairs on the smoking deck and we all piled onto the side of the bus where we could see them and shout abuse through the windows. The skins started shouting their own abuse and giving us the wanker sign as the bus pulled away. We were all fired up and excited over it. This was the first time we had come across another teen subculture outside the estate and the instant animosity was to set the tone for all future contact. Moving around in a group that had a distinctive look gave me a good feeling of belonging. This was my gang. We were into the 1950s and were declaring it loud and clear with our hairstyles and clothing, and if you didn't like it, well fuck you! And if you belonged to a distinctly different subculture you were an instant enemy even though I did not know you. It was strange how we all just seemed to arrive at that point at the same time; not just us, but the skinheads, soul boys and smoothies as well. Perhaps it had always been this way for teenagers, and you could certainly see the same attitude in mods and rockers of the early 1960s, but in 1976 I think the lines were being drawn more clearly. If you were not with us then you were definitely against us, and that seemed to be our creed.

I was very nervous about entering The Edwardian Club for the first time and didn't know what to expect. As we walked down Loughborough Road we were passed by a big 1957 Ford Zephyr in two-tone pink and black, which seemed to be packed out with Teddy boys all hanging out of the open windows. As they passed us they sounded the horn, which played the first few bars of 'Dixie', and waved to us. We didn't know them and they didn't know us, but we were fellow travellers close to the same destination so we waved back. The Loughborough Hotel was on the corner of a side street with the front of the pub facing out onto Loughborough Road. To get to The Edwardian Club we had to turn down the side street and go to the rear of the pub. When we turned the corner I was overtaken with delighted excitement. On that warm summer's evening that backstreet in Brixton looked to me exactly how I imagined it did in the 1950s. There were classic cars parked on each side of the street – Ford Zodiacs, Zephyrs and Consuls, Vauxhall F-Type Victors and Crestas, Humber Super-Snipes and Hawks – mostly in bright two-tone paint jobs and all polished and gleaming in the evening sunlight. There was a row of about eight motorbikes, Triumph and BSA being the favoured marques, parked next to each other like horses outside a Wild West saloon.

Groups of be-quiffed Teddy boys and leather-jacketed rockers were standing around as though they owned the street. As we stood there, taking it all in like a bunch of yokels seeing the big city for the first time, a bright pink Ford Anglia pulled up and four of the most gorgeous girls I had ever seen got out. They were dressed up in circle skirts with petticoats, black stockings and stiletto shoes that clicked loudly on the pavement. I whistled softly and looked at Dave as the girls made their way across the pavement to the club entrance. Dave straightened his slim-jim tie and swallowed. 'Wow!' he exclaimed. And I felt the same way.

To get into The Edwardian Club you had to go up a wide concrete staircase and onto a narrow landing. From the bottom of the stairs we could hear the music, loud but distorted in the cavernous stairwell, as though it was coming from under water. Outside the doors that led into the interior of the club was a table at which sat Lynne Hogan and a couple of burly Teddy boys with hard faces. Lynne was tall and blonde and looked very 1950s in her leopard-print blouse and bird-wing glasses. She reminded me of one of The Vernon's Girls, the backing singers on that old 1950s TV programme *Oh Boy!* and she had a real cockney barrow-girl charm about her. 'Hello boys,' she greeted us cheerily. 'Good night tonight. We've got a decent band and plenty of Johnny Kidd on the disco. £1 each, lads.' We paid our entrance fee and walked through into the club.

The interior was dimly lit and packed with people. The bar was right next to the entrance and we made that our first stop. As I waited to be served in the throng around the bar, I looked around and took it all in. The ceiling was high and domed and there were light sconces around the walls at regular intervals above head height but they didn't seem to give off much light. The tables and chairs were situated around a large hardwood dance floor with a good-sized stage area towards the back of the room. I got my pint of light and bitter and made my way through the crowds to the edge of the dance floor. I wanted to see everything. Tommy Hogan himself was spinning the records from a set of decks in one corner of the stage and I spotted Bopper up there behind him going through a record box. The rest of the stage was set up for a band, with instruments, amplifiers and microphones all ready, though no sign of the band. The dance floor was packed with jiving couples and bopping singles. I watched, utterly fascinated, as the jiving girls were spun around at high speed, exposing their knickers and stocking tops for a split second. I didn't yet know how to jive but I was looking forward to learning. We all did a version of the bop that we had picked up mainly from watching '50s impersonation band Showaddywaddy on *Top of the Pops*, but it was nothing like the dance I was seeing here. It looked as though my practiced dance moves would need a drastic revamp if I didn't want to embarrass myself. Big Nose Eamon sidled up to me, pint in hand and eyes glowing in the dimness. 'This is fucking great!' he shouted in my ear above the music. I smiled and nodded. It was just what we had been looking for and expecting.

The record that was playing approached its end and the dancers slowed down before it segued smoothly into another song and they renewed their efforts. Bopper must have spotted me from his vantage point on the stage and came down to see me. He looked immaculate, as usual, in a blue three-piece drape suit and blue creepers. He took me up on stage to meet his dad. Tommy Snr was as immaculately dressed and coiffured as his offspring and shook hands warmly with me. I liked Tommy straight away and was impressed with the way he could work the complicated-looking decks while shouting encouragement to the dancers through the microphone and carrying on a conversation with me. He asked me if I had any requests I wanted playing and on the spur of the moment I asked him to play 'Rave On' by Buddy Holly and to dedicate it to the Sinclair Mob. The band came on stage at 9.30 but just before they did Tommy played my request. I was made up and so were the rest of the lads. It felt as though we had finally made it and arrived on the rock'n'roll scene..

The majority of people at The Edwardian Club were a lot older than us and seemed to be either drape-suited Teddy boys or leather-jacketed rockers with little in between. Me and my mates were dressed in a 1950s style at least, which I think is why we were tolerated, but there wasn't a drape or a leather jacket between us, which made us stand out a bit. I made up my mind that I was going to steal enough money to get a drape suit made before I came to the club again. I wanted to immerse myself. That night I came across a phenomenon for the first time that would always make me feel slightly uncomfortable in rock'n'roll clubs. When the records were playing the dance floor was full of dancers, but as soon as the band came on everyone would either head for the bar or outside the club for a breather, leaving only a handful of people in front of the stage. No one seemed to want to dance to the live music, only the records. I don't really know why this was because some of the better bands could produce a sound that was so close to the original as to be almost indistinguishable. It had just somehow become the tradition that no one danced to the band, but if the band were exceptional then plenty of people would gather in front of the stage to watch them perform. I sometimes felt sorry for the bands, particularly the young ones, as they gave their all for an ungrateful and undemonstrative crowd, but that was the tradition.

Around 10.30 I was feeling pretty drunk and happy. I even ventured onto the dance floor to hop about a bit when Tommy played Johnny Kidd's 'Please Don't Touch', which was my particular favourite. I noticed that Dave spent most of the evening chatting to a couple of giggling Teddy Girls in one corner of the club and seemed to be getting on famously with them judging by their body language. The heat was stifling inside the club and I decided to pop outside for a couple of minutes for a bit of fresh air. The stairwell was crowded with couples sitting talking or kissing and I had to step over people to make it to the street. It was dark outside now and a bit cooler, but the streetlights cast a warm orange glow over everything. I lit up a cigarette and saw Big Nose Eamon and John Carey talking to a mean looking biker with 'Road Rats MC London' on the back of his cut-down denim jacket. I walked over to take a listen and found they were talking about motorbikes. The biker was very well spoken, which seemed completely at odds with his huge straggly beard, tattoos and oil-stained denims. I was later to find that this was the case with a lot of bikers: they were not all wild-eyed criminals and some of them held down very well-paid day jobs. I was admiring the sleek lines of a jacked-up Ford Zodiac that was parked along the street from the entrance to the club when I became aware of raised voices down at the corner of the street. Three young Teds came bombing around the corner at top speed and shouting an alert. 'The niggers are coming! The niggers are coming!'

Brixton was a predominantly black area and since the Notting Hill riots of the 1950s there had been no love lost between black people and Teddy boys. Having a Teddy boy club in what was essentially the heart of Brixton was a bit too much for a lot of the young black kids on the surrounding estates and sometimes there would be trouble. Bopper had told me that the week before the Johnny Kidd night a couple of Teds from Shepherds Bush had beaten up a Rasta in one of the cab offices after leaving the club. Now it seemed there was a gang coming for revenge. I didn't know what to do. One of the Teds ran into the club and within about a minute crowds of Teds and rockers were piling down the stairs and out onto the street. I got carried along with the excitement of the crowd as we spread out across the street and began marching up towards the junction. I noticed that a lot of people had produced weapons and there was everything from sheath knives and cut-throat razors to motorbike chains and broken pool cues. I felt a bit naked without a weapon of my own but I was up for a punch-up. There must have been about 60 or 70 of us by the time we reached the junction. I noticed Eamon, John, Lee and Peter in the crowd, faces glowing with drink and excitement, and the only one who was missing was Dave, who was still inside the club chatting up the girls. I had been in gang fights before but nothing on this scale or with this amount of weaponry on show. My heart was racing and my mouth was dry but I was eager. This was it; we were going to show these fuckers that you couldn't mess with the Teds. As we turned the corner I saw a group of about 40 blacks, all armed with sticks, bats and knives, and my excitement reached fever pitch. Someone had found a plastic crate full of milk bottles outside one of the shops and was passing them to those in our crowd who didn't have a weapon. I grabbed two bottles, one in each hand, and holding them by the necks I stood shoulder to shoulder with my people. This was what it was all about, a brotherhood, us against them; it didn't matter who the enemy was, if they weren't us they weren't anything.

The two groups stood facing each other over about 20 feet of street. A big Teddy boy, whom I later found out was called Cut-Throat John, stepped forward and shouted towards the blacks, 'You fucking golliwogs! You fucking want some? Come on then!' He then ran towards the blacks with a roar and waving a cut-throat razor above his head. The Teds followed suit, roaring and running up the street towards the enemy group. The blacks hesitated for a moment and then, realising that they were outnumbered, broke ranks and began running back the way they had come. In their panic to get away, a couple of blacks tripped and fell and were quickly swamped by kicking and slashing Teds. I heard the screams above the rest of the noise but I carried on running with the crowd. As we realised that the blacks were getting away, the crowd began to slow down. I launched my milk bottles, one at a time, over the Teds in front of me and heard them smash on the road behind the retreating blacks.

The walk back to the club was the march of a triumphant army, all backslapping and laughter at our victory. We had 'run' the Brixton blacks and that was worth savouring. Even I, novice as I was, knew that at some stage, maybe next week or next month, they would be back in even greater numbers and things might not go our way then. But for now the Teds were riding high. I noticed a pool of blood on the tarmac near the junction and knew this was where one of the black gang had been caught and battered. As I walked by, the orange streetlight was reflected in the blood and it made me feel slightly sick. I wondered where the owner of that blood was and how badly he had been hurt. Then I was caught up in the moment again and dismissed the blood and any thought of the victims. I caught up with Eamon, John and Peter who were in very high spirits and we all went back into the club to take the piss out of Dave for missing all the excitement.

Looking back, I realise that the Teds were what would now be described as 'institutionally racist'. In those days a lot of people were and, if the truth were known, a lot of people still are, and not just white people either. I think we've just got better at hiding it these days. I'm not a hypocrite and I won't sit here and pretend to have an attack of the vapours because I fought and verbally abused black gangs when I was younger. It happened, and I took plenty of stick from the other side as well. The '70s was a pretty confused decade. You could hear the words 'nigger' and 'honky' on television most weeks and the National Front (NF) was openly recruiting and marching our streets and football terraces, as was the Anti-Nazi League (ANL). A lot of the Teds were NF members, and a few were members of the ANL, but I never joined any of these organisations. My reason for not joining any of the right-wing groups was because both my parents were Irish and the likes of the NF had plans to kick the 'paddies' out of England as soon as they had dealt with the blacks and Asians. I had a couple of black friends and there were even a few black Teddy boys, such as Black Bill of Tooting, Olly the Cat of Streatham and Jester of the Shepherds Bush Rebels. So, although I may have been casually racist, my loyalty was to rock'n'roll and my hatred was for anyone outside of that sphere, whether they were black, white or brown.

The Johnny Kidd Memorial Night at The Edwardian Club will always live in my memory as a golden time. I was on the verge of getting into something to which I felt I belonged. I believed that rock'n'roll was here to stay and that, like Tommy Hogan and the rest of the originals, I too would be bopping and jiving my way into middle age someday. I was proud to be part of it all and to have met such great characters and been accepted at face value. We all ended up pissed that night and singing rock'n'roll songs at the tops of our voices as we made our way home. It was a great summer to be a teenager.

All the Fun of the Fair

Every summer a travelling funfair pitched up on Tooting Bec Common and the bright lights and loud music attracted every kid within a ten-mile radius. The fair should have been a happy place, full of laughter and enjoyment, and sometimes it was, but it could also be dangerous. In 1974 there was a pitched battle at the fair between the Sinclair Mob and a gang of kids from the Phipps Bridge Estate in Mitcham. We fought all-out with fists, feet and whatever tree branches happened to be lying about, and it ended with a lot of bloodied noses and sore heads. In the end we ran the Phipps Bridge gang off the Common and went home happy. Because of our young age we visited the fair in the daylight hours and missed the worst of the violence, which occurred in the evenings. In 1975 two teenagers from Streatham were stabbed in a fight between rival gangs just outside the fair after an evening session. Apart from all the different gangs who visited the fair on its two-week stay, there was also a tasty little firm who worked on the fair and weren't shy about getting into a good tear-up. And the fair, unlike East Street market, was not considered to be neutral territory by anyone, so if anyone wanted to start a bit of trouble there was little to stop them. The trick with the fair was to go there mob-handed just in case.

To get to the fair from Sinclair Estate meant a trek across about a mile-and a-half of common land, under a railway bridge and across Bedford Hill, which cut through the centre of the common. The fair always pitched on the side of the Common closest to Mitcham, and next to the Tooting Bec lido. The only good thing about getting there was that we didn't have to cross anyone's turf. The closest gang to our route was a skinhead firm called the Balham Boot Boys who lived on an estate at the top of Bedford Hill at the edge of the Common. But we still planned our visit to the fair like a military operation and all went together. After our exploits at The Edwardian Club we had all become that little bit more serious about ourselves. I had managed to nick a nice few quid by burgling an off-licence with Peter Mayne, and he and I had bought our first drape suits with the proceeds. My suit was black with black velvet trim and half-moon pockets, and Pete's was light blue with black velvet. I also bought myself a cut-throat razor from a second-hand shop. I sharpened the round end of the blade by rubbing it vigorously on a lamp post and taped it about an inch from the end, Teddy toy fashion, so that the blade could not go too deep and kill someone accidentally. I practised flicking the razor open and making slashing movements until I was pretty good at it, but I had no plans to slash anyone; like my Commando dagger it was just for show. If it came to a fight I would rely on my punching, kicking and head butting. Or that's what I told myself. We now had a pretty sizeable gang and I felt good as we gathered in the porch on that warm summer's evening. There was me and Pete, Big Nose Eamon, Dave Wall, John and Lee, Tony Brooker, Mark Ishmael, and Alan Budd. There was also what I thought of as our junior contingent, the younger brothers who were trying to emulate our dress and actions. There was my own sibling, Mick, Dennis Budd, Harry Mayne, and Adrian and Vince Street who lived in the houses up the road from the estate. The junior contingent were all around 13 or 14 and had greased their long hair into a parody of 1950s hairstyles and, in some cases, tucked their flares into their socks, but at least they were making an effort and we were glad to have them as they swelled our ranks and made us look that bit more scary. There were a small group of Teddy Girls on the estate: Pete and Harry's sister, Marina, a girl called Debbie Lee and another called Christine, but they would go to the fair with the '70s girls and would not be part of any fighting that might develop. The girls who liked rock'n'roll didn't really have a gang mentality like the boys did. It was easy for them to become Teddy Girls as they could pick up pencil skirts, petticoats and circle skirts quite cheaply, and then it was just a matter of putting their hair in a ponytail and they were ready to rock. Plus they never seemed to fall out with the '70s girls over it. There were never any fights between them and they would still hang around with each other. The girls seemed to think it was all a great laugh, while the boys took everything more seriously.

The '70s kids from McGregor porch were also going to the fair but they set off before us. Relations between us were still a bit strained after the split, but we had reached a point where we could have a bit of good-natured banter with each other. We were no longer the Sinclair Mob; the estate was clearly split into two separate factions and would remain so. Some of the '70s kids were finding their own level. Some, like the Finn brothers, Joey and Derek, and Gary O'Donahue, were budding soul boys, while Terry O'Donahue and others started getting into some weird shit like Pink Floyd and Tangerine Dream. Others remained what the retro section disparagingly referred to as 'smoothies' or 'squares', those with no discernible sub-cultural identity. Smoothies were the chameleons of the teen world, content to wear the fashions of the day and listen to whatever music happened to be popular at the time. When fashion changed they changed with it, like a herd of sheep. In 1974 they were raving about Gary Glitter and the Bay City Rollers, and by 1976 it was Abba and 10cc. By the early 1980s most of them would be sporting wedge haircuts and wearing frilly pirate shirts. Big Nose Eamon had his tape deck with him that evening and we sat on the wall around the south end of the estate and watched the '70s kids set off up Thornton Road towards the Common. It was around 6.30 in the evening and still hot. I felt very warm in my new drape suit and wished I'd worn casual clothes like most of the rest of the boys. Me, Peter and Dave were the only ones wearing suits; the others were in jeans, T-shirts and boots. I was made up with my suit and had hardly taken it off since I'd got it. Peter and I had gone together to a little tailor's shop on Camberwell New Road to get measured up and pay our £20 deposits. We thought we were the dog's bollocks in our Teddy boy gear. I got a lot of attention from people when I wore my suit: older people would smile and nod or stop me to tell me how great it had been in the 1950s, but I got a few dirty looks from older black people who probably remembered Teddy boys in a different light. I didn't give a fuck; I was a Ted and proud of it.

One time, Peter and I were on a bus coming back from Streatham when a black bus conductor who was taking our fares kissed his lips at me and we got into a slanging match. He had taken offence simply because of the way I was dressed and kept calling me a 'Teddy gangster'. We were on the top deck of the bus and I stood up and flicked my razor out so he could see it. I wanted to frighten him. 'You fucking sambo, I'll cut you,' I told him, and he backed off. Peter and I jumped off at the next stop and as the bus was pulling away the conductor was on the open platform shouting that he would kill us the next time he saw us. We pretended to chase after the bus and the conductor ducked back off the platform. It was just a laugh to us but the way we dressed could upset some people.

The walk to the fair was pretty uneventful and we hardly saw anyone. When we got to the part of the Common where we had to cross Bedford Hill we were on alert for any sign of the Balham Boot Boys, who lived further down the hill, but we saw no one. You could hear the fair long before it came into sight: loud pop music mixed with the screams and cries of people excited by the rides. Then you could smell it: frying onions from the burger stall and the sickly sweet aroma of candyfloss. Finally we came over a grassy hill near the fishing pond and there it was: caravans, tents and big trucks with generators hooked up behind them.

The concourse was crowded with people in their summer finery taking in the sights and sounds and queuing for rides. We headed straight for the rifle range as we all thought we were great shots, and so we should have been after the amount of practice we'd had with air guns. Peter went off to get a hot dog and was back five minutes later and telling us that he had seen about 20 of the Balham Boot Boys over at the dodgems. Even allowing for Peter's tendency to exaggerate, it sounded like too many. The younger members of our gang had already split off from us and were enjoying the rides. We decided that if the Boot Boys were here in force it was probably all going to end up in a ruck as we had no intention of leaving.

Sticking together, we went for a walk through the fair to see what was what. I was feeling a bit nervous about a confrontation with the Balham Boot Boys. We had never clashed with them before but they had a major reputation for tear-ups. A few of them were from the Zennor Road Mob and the rest were skinhead football hooligans who mainly worked in Balham Market as barrow boys. I had been at primary school with a couple of them and even then they were considered to be hard nuts. They were used to fighting mob-handed at the football and they also clashed regularly with the Asian gangs in Tooting. There was no question that as soon as we laid eyes on each other there would be a ruck. We were Teds and they were skinheads and that's just the way it would be. I also remembered that it was rumoured that they all carried Stanley knives.

As we came up to the dodgems I saw two skinheads dressed in Ben Sherman shirts, rolled-up jeans with braces and oxblood Doc Marten boots. I looked around the crowds surrounding the dodgems but didn't spot any more of them, but that didn't mean they weren't there somewhere. I led my crew over to one end of the ride and we stood there watching the crowds and the cars bumping each other. The two skins had spotted us and didn't look at all perturbed. That was a bad sign. If I had been on my own and had seen a gang of skins nearby I would have been at least a bit jumpy. My mouth went dry. There were around 15 skinheads standing there and looking at us. I reached into the pocket of my drape and gripped my razor. I turned as casually as I could. 'Let's see if we can round up the juniors,' I said. 'We might have to make a quick getaway here. There's fucking hundreds of them!'

We moved away from the dodgems as a group. I didn't dare look back – I was absolutely shitting myself – but Peter did and his words chilled my heart. 'They're coming.' This was it. I was thinking fast. If we legged it we would never live down the embarrassment of it, and they would probably catch us anyway and then we would get a kicking. If we faced them we would probably get a kicking anyway. As we walked towards the open ground at the back of the fair I took a quick glance back over my shoulder and saw that they were definitely following us. It was Peter who made up my mind for me; big mad Peter, who definitely had a screw loose and was game for anything, god bless him. 'I ain't fucking running,' he said, firmly. I felt calm then; it was that moment when adrenalin has flooded into your system and needs a release. 'We ruck, then?' I said, but no one replied. As we reached the outskirts of the fair I turned around and so did the rest of the gang. The skins looked like a fucking army. I didn't see any weapons on show and I wondered whether I should pull my razor, but the thought passed quickly as one of the skins pointed at Peter and shouted, 'You fucking long streak of piss, who are you looking at? You fucking want some?' Peter nodded. 'Yeah, you bald-headed cunt, I'll have you!' And then it was all off.

One minute I was standing still and the next I was charging into the skins and throwing punches and kicks at anyone who moved. I didn't even think or make any sort of conscious decision, I was just in there flailing like a berserker. I got a good hard punch in the ear and went down onto the grass and then the boots came in hard and fast. I curled up into a ball and covered my head with my hands. I remember worrying that I might get grass stains on my suit, and then no one was kicking me anymore. The skinheads had done us, that was for sure, but at least we had stood our ground and they hadn't run us. We could take a lot of comfort from that. All our gang were bruised and dishevelled and Peter had a bloody nose, but, as kickings go, it hadn't been too bad. The skins had gone back to the fair. We checked each other for damage and decided to head back to Sinclair. Peter wanted us to go and get tooled up and come back and start all over again, but for the rest of us one kicking per night was more than enough. As we limped back across the Common I put my hand into my pocket and felt for the razor. A lot of fucking good that had been! I doubted whether I would have had the bottle to use it on someone even if I had pulled it out. I wasn't a tool merchant, I'd always been a fist fighter. I just wished some of the Teds from The Edwardian Club had been with us at the fair, then we would have kicked the shit out of the Boot Boys. By the time we reached Sinclair we had all convinced ourselves that there had been over 30 skinheads and that we had more than held our own against them, only being overwhelmed by their superior numbers at the last minute. Big Nose Eamon compared it to the film *Zulu*. We all agreed that the next time we met the Balham Boot Boys on the field of battle there would be a different outcome and we would come away the victors. We were to clash with the Balham Boot Boys again sooner than any of us had dreamed. We were about to expand our turf and our horizons, and the rest of the summer would be spent making our mark. The kids' stuff was coming to an end and it was all going to get very bloody.

Making a Name for Ourselves

Stanford House Juvenile Remand Home, in Goldhawk Road, Shepherds Bush, was a kind of kiddies' prison for petty offenders. There was a 12-foot fence around it but it was chain-link and easy to climb for any kid who was really determined to escape. Run by the probation service and local authority, it took boys aged between 13 and 17 who had been remanded in custody by the juvenile courts or given care orders. As places of juvenile incarceration go, it was pretty low on the army-style discipline that was popular in those days and not a bad place to do your bit of bird, if you had to. The uniform at Stanford House was a T-shirt, jeans and plimsolls, and the colour of your T-shirt indicated which house you were in. Church House took boys aged between 15 and 17 and their T-shirts were red. Hanvey

House was for the really young kids of 13 and 14 and they wore yellow T-shirts. O'Hare House dressed in blue tops and held the boys who had been sentenced to care orders and were awaiting assessment to go to other children's homes. There was also a closed unit which held those boys who had committed more serious offences and were awaiting trial at the Crown Court, and also held those who had tried to escape or had kicked off whilst at Stanford House.

Throughout the summer of 1976 I was in and out of Stanford House on a few occasions, mainly due to my propensity for petty offending. I couldn't resist stealing motorbikes, and, together with Peter Mayne, I funded my Teddy boy lifestyle by breaking into shops and nicking anything that wasn't nailed down firmly. On the yard at Stanford House I met up with other Teddy boys from all over London. The Shepherds Bush Rebels were always well represented as they were local, and it was on the yard that I first came across Stud. He was the leader of the Bush Rebels, a gang of Teddy boys who were fast gaining a reputation as the kind of cats you wouldn't want to fuck with. They had West London sewn up as far as other subcultures were concerned. The Bush Teddy boys were around 30-handed, more if you counted their affiliates, and they would battle with anyone. It was to be a while before West London became infested with punk rockers, but in 1976 the main enemies of the Bush Rebels were soul boys, smoothies and black gangs. In the summer of 1977 the Bush Rebels would be heavily involved in the fighting with punk rockers on the King's Road, but Stud himself was out of it, serving a ten-year sentence for stabbing a punk rocker in the neck with a screwdriver in January. Another regular in Stanford House was Bopper Hogan, usually nicked for TDA (taking and driving away) or attempted theft from tourists' pockets.

There was also Putney Steve, who had 'Gene Vincent & the Blue Caps' tattooed around his neck. Then there was Kidd, a black Teddy boy from Stockwell. He got a lot of stick from the black kids about being a Ted, particularly from the soul boys and young Rastas, but as far as we were concerned he was one of our own and all Teds stuck together. There were a few black and even a couple of Asian Teddy boys and they rarely got any trouble from the young Teds; it was only the originals who looked down their noses at them. Of course they got a barracking and occasional violence from kids of their own race and were called 'Bountys' after the chocolate bar that's dark on the outside and white on the inside. Kidd was one of those lads who didn't give a fuck what people thought of him, he was having a great time. Kidd could have a tear-up and had a great sense of humour, so he would give as good as he got in any exchange, be it verbal or physical. When I got into it I thought that the Teddy boy world was a small one, but through places like Stanford House and The Edwardian Club I started meeting up with Teds from all over London. I heard about other rock'n'roll clubs like Bobbysox in Neasden and The Lyceum in The Strand, where the growing retro scene flourished and it seemed as though it was growing by the day. Every time I went over the fence at Stanford House, which was a lot during that summer, I brought news of what was going on in the world to our little enclave in South London: which gangs were forming where, what records were popular in the clubs, and places where we could buy clothes. I discovered that there was a record shop in Camden Town that sold a lot of deleted rock'n'roll albums and singles, and that there was a shop inside Victoria Market that stocked everything that might be needed by the well-dressed Teddy boy, from bootlace ties to brocade waistcoats. It was all a learning process for me and being remanded in custody every now and again helped me to keep my finger on the pulse of the Teddy boy scene.

Battersea was a big Teddy boy area and particularly the Patmore Estate just off the Wandsworth Road. The Hogan family lived on Patmore and were a big influence on a lot of the kids on the estate as far as rock'n'roll was concerned. The graffiti on Patmore seemed to consist of two words: 'Teds Rule'. The Battersea Teds, as they were known, were a mixed bunch of original Teds and youngsters, with the Hogans basically setting the standard. Tommy Jnr led the youngsters when Bopper was in jail, as he invariably was, and they were all good fighters, good dancers and well-dressed coves. Just as Sinclair Estate had become the mecca for retro kids and Teddy boy wannabes in SW12, Patmore was the same in SW11. Down in Balham the retro movement was also starting to take off in a big way. My cousins on my father's side, the Regans, lived in a house on Carmina Road in the heart of Balham, just a few streets away from Bedford Hill. There were 14 Regan kids in all, but it was only the older ones who got the rock'n'roll virus in the summer of '76. Ronnie and Eddie had been up to Sinclair Estate to see us and I had stayed at their house during one of my short periods on the run from Stanford House at the start of the summer. Both Ronnie and Eddie, and their older sister Sylvia, took to the early Elvis look and sound and all became Teds. As the Regans were well known and well liked in Balham, other kids took the lead from them and soon there was a little gang of Teds down there who called themselves The Wanderers. They came by their gang name because Eddie was always playing Dion's 'The Wanderer' on his tape deck, but, by coincidence, in 1979 a film was released that was to have a major influence on London gangs and this was also called *The Wanderers*.

The Balham Wanderers were way ahead of their time. The good thing about the Balham Teds being my cousins was that we now had a good excuse to move in on Balham and claim it as a joint turf between the Sinclair Mob and The Wanderers as we were all Teds and retros. This opened up our turf and made us that bit more powerful to the other gangs. But the truth of it was that there was nothing of any interest in the quiet residential streets between Sinclair Estate and Balham Market. It was a dead area and the only ones who had previously had any claim on it were a square mob led by one good fighter named Mick Garry. Mick could have a ruck and he and I had fought each other on a few occasions when we were growing up, but as he lived on one of the side streets and not on an estate he didn't have much of a gang available to him. So he wouldn't be able to stop us trampling over his turf on our way to and from Balham.

One other little problem about Balham was the Balham Boot Boys, the skinhead gang who had given us a trouncing at Tooting Bec fair. They lived mainly on an estate at the top of Bedford Hill, just before the Common starts, but some of them worked in the open-air market on Hildreth Street and as Balham was their home turf they could pop up anywhere. But as we were now affiliated with The Wanderers we had nearly equal numbers to the Boot Boys and we would just have to be prepared for trouble wherever we met it. The Wanderers had started to frequent a pub on Garratt Lane called The Fountain, which held a rock'n'roll night every Friday. The Fountain had become a popular hangout for the Road Rats MC, a motorcycle gang who had a charter from the American Hell's Angels and were well known for their outlaw violence. The Road Rats had always co-existed with the retro and Teddy boy scene without much trouble and you could see quite a few of them at The Edwardian Club and other rock'n'roll venues. I think it may have been because the outlaw biker gangs had evolved from the mod-hating rockers, many of whom had evolved from the original Teddy boy movement of 1954. Anyway, they were fond of a bit of rock'n'roll.

The DJ at The Fountain was an original Ted who went by the name of '50s Flash and he played some great music. There was a beer garden at the back of the pub on Fountain Road where the Road Rats parked their bikes, and when the back doors of the pub were open, as they were during that long hot summer, you could hear the music as clearly as if you were in the pub. The Fountain was great. Although we were underage we had no trouble getting served with drinks and there was also a pool table in there. A lot of the Battersea

Teds came down to The Fountain on a Friday night to bop and jive to the music and show off their latest bit of clobber or footwear. There was also a Ted/rocker gang from Tooting who called themselves The Pharos after the gang of JDs in the film *American Graffiti*. The Pharos were pretty tough and often fought with the Mitcham Skins and the black gang from Tooting Broadway arcade. All the Pharos wore black leather biker jackets with 'The Pharos – London' painted on the back panels. I was really impressed by this and started thinking that it was about time the Sinclair Mob had a real gang name.

The rock'n'roll bands I remember seeing around this time were CSA and The Rocking Devils. CSA were brilliant and could play Gene Vincent stuff just like the Black Leather Rebel himself, and I particularly remember that their version on the Santo and Johnny instrumental, 'Sleepwalk', would always bring the house down. The Rocking Devils, on the other hand, were a bit of a strange band. There were three of them but one was a midget and this earned them the nickname of The Rocking 2. They did a lot of their own songs and I remember that my cousin Ronnie bought a couple of their LPs. I'd guess they were the only ones they ever sold, but they did do a very funny song called 'The Middle-Aged Teddy boy's Lament', which was much loved by the original Teds. But the real darling of the Ted bands was a bunch of mad Welshmen called Crazy Cavan and the Rhythm Rockers. Crazy Cavan had been plugging away since the mid-1960s, playing every backstreet pub and dingy club where the surviving Teddy boys gathered. In 1976 they had a recording contract with a West London label called Charly Records and had released a couple of singles and albums. One of their singles had been a minor hit, troubling the back end of the top 100, called 'My Little Sister's Got a Motorbike'. Crazy Cavan were definitely the best of the Teddy boy bands of that period. They laid down a tough and menacing sound that appealed to Teds, rockers and retros alike and you could also bop to their stuff. They were closely followed in the Ted popularity stakes by a band called The Sunsets. The Sunsets were also fronted by a mad Welshman, by the name of Mike Barratt. He could move on stage just like a young Elvis and had a lot of style and chick appeal. I remember seeing him miming to a song called 'I'm a Nut' by Vern Pullens on my one trip to The Lyceum and he was about the only one who could have pulled it off and still look cool. Eventually Mike changed his name to Shakin' Stevens and the band was known as Shakin' Stevens and the Sunsets until their lead singer auditioned for the Elvis stage show and became a star in his own right. Another good young Ted band were Whirlwind, a four-piece out of West London who favoured gold and silver lamé drape suits and hopped-up Billy Fury covers. There were also The Wild Angels, The Flying Saucers and Johnny and the Jailbreakers.

The Fountain became a regular haunt for us as it was only two steps away from Balham on the Northern Line of the tube. Sometimes we would drive down there on stolen motorbikes and pull off wheelies and wheelspins in the park, much to the amusement of the Road Rats. We also started to use the tube network to get to pubs and clubs on the other side of London. We made trips to the Adam and Eve in Hackney, which had the best selection of rock'n'roll records ever seen on a pub jukebox, and The George, a rock'n'roll pub at Shepherds Bush Green that was frequented by the Bush Rebels and the White City Wild Cats. We went to Neasden to enjoy the delights of Bobbysox with '50s Flash spinning the wax, and The Lyceum in The Strand to see The Wild Wax Roadshow, which consisted of DJs named Jailhouse John, Runaround Stu and Rocking Roy. Our musical knowledge was growing and we started to notice that certain records were guaranteed to fill the dance-floors. There was a lot of stuff I had never heard before. It was kind of rock'n'roll but had a harder and rawer edge to it. I found out it was called rockabilly. I asked Tommy Hogan Snr to play a rockabilly record I had heard at Bobbysox called 'Pegged Pants' by someone named Bill Beech, and he got a sour look on his face. 'That's all that 'billy shit, ain't it?' he asked. From this I learned that the original Teds viewed rockabilly with disdain. The trouble was that most rockabilly recordings pre-dated rock'n'roll by a couple of years and had never been widely available in the 1950s outside of small-town America, so to the Teds this was a 'new' music and they weren't happy about it encroaching on what they considered their own musical territory. Some Ted DJs would happily play rockabilly in their sets and others refused point blank.

There was a Ted DJ from Tooting called Moses, who ran a disco that sometimes played The Fountain on Wednesday nights and was called Transistor Twister, and he refused to play rockabilly requests on his deck. It was a bit strange because the Ted DJs would gladly play the rhythm and blues records that also pre-dated rock'n'roll in some cases, but I suppose it was because they were very close to rock'n'roll in sound and they were great for couples to jive to. Records by the likes of Big Joe Turner, Wynonie Harris, Roy Brown and Louis Jordan were regulars at Ted discos and these men were all basically blues shouters. But the rockabilly sound was becoming very popular amongst the younger crowds of Teds and retros.

Back in Balham I no longer wore my drape suit every day, saving it just for nights out. It was awkward for me as I couldn't live at my parents' flat because most of the time the police were looking for me due to my going over the fence from Stanford House and committing various other crimes. Instead, I kept my clothes at Peter Mayne's ground-floor flat, 1 Ingle House, and I slept most nights in an old Triumph Herald car that Peter's dad owned. The car was parked right next to the porch where we all hung out, so I was never short of company in the evenings. We would hang around listening to music from portable tape decks, bopping and jiving with the girls and drinking cider mixed with gin or vodka straight from the bottle. Most of the teenagers on the estate had to be in by 10 o'clock in the summer, except at weekends, but the wilder cats like me and Peter could do what we liked. Peter's younger brother, Harry, was a soul boy through and through but he had still hung out with us until he got nicked for chinning a copper and got sent to borstal. I was bang in love with his sister, Marina, and sometimes she would sneak out of her flat and come and sit in the car with me and we would have a bit of a kiss and a fumble. I loved the freedom of being on the run and not having to report to anyone, but I had to steal every day in order to keep going. I would have a bath at Peter's flat when his dad was out or I would take a walk up to Streatham and have a wash in the public toilets, and there was also the public bathhouse in Tooting Broadway. I did okay; I was young and fit and doing what I liked. And the weather was fucking great!

Our next meeting with the Balham Boot Boys came about three weeks after the beating at the fair and this time we were more than ready for them. We had been hanging out on a piece of open ground near the health centre on Bedford Hill, just shooting the shit and drinking from the bottle, when we spotted three skinheads on the other side of the hill. Peter said, 'Here, that's one of the mugs from the fair. I recognise him by the tattoo on his neck.' We were across the hill before they spotted us and we surrounded them and brought them to a halt. It was gratifying to see that the skins looked worried now that they were outnumbered. Peter poked the tattooed one in the chest. 'Remember me, you baldy cunt?' The skin tried to make out he didn't remember anything and that he had never seen us before, and his two pals swore the same. Peter smacked him in the face and he hit the pavement as though he'd been pole axed. That was the signal for us to steam in and we started punching and kicking the skins. I caught one of them on the jaw with a lovely right-hander and then kicked him as hard as I could in the back when he went down. We made short work of the three skinheads and, getting carried away with the excitement and bloodlust, we decided to march onto the Bedford Hill Estate and get the rest of them. I wasn't carrying my razor but Ronnie had a bicycle chain and a few of the boys had bits of sand-filled lead pipes that they carried as coshes. As we marched up the hill those of us who didn't have weapons ran in and out of the gardens of the houses looking for things to use to bash our enemies. We were like wild men, buoyed up by the beating we had given the first three and hungry for revenge against the firm who had humiliated us at the fair. No one had to say much, it was as though the beating had rankled and festered in our collective minds and now we saw the chance to avenge it and we didn't need to discuss it. It was funny; one minute we had just been wasting away a summer's afternoon, and the next we were like a howling mob marching on Dr Frankenstein's Castle with murder in our hearts. They say the young can be impetuous and impulsive but that's an understatement. I found an old starting-handle in one of the gardens, Peter had a shovel handle with the blade snapped off, and a few of the lads had milk bottles, the old standby in a street fight.

One of The Wanderers, a mad-looking Ted called Blue, had what looked like a machete. Blue, so called because he wore a sky-blue drape suit, had a reputation as a bit of a loose cannon even among the slackest of big guns. Some of us had been at junior school with Blue, though he had been plain Mickey in those days, and knew how off-key he could become around a bit of violence. His mum was Irish and his dad was Maltese and he had slightly protruding eyeballs, which led to his being teased from a young age. At school he was called 'Marble Eyes', but not for long as he would steam into anyone who even looked at him sideways (forgive the pun) and we soon learned that you didn't take the piss out of Mickey if you wanted to keep all your teeth in your mouth. When I heard that he had become a Ted I was delighted. As the old saying goes, it was better to have him inside your tent pissing out than outside pissing in.

When we reached the top of Bedford Hill we spotted five

skinheads sitting on the wall outside their estate smoking. When they caught sight of us coming up the hill they legged it pretty smartish into the estate. We chased them but they soon lost us over ground that was familiar to them. We raged through the estate for about ten minutes, looking for anyone over the age of 14 and with a shaven head that we could take our violence out on, but they had deserted the gaff. We had run the Balham Boot Boys on their own turf and now we would be even more of a force to be reckoned with. Eddie used a thick marker pen to write 'The Wanderers and Sinclair ran the Boot Boys!' on one of the chute doors, which was already marked with the names of various members of the Boot Boys, and then we marched back down the hill feeling triumphant.

Over the rest of that summer and throughout the next four years we would fight a guerrilla war with the Balham Boot Boys. They would catch a couple of ours and give us a hiding and then we would catch a couple of theirs and do the same. We would fight our last and decisive battle in the spring of 1980, but we would always be natural enemies. In the meantime I decided that the Sinclair Mob needed a proper gang name. After all, we were no longer the Sinclair Mob as the original mob was split into two factions. We sat down and thought about it one evening and, after rejecting the more outrageously silly names, we settled on the Balham Wild Cats. The members of the original Wanderers voted to keep their own name, even though we all hung out together now, but gradually we all became known as the Balham Wild Cats. Now we were a real gang.

Summer Comes to an End

Having noticed that a lot of the original Teddy boys had their left ear pierced with usually a gold sleeper earring, I decided that I would have the same. I was talking about it one night on the porch when Marina's younger sister, Jenny, said she would pierce my ear for me. Not wanting to appear cowardly at the thought of having a sewing needle pushed through the flesh of my ear lobe, though I did not fancy it in the slightest, I suggested that I should wait until I had an earring to put in the hole. The sweet and ever-helpful Jenny was quick to offer me one of her own gold sleepers and so it was settled. Whilst Jenny nipped into her flat to get the needle I managed to neck half a small bottle of vodka that was being passed around, in the hope that it might dull any pain. I was nervous as I watched Jenny hold a lighted match to the end of the needle in order to sterilise it and I was close to fainting as she gripped the bottom of my ear lobe and pulled the skin tight. There was a slight sharp pain as she pushed the needle through, but nothing near as bad as I had been expecting. Within minutes Jenny was wiping my blood from her hands and I was proudly sporting a small gold sleeper in my ear. Once again the gang were slightly in awe of me as I had been the first with an earring. Others would soon follow.

Now that I had the earring my next move was to get a tattoo, preferably in a place where it could be seen. Peter, who had been in borstal and knew about these things, brought out another needle and a bottle of Indian ink. He went through the same routine as Jenny had for my ear piercing, burning the end of the needle with a lighted match, and then he wrapped a lot of thread around the shaft of the needle near the point. Rather like the way we taped our razors, the thread was to stop the needle going too deep into the flesh. Peter dipped the thread end of the needle into the small bottle of ink and, holding my hand firmly on the bonnet of his dad's Triumph Herald and watched by a crowd of open-mouthed Teddy boys and girls, he proceeded to jab the needle into my left wrist. At first it hurt like fuck and I had to use all of my self-control to stop myself pulling my hand away. It felt exactly like what it was – a sharp, pointed piece of steel being plunged in and out of my wrist until it drew blood. The ink from the thread on the needle was black and stained my wrist so that the blood was barely visible, but as soon as Peter wiped the wrist with a paper hankie to see what he was doing you could clearly see the blood bubbling up out of the holes in my wrist. There were oohs and aahs from the onlookers but I forced a smile and winked at Marina.

My first tattoo was a bit wonky but I wore it with pride, as it showed my absolute commitment to my lifestyle. It was the letters 'S.T.U.D.', which was our motto and stood for Stay Ted Until Dead. I would have many more tattoos over the years but none was as excruciatingly painful as that first one. Now that I had been pierced by cold steel myself, I was to find it easier to pierce others.

One Saturday night we were at The Edwardian Club, where I was now a regular, when the word went round that a load of soul boys were coming down from a pub near Brixton market for a ruck. The rumour about the impending rumble was persistent and by 11.30 a lot of the lads in the club, including me, were getting wired and ready. But by closing time the soul boy gang had still not material-ised and people started to relax. A lot of the crowd had left and I was outside the club talking to Bopper and a Ted called Shades when I heard a shout and looked up to see a crowd of about 15 soul boys, both black and white, running up the street towards us. They were on us before we had a chance to move and I found myself dodging a cosh that was swung by someone at the front of the group. The first few runners passed me and then I was faced with being stuck in the middle of the crowd and I began to be hit.

In a situation like this you rarely feel the pain of the blows though the shock of each one tends to register. Someone punched me in the nose and my head seemed to explode. I fell forward with both hands on the pavement, but I quickly managed to get back upright and took another punch to the side of my face. It was all very confusing for a minute, as I was being hit by people who were running past me. Then I was faced with a kid about my own age who threw two punches at my face in quick succession. I was starting to regain my senses and managed to dodge the first punch and twist so that the second hit me in the shoulder. I threw a punch of my own and missed completely. I was off balance and backed up against a window of the Loughborough pub and this kid really started unloading punches on me. I was taking a beating and then, somehow, I had my cut-throat razor in my hand. I struck out with the blade and felt it hit something, so I jerked my wrist down and back just as I had practiced so many times in front of the mirror. For a moment nothing happened and then the kid stopped throwing punches and stepped back. I could clearly see by the light coming from the pub window that I had left a mark down his face all the way from forehead to chin. Then, as if in slow motion, his face seemed to fall apart and the blood gushed down his chest. The soul boy screamed and staggered away, holding his face together. To be quite honest I was shocked and sickened by what I had done. I wanted to take it back, run after the kid and say I was sorry. I looked down at the razor in my hand and there didn't even seem to be any blood on the blade. My heart was racing and I felt like crying. Then I felt a clump on the back of my head and turned and saw I had been hit with half a pool cue. Without thinking I struck out again with the razor and missed the kid who had hit me by about an inch. There was still fighting going on and I saw that two soul boys had Shades on the ground out in the road and were kicking lumps out of him. I slipped the razor into my pocket and drop-kicked one of the lads who was doing Shades.

Then, as quickly as it had started, the fight was over and the soul boys were legging it back up to Brixton Road. There were a couple of Teds lying in the gutter and moaning in pain and someone had put the windscreen through on one of the classic cars. The soul boys had retreated when a handful of bikers, who had still been inside the club finishing their drinks, had clattered down the stairs sounding like an army of elephants. I found out later that nearly all of the soul boys had been armed. Though no one on our side had been stabbed, a couple of Teds had head wounds from being coshed and Shades had a bad limp from being kicked in the legs when he was on the ground. I looked over at the pavement where I had used my razor and saw a dark spatter of blood on the dusty concrete. I swallowed some bile that had quickly worked its way up my throat and turned away. I was grabbed around the shoulders by a Ted called Johnny Virgo who was very excited. 'Fuck! You cut the fucking face off that geezer! Nice one Cyril!' Everyone was looking at me and I shrugged. One of the older originals gave me a little pat on the cheek. 'Well done, young 'un,' he said. 'You stood your ground.' I shrugged again. 'He didn't even have a tool,' I muttered, still feeling sick at what I had done. I could clearly picture the moment when his face seemed to fall apart. The older Ted lifted his shirt and displayed a terrible-looking scar that dissected his stomach. 'That's what those fucking soul boys did to me last time,' he said, vehemently. 'Stuck a fucking bayonet in my guts and left me for dead. I was with my bird at the time and they were mob-handed. I'd be happy if you slashed every one of the cunts!' I seized on this justification to help salve my conscience. He was right, it could just as easily have been me who was cut in the heat of battle. The soul boys hadn't rushed us for any reason other than to do us violence. I rationalised it for a while and soon it seemed more of an achievement than a badge of shame. In a short while I was lapping up the praise and the pats on the back.

The next week I turned up at The Fountain and a few of the lads who had been at The Edwardian Club were there. 'Want a pint, Razor?' I was asked. And from then on everyone called me Razor Smith. I had earned my nickname. The first cutting had been the hardest and most traumatic for me but after that it came easy. I began to carry my razor everywhere and would flick it out at the slightest sign of trouble. I became almost manic in my quickness to lay the blade across someone's face and I thought very little about the damage I was doing. All I knew was that my reputation on the Teddy boy scene was growing and I was happy with that. The summer became a blur of travelling to Teddy boy pubs and clubs, getting steaming drunk, pulling birds and fighting anyone who didn't have a quiff. The heat wave held out until the middle of September and then, one afternoon as Peter, Big Nose Eamon and me were hot-wiring a stolen Honda 250 motorbike on the Sinclair Estate, the rain came. It seemed to come out of nowhere, big fat raindrops that burst on the parched dry earth and the dusty concrete and stained them dark once again. I remember we were all wearing cap-sleeved T-shirts and jeans and we stood there with our arms and faces raised to the sky whooping like a trio of lunatics as our clothes became soaked through and the rain bounced off our faces and filled our mouths. The Long Hot One was finally over.

For me that summer of 1976 marked the end of something – and the beginning of something else. At the start of the summer I had been a long-haired trendy virtually unknown outside my own estate and with the idea that I might like to be a Teddy boy, and by the time the rains came I was a slick, strutting demon with a reputation as a blade merchant and with a gang of like-minded kids behind me. Not only that, I had upped my criminal activity and had started committing armed robberies along with Peter. There was no way that I wasn't heading for trouble and plenty of it. I was going to be leaving the scene for a while, but the movement that I had played a part in reviving would carry on without me and grow.

In February 1977, Peter and I were arrested for armed robbery, possession of firearms and grievous bodily harm. We attended the Old Bailey in May of that year, dressed in our drape suits, and we were each sentenced to three years imprisonment. In June the newspapers were full of the fighting between Teddy boys and punk rockers on the King's Road in West London. Many of the Balham Wild Cats were involved. I was only sick that I had missed it. I was sure that by the time I came back the scene would be dead and gone. I had no idea that it was to grow and grow, but also that I would play a major part in the violence that would eventually kill it off.

Part Two

The Rebel Teds

Rebel reb (a) l, n – someone who refuses to conform to the generally accepted modes of behaviour, dress, etc.

Return of the Rocker

The South London I came back to in May 1979 after 27 months of incarceration in the juvenile prison system looked a bit different, but then so was I. Now taller, broader, fitter and meaner than when I had gone away, I had spent my time fighting the system and trying to escape at every opportunity. I had been beaten, drugged, put into a straitjacket and forced to endure months of solitary confinement. Now I was close to actual release and had been given a seven-day home leave in order to acclimatise myself with the outside world. I had gone in as a fairly violent kid, and I was coming out as a seriously disturbed young man who was determined to catch up on all I had missed. As I stepped off the train at Streatham Hill station I noticed a spray-painted symbol on the wall facing me. It was a big letter 'A' enclosed by a circle with the word 'Punks' below it. I knew what the symbol meant: it was the punk rockers' sign for 'Anarchy', which seemed to be their battle cry. I had come across punk rockers in jail and had fought them at every meeting. Ever since they had burst onto the teen scene in a rain of gob and expletives they had proved themselves the natural enemy of the Teds.

My first sight of punk rock had been in November 1976 when the *Sun* newspaper had run a centre-page spread on the new fashion. They had spiky-haired models dressed up in bondage trousers and ripped T-shirts and with safety pins for earrings. The *Sun* said they called themselves punk rockers because the American word 'punk' meant 'something worthless' and they classed themselves as 'outcasts of society'. I almost pissed myself laughing at their outlandish dress and I remember thinking it was too ridiculous ever to catch on.

Then, in December, a bunch of punk rockers, including the members of a punk band called The Sex Pistols, appeared on a live-broadcast, early-evening television news show to be interviewed by Bill Grundy. Grundy, who looked a cranky-faced fucker at the best of times, seemed to take an instant dislike to the punks and wound them up until they committed that most terrible of television sacrilege and said the word 'fuck' on prime-time TV. The *Sun*, which only weeks before had been happy to announce the arrival of punk rock, suddenly went all moral outrage, like a Victorian schoolmarm catching sight of an uncovered male ankle, and it gave them more front-page publicity than they could ever have dreamed about. Within a month there were more green Mohicans in London than in a South American parrot sanctuary. The first bit of trouble between punks and Teds started in West London, STUD's stomping ground, when the local Teddy boys spotted punk rockers wearing drape jackets with badges and pins stuck all over them. Not content with this, punks also seemed to favor the infamous brothel creepers as footwear. Hijacking the Teddy boys' gear and then treating it with this sort of disrespect was never going to endear the new subculture to the old. So the punks were promptly thrashed. From then on the punks became fair game to the Teds and vice versa. The original Teds, though outraged enough at what they saw as the theft of their own unique style, were also incensed at the punks' treatment of the Queen. When The Sex Pistols released their recording of a song called 'God Save the Queen', in the spring of 1977, they compounded their error by promoting the single with T-shirts showing Her Maj with a safety pin through her nose. To the mainly right-wing and ultra-royalist original Teds this was like a gob in the face of all they believed in. Punk rockers moved to the top of the hate list.

The trouble between the Teds and punks came to a head in June 1977 in the much-publicised battle of the King's Road. The King's Road was well known for its up-market boutiques and expensive properties and it was where the con artist who was behind The Sex Pistols, Malcolm McLaren, had a clothes shop called Sex. Vivienne Westwood designed many of the clothes that McLaren sold, and punk rockers were always hanging around at the shop and in the local cafes and pubs. The punks had made the King's Road their meeting place during the early summer months, so the Teds knew where to find them. A gang of Fulham Teddy boys, incensed that the punks were on what they classed as part of their manor, descended on SW1 one Saturday afternoon in June and, after the insults had been traded back and forth for a while and a few bottles had been thrown, they commenced battle. The actual fighting was short and bloody and was soon broken up by the arrival of the police in great numbers, but it attracted the attention of the news media and made the daily papers.

By the following Saturday word had spread through the Teddy boy clubs all over London that the punks were going to have a show of force on the King's Road and that they were gagging for a tear-up. The Teds took up the rumoured challenge and Ted gangs from Brixton, Chiswick, Shepherds Bush, Acton, Poplar, and Islington and, of course, Balham arrived in SW1 fired up and ready to rumble. There was the odd skirmish but it was generally agreed that the punks had shit themselves and stayed away. The few punks who were on show had to be protected by the police who, hearing rumours of the impending battle, showed up in force.

Once again the newspapers lapped it up and told of 'terrified tourists', 'snarling punks' and 'baying gangs of Teddy boys armed to the teeth with razors, bike-chains and knuckledusters'. From then on the Teds vs Punks saga became a regular column filler in the tabloids and local papers. On Tuesday 26 July the front page of the *Sun* newspaper was taken up by a picture of Fulham Teddy boy, Jimmy Smart, resplendent in drape jacket and brothel creepers and carrying a brick in each hand as he marched down the King's Road in search of punks. The headline read 'King's Road Warrior Caught In The Act'. On page five Jimmy eloquently explained why he hated punk rockers: 'A couple of them stabbed my mate a few weeks ago … they're skinny little bleeders and half of them are queer.' Also in the same paper was an old mate of mine from Clapham who had been arrested along with 12 others on the same day. Paul Hardings, also known as Cut-Throat Paul because he was reputed to carry a gold-plated cut-throat razor with his initials engraved on the handle – now that's Teddy boy class – had come down to Sinclair a few times in 1976 and was a regular at The Edwardian Club and The Fountain. Paul told the *Sun* reporter, Keith Deves: 'There was about 60 punks and they came at us with knives, belts and iron-bars. We will have another go at them, make sure.' On 30 July the *Melody Maker*, a music paper, had a two-page spread headlined 'Fighting In The Streets' by Chris Welch, in which they investigated the cause of the, by now, weekly battles. A Teddy boy called Rebel Eddie, described as the 'operator of a Teds' disco', stated, rather disingenuously, 'I just cannot stand punk rockers. Why they can't find something original beats me.' His mate, Big John, explained how the aggro around Sloane Square and the King's Road was organised by announcements made over the PA systems at gigs and discos. The punk side of the argument was given by two punk rockers, one of whom was the editor/writer of punk fanzine *Sniffin' Glue*, Danny Baker, who went on to become a media personality in the late '80s. He said: 'The Teds only attack punks to get their names in the papers. The last time they had any publicity was in '58 or something, for wrecking cinemas.' The gulf between the Teds and punks seemed insurmountable.

The fighting, if you could really call it that, went on throughout the summer of 1977, but there was such a police presence on the King's Road every Saturday that it normally came down to Teds and punks standing on opposite sides of the street shouting threats and insults at each other. This spectacle received so much publicity that before the summer was out it had actually become a tourist attraction: see the Houses of Parliament, the Tower of London, Big Ben – and the Teds and punks kicking off on the King's Road. But the real fighting was being done out of the gaze of the police, reporters and tourists. Blood was being spilled in the backstreets, in the parks and outside the pubs and clubs, mainly after the sun went down. The King's Road was the front, a smoke-and-mirrors trick to take attention off the real war.

On 16 August 1977 the Teds suffered their worst blow since Eddie Cochran had been killed in a car crash in April 1960, when Elvis 'the King of rock'n'roll' Presley dropped dead at his home in Memphis, aged 42. Although the Elvis of the 1970s was a long way from the snake-hipped 'Hillbilly Cat' of the early 1950s, and the music he had been recording for more than a decade could in no way be described as rock'n'roll, the Teds of England felt his passing most keenly. The early, young Elvis was rock'n'roll and had always been a god to the Teds: his 1950s recordings, his style of dress, his pink Cadillacs and – oh wow! – his hair! So far as a lot of Teds were concerned, Elvis was 'the man' and to lose him now, though he be only a rather substantial shadow of his younger self, caused an outpouring of genuine grief in the Teddy boy community. And, of course, the reporters and photographers from the tabloid press were there to catch the Teds at their most vulnerable moment and plaster it all over the front pages of the newspapers. How the punks chuckled to see their hated enemies in tears and wiping the snot away, as they grieved for their dead god.

The death of Elvis at the height of the war between Teds and punks did plenty to fuel the enmity between the two groups. Punks began spray-painting walls around London with messages designed to incense Teds, such as 'Elvis rocks ... in his box' and 'The king is fat ... and dead!' The violence between the Teds and punks got so bad that not even high-profile punk rockers were exempt. Both Johnny Rotten and Sid Vicious of the Sex Pistols, were attacked by Teds wielding iron bars. The girlfriend of Sid Vicious, Nancy Spungen, was arrested for having a truncheon in her handbag and charged with carrying an offensive weapon. She told Horseferry Road magistrates court that she had it 'as protection against Teddy boys' because she was a punk rocker. She was fined £20 plus £25 costs. The fighting continued.

The posturing on the King's Road carried on as Teds and punks were battling it out all over London. The only difference was there were no newspaper reporters and photographers to record it all. Some of the fighting was vicious and I was to see the results of it in the borstal system as magistrates and judges began to take a hard line with the combatants. I met a couple of French Teddy boys in Ashford who had crossed the channel specifically to fight the punks and ended up jailed for their troubles. They had been fighting the punks and skinheads in France and, in a true spirit of international Teddy boy solidarity, had come with a gang of their countrymen to help out their rock'n'roll brethren in London. In the *Sun* of 26 July 1977 the headline was 'Britain Is Invaded By Les Teddies' and the article went on to report that port officials had been warned to be on the lookout for gangs of French Teddy boys, known as Les Blousons Noirs (The Black Leathers) who were coming to London for the fighting. Fining a French Teddy boy £5 for carrying a cut-throat razor on the King's Road, a Chelsea magistrate warned that in future he would be handing out immediate detention orders to young people, from England or abroad, for carrying weapons.

The borstals in the south began to see a steady trickle of Teds, punks and skinheads who had received their sentences for fighting each other. Many of my old friends were to join me in incarceration for a while, including Bopper Hogan from Battersea, Stud from Shepherds Bush, The Duke of Earl, a huge Teddy boy who used to work behind the bar at The George pub in Hammersmith, Johnny Virgo from Brixton and Gene Vincent Steve from Putney, all jailed for fighting punks and skinheads. For a while borstal was a micro-cosm of what was going on in the outside world as violence and vendettas between the subcultures carried on as usual. The news from my own manor was that the juniors were now coming of age and all well involved in the rock'n'roll scene. My brother Mick, or Rocky as he was nicknamed, Harry Mayne, now known as Mad Harry for his all-in fighting style, Dennis Budd, Adrian Street and a bunch of kids from an estate further up Thornton Road had joined with the remnants of the Balham Wild Cats and The Wanderers to form a formidable gang. The main enemy was now the punk rockers but the skinhead gangs were also on the rise as the National Front embarked on a major recruiting campaign. Race-hate organisations like the NF and the British Movement loved the skinheads because they were mostly young, stupid and had the balls to do their dirty work for them. Most of the skinheads had no idea how they were being manipulated by right-wing organisations into being their military arm.

The original skinheads of 1968 had been an integrated subculture who followed the ska and reggae music of Jamaica and were welcomed as friends by the black youths to their pubs and clubs. But the new breed of skinheads had come out of the football hooligan culture and were into violence more than music. Some of them still listened to reggae but they justified their racist stance by claiming they were against 'the Pakis' rather than the Jamaicans, as though there were certain degrees of racism that they would not go to. I don't know if it came as any surprise to anyone when on 4 July 1978 the front page of the *Daily Mirror* exposed the National Front as a 'racist organisation', but I'd lay odds that the skins already knew it.

Some of the Teds also dabbled in racist organisations but not to the extent that they would go to meetings or on marches with their old enemies the skinheads. The Teds were more institutionally racist; they would be racist if the opportunity presented itself but they would not go seeking the opportunity. A few of the Battersea

Teds openly sported British Movement T-shirts or badges but they mixed with black and Asian Teds and there was never any trouble between them.

In 1978 the film version of the musical *Grease* was released and became very popular. It starred a be-quiffed John Travolta as the leather-jacket wearing leader of the T-Birds, a gang of comical juvenile delinquents at a 1950s high school, and Olivia Newton-John as the hottest co-ed ever to spray on a pair of pedal pushers. The music wasn't very '50s rock'n'roll but several songs from the film made the British top ten, including a couple of number ones, and the showing of extracts of the film on *Top of the Pops* to accompany the records did much to recruit a new army of kids for the Teddy boy/retro movement. The newspapers, and the *Sun* in particular, did much to promote the relative wholesomeness of the 1950s fad. In November 1976 the *Sun* had featured a centre-page spread of models in punk gear, but in June 1978 it was rooting for the Teds with its centre-page layout of models in rock'n'roll garb, including information on where to get the clothes. The popularity of *Grease* swelled the ranks of the rock'n'rollers but, though on the wane, punk was far from dead. So, once again, in the summer of 1978 the Teds and punks invaded the King's Road for what was fast becoming the annual summer punch-up and the press were waiting.

By May 1979, as I was stepping off a train at Streatham Hill station in my ill-fitting Teddy boy suit, the lines had been clearly drawn but the war was starting to drag its feet. The shouting and wanker signs of the King's Road were the front, but it was all about skirmishing in the backstreets and keeping off other people's turf. The spark was starting to go out of it and if we weren't careful it could be all over by Christmas. I had been away for a long time and felt that I had been missing out on all the excitement. Now I was back and I was determined to liven things up. I had been in at the start and I was going to be in at the end – no matter what the cost.

The Rise of the Rebel Teds

Sinclair Estate seemed to shimmer in the mid-May 1979 sunshine as I looked down the slight incline of Thornton Road. The heat was pretty intense and it was only 11 in the morning. For just a second it was as if I had never been away and this was still the summer of '76. I was sweating in my too-tight suit and grubby shirt. My clothes had lain in a storage box since May 1977 and had not been washed or cleaned in all that time. I took my drape jacket off and slung it over my shoulder as I walked the last 100 yards to the boundaries of the estate. Top of my list was to get into some more comfortable clothes and I hoped there was something that still fitted me left at my parents' flat.

The first familiar face I saw when I entered the estate was my old pal Joey Finn. Joey had shot up while I had been away and he was now a shade under six feet but still skinny. He greeted me with a big smile and a pat on the back. Joey had been one of the '70s kids who had moved to McGregor porch when the estate split in 1976 and I noticed that he was still a square. At one stage he had been talking about becoming a skinhead but I was glad to see that he hadn't made good his threat. It was bad enough having squares and soul boys on the estate without having to put up with the baldy firm as well. Joey was on his way up to Streatham and said he'd catch me later. There didn't seem to be anyone else around so I carried on down to Sinclair House. The lift still smelled of piss – some things just never change – and I was glad to get out on the third floor. My mum greeted me at the front door and I was welcomed back into the family home. My sister, Samantha, was at school and Mick was living in a probation hostel at Tulse Hill as a condition of his bail on a charge of car theft, but my dad was there and glad to see me back. Mum and dad told me how Mick had come to be in a hostel. It turned out that he and Harry Mayne had been caught after a car chase with the police in a stolen Cortina. Mick had given false details and, as it was his first nicking, the police had accepted them and bailed him to the hostel. So he had taken it as the opportunity to leave home. He was hoping to get a flat of his own once he had finished his time at the hostel. After a huge fried breakfast cooked by my mum I went to the bedroom that Mick and I had once shared to look for some clothes. I found an old white cotton shirt that still fitted me and borrowed a pair of Mick's jeans that I found in the wardrobe. I also found my old Commando boots, a bit battered but nothing a lick of polish wouldn't sort out. On the inside of the wardrobe door Mick had sellotaped newspaper cuttings from the Teds vs punks battles on the King's Road and I read them with great interest. I had never seen the newspaper reports, as we had no access to papers in the borstal system. I had only heard about the fighting from some of the people who had been nicked for it, so I was surprised at just how much news coverage it had been given.

After taking a bath, to wash the prison smell off me, and dressing in my fresh clothes I was delighted to find that Mick had left behind a pretty decent record collection and a box Dansette record player. I noticed that Mick had quite a few rockabilly LPs and a lot of stuff that was new to me, so I put a record called 'Capitol Rockabilly' on the deck and had a listen. In the borstal system I had been able to borrow a transistor radio now and again, but it had been pretty hard to find any decent music on any station. Then, as a direct result of the rock'n'roll protest march of 1976, the BBC had relented and given a rock'n'roll DJ named Stuart Colman a regular one-hour slot on Radio 1 on Saturday evenings. The show, called *It's Rock'n'Roll*, was the only place on the airwaves that catered to lovers of real rock'n'roll and I became a regular listener. It was by listening to Stuart Colman's show that I was able to hear records like 'Black Slacks' by Joe Bennett & The Sparkletones and 'Leroy's Back

In Jail Again' by Jack Scott and others that were being played in the rock'n'roll clubs. This was the only way I had been able to keep in touch with the music, so I had a lot of catching up to do.

I found the rockabilly sound much edgier than rock'n'roll and the best recordings had a hypnotic, echoey, slapped bass in the background that was infectious and made me want to dance. I had heard that rockabilly had taken over a lot of the clubs and that there were now people who actually called themselves 'rockabilly rebels' and had their own style of dancing and dressing. I was keen to see what that was all about and how this new style differed from the Teds. Though I had started to get into the rockabilly sound towards the end of the summer of '76, I still classed myself as a Teddy boy and I had yet to see anything that might make me change from this.

After listening to a bit of music I decided it was time to get out and about and see what was cooking with the old gang, so I greased up my hair and spent some time getting my quiff to hang right before going anywhere. Mum and dad told me that Peter and Harry Mayne now had a flat down at Poynders Gardens near Clapham South and that a lot of people went there, so I would probably get to see Mick there as well. Dad slipped me a few quid for walking-around money and I set off in the bright May sunshine. After my long months in underground solitary confinement cells and marching the concrete yards of borstal it felt really great to be home again. Just walking down a quiet street with my hands in my pockets was a buzz and I was going to enjoy every minute of my seven-day release.

The streets were quiet and I was walking along whistling when I heard a loud screech of tyres behind me and a big car skidded up to the kerb. For a second I panicked. I wasn't used to cars and I thought there had been an accident. I stood there looking at the car, which had stopped a couple of feet away from me, and was wondering what to do next when the horn sounded with two loud blasts, making me jump again. Then Big Nose Eamon poked his head out of the driver's window with a large smile on his face. 'Razor! I thought it was you. Mickey said you might be getting out today!' I went over to the kerb and Eamon reached across and opened the passenger door. 'Jump in,' he said. It was great to see Eamon again and he hadn't changed much except for the fact that he was now a '50s hoodlum in a car instead of on a pushbike. 'Oh, wait till the lads see you! You've been away for fucking years!'

The car, a nearly new Vauxhall, belonged to Eamon's dad, but once he had passed his driving test the old man had insured him and let him drive it. He told me that he was working in a factory but he had taken the day off and had been hanging around the estate in the hope of seeing me. Joey Finn had told him that he'd seen me leaving the estate. Eamon filled me in on a bit of what had been happening since I had been away, though I knew some of it. Peter Mayne, who had been sentenced to three years with me at the Old Bailey, had been released early on compassionate grounds when both his parents died in quick succession. The council had given him a three-bedroom flat on Poynders Gardens Estate and he had been granted custody of his brother, Harry, and his two sisters, Marina and Jenny, who were in their teens. His two younger brothers, Robert and Timmy, had been taken into care. The flat had quickly become the meeting place and unofficial headquarters for the old Sinclair gang and the place to be if you were into the 1950s scene. Eamon told me that Peter had gone even further off the rails since his parents had died and was considered to be slightly crazy, even by the people who had known him for years. Just before I was released he had shaved his hair into a Mohican and tried to form a rockabilly gang called the Mohican Warriors. So far he'd only had a couple of takers, including my old Teddy boy pal Johnny Virgo, but he had even designed his own gang logo of a laughing skull with a Mohican haircut and they were wearing it on their jackets. The Mohican Warriors spent their days pissed and their nights out thieving, burgling shops, offices and factories. Johnny Virgo was a good car thief and they stole a different car every night.

Mick, Harry, Alan, Dennis and a few others had formed a loose gang and were calling themselves The Mustangs and were heavily into the rockabilly scene, though they actually called themselves 'rebel Teds' rather than rockabilly rebels. The older lot who used to be the Balham Wild Cats and The Wanderers still hung out, but most of them were working now. They could be counted on if there was any serious trouble with other gangs, and they still turned up at the pubs and clubs on Friday and Saturday nights, but they were no longer really a gang. I heard that The Edwardian Club had closed down in 1977 but that other clubs were now taking its place. Tommy Hogan Snr was still dee-jaying, but at a pub in the Elephant & Castle called The Duke of Clarence, or The Clarence for short. The top club now was the Chick-A Boom, held at The St Helier Arms in Carshalton on Wednesday and Saturday nights. I asked Eamon about the rockabilly thing I'd been hearing about and he smiled. 'It's the bollocks!' he said, enthusiastically. 'Forget Teddy boys, they're fucking old hat, mate. All that paying out fortunes to get suits made and dancing to Connie Francis records, fuck all that! The rockabillies wear '50s box suits at £3 a throw from charity shops, just like we did when we started out, or leather jackets, jeans and boots. Some of them wear donkey jackets! The fucking Teds hate us for it, but there's more rockabillies and rebel Teds now than there ever were Teddy boys, they're outnumbered, so there's fuck all they can do about it.'

My loyalty to the Teds was still strong, but I was intrigued by rockabilly. It turned out that the rebel Teds were a kind of way station between the new and old subcultures; a stop-off point for those who had been Teddy boys but also fancied the idea of rockabilly. They kept their drape suits and brothel creepers, wearing them for special occasions, but also wore the drainpipe jeans and leather jackets of the rockabilly rebels as casual wear. There was also a difference in the hairstyles. The Teddy boys favoured the old Tony Curtis look with a quiff at the front and a duck's arse (or 'ducktail' as the rockabillies called it after the Joe Clay classic 'Don't Mess With My Ducktail', which was filling the dance floors at the time), whereas the rockabillies went for either the 'GI', i.e. shaved back and sides like the American army, or the Mac Curtis, which is a flat top with the hint of a quiff. Mac Curtis was an obscure rockabilly singer from Texas whose records the rockabillies had taken to their hearts and whose hairstyle was visible on the cover of those records. The rebel Teds, whilst willing to don rockabilly duds and dance to their music, usually kept their Teddy boy hairstyles. But to outsiders and other subcultures these subtleties were lost and the rocking crowd were all classed as Teds. Eamon pulled out his wallet and handed me a frayed newspaper cutting from the *Daily Mirror*. 'That's us!' he said, proudly. The headline read 'Teddy boys Are Back In Gang Battle' and went on to explain that 'Gangs of "new style" Teddy boys' fought a pitched battle at Margate on Bank Holiday Monday and 21 people were arrested. A police spokesman said: 'There has been a revival of the Teddy boy cult.' However, the 'Teddy boys' were in fact rockabillies and rebel Teds.

Musically the rebel Teds had the best of both worlds. In the clubs there were certain records that brought the Teds out onto the dance floor and others that brought the rockabillies out, and it wasn't unusual to see either camp leave the floor in disgust if the right tunes weren't played. The rebel Teds could dance to anything, and they did, from 'Mister Lee' by The Bobbettes to 'One Hand Loose' by Charlie Feathers. In 1979 the dance-floor fillers for the Teds were jivers from Bill Haley and boppers from Eddie Cochran and Jerry Lee Lewis, and the rockabillies were big on Gene Vincent who, despite being an original Ted favourite, was considered wild enough for the rockabillies, and The Johnny Burnette Trio. But you could hear a wide spectrum of rock'n'roll-type music in the clubs from 1940s blues shouters to early 1960s surf music. There was something for nearly everyone. I would learn more about rockabillies and rebel Teds in the next few days but for now it was time to meet the gang.

Eamon pulled in through the main gates of a dirty-looking red-brick estate adjacent to Agnes Riley Park and drove around a winding road until he spotted a parking space between a burned-out Ford Corsair and a battered-looking transit van. Poynders had always been a bit of a rough estate when we were growing up and it hadn't changed much. I remembered that one of the best fighters on Poynders when we had been kids had been a tough little ginger-haired kid called Lawrence O'Brian. I had fought LOB, as he was known, in Agnes Riley Park one day and he kneed me in the face. That was the first time I'd had my nose broken, though not the last, and I was ten years old. As we got out of the car I reminded Eamon of LOB. 'Yeah, he still lives here,' he said. 'He comes over to the flat sometimes to hang out.' I shook my head in wonder. 'Don't tell me LOB is a Ted?' I asked. Eamon laughed. 'Nah, he's a smoothie. But we get on okay. Mick Garry sometimes comes around as well.' Mick Garry was another one of my old sparring partners. How times had changed.

As we walked from the car I could hear loud music coming from one of the flats. It was Johnny Restivo singing 'The Shape I'm In', and I noticed a huge Confederate battle flag draped across the open window of one of the ground floor flats. The flag was rippling and, as there was no breeze to speak of, it could only have been the bass from the speakers that was causing it to move. I stopped in front of the window and began to bop, my steel-toed boots kicking up a bit of dust from the dry earth, and Eamon joined in. The record came to an end and in the relative silence I shouted at the window, 'Oi, you fucking greasers! Turn that shit off and stick a bit of Johnny Rotten on!' There was an outraged roar from inside the flat and then three figures leapt through the open window with all the gymnastic panache of Errol Flynn in a pirate epic. Harry was shirtless and wearing Commando boots and drainpipe jeans with a heavy

Triumph motorbike drive-chain as a belt, and carrying a small camper's axe. I didn't know the other two lads but they were similarly attired and both waving bicycle chains. I stood there for a second and then spread my arms wide. 'What, only three of you?' I asked. 'What sort of gang is that?' Harry's mouth dropped open for a second and then he whooped, dropped his axe and threw his arms around me. 'Razor! You cunt! It's great to see you out! Fucking hell! We thought it was the skins from Cubbitt House.' He turned to the other two, who had relaxed now, and said, 'This is Razor, Rocky Mick's brother. He's been away in borstal for years!' The other two put their weapons away and came and gave me the rebel handshake (hands clasped around each other's thumbs). Harry introduced us. 'This is Gordon, he's out of Redskin Village, and this is Perry, he's living with us in the flat for a while.' 'Redskin Village' is what some people call Mitcham, an area on the outskirts of South London heading into the Surrey postcode, because of the number of retired travellers living there. It was also called 'injun country' because it was hard to pass through without getting yourself scalped. 'Hello stranger,' I heard, and I looked at the open window that the lads had jumped from. There were a couple of girls leaning out of it and one of them was Marina, my old girlfriend from '76. I didn't recognise the other girl but she looked like a young Liz Taylor, all jet-black hair and dark flashing eyes. I winked at the girls and they both smiled back. Harry slapped me on the back. 'Let's get inside,' he said. 'It's party time!' It was good to be home.

The Party Lights

My coming-out party was a raucous event and I got to meet a lot of old friends and make a few new ones. The interior of the flat at Poynders Gardens was clean and well furnished, which I put down to the girls who were living there. As well as Harry's two sisters, Jenny and Marina, there was also the Liz Taylor lookalike I had seen at the window, whose name was Elaine. It turned out that Elaine was living at the flat because she didn't get on with her mother and had tried to strangle her on one occasion, which meant that she had to leave home. She was half Sicilian and had the fiery temperament that goes with that heritage, and I liked her. Marina looked pretty much the same as she had when I went away. We had written to each other for a few months at the start of my sentence, but then her letters had tailed off and I found out that she was going out with a Brixton Ted named Boogie. He had dumped her after a couple of months and that was the last I had heard, but from the looks I was getting from her I guessed she would be amenable to taking up where we had left off. The biggest surprise for me was Jenny. When I had gone away she had been just a little kid with a ponytail and an attitude. She used to hang around with my little sister Samantha and they were an annoyance more than anything, always wanting to knock about with us. But now Jenny had grown into a beautiful young woman. She was going out with Gordon, the rebel Ted from Redskin Village, and they made a good couple. Harry's girlfriend, who turned up at the flat later, was like a sexier version of Marilyn Monroe, if there could be such a thing, and her name was Kim. Perry, the other rebel Ted who had jumped out of the window at me, was also staying in the flat as he was on the run from the police for some petty thievery and jumping bail on an assault charge relating to a gang fight with the Clapham skins and he was in an on/off relationship with Elaine. I was also surprised at the number of rockabillies and rebel Teds who turned up at the flat during the day and into the evening, and they seemed to be coming from all over South London. There were Mitch and Snapper from the Streatham Teds, Little Roy and his girlfriend Billie from Clapham Junction, half-caste Lloyd, Little Bopper and Steve the Spiv from Battersea, and Moses, an original Ted and DJ, from Tooting. Moses always had a fat Teddy Girl in tow I was to find out, though not the same one but a succession of them. It was also at this party that I was to meet a rockabilly by the name of Joe Kennedy who would become my good pal throughout many battles and punch-ups over the next few years.

The music was blaring, the drink was flowing and couples were jiving in a cleared space in the front room. I was getting fairly drunk but feeling great to be back amongst what I classed as my people. The front door of the flat was always open and it seemed as though I was shaking hands with someone new every few minutes. Just as it was getting dark I made my way out of the front door and onto the balcony to clear my head with some fresh air. A couple of the Battersea mob were out there already puffing on a joint. I knew nothing about drugs and had only met one other person who smoked cannabis and that was a hippy bloke in borstal. The Battersea lot were pretty casual about their drug use. They smoked cannabis, which they called 'draw', and also 'bombed speed', which meant wrapping amphetamine sulphate in a cigarette paper and then swallowing it with a drink. They asked me if I wanted a puff on the joint but I shook my head. As far as I was concerned, drugs were for pill-popping skinheads and glue-sniffing punk rockers and I didn't want to go there. I suppose it was safe to say that I disapproved of all drug taking, as I had grown up in the company of Irish Catholic hard drinkers who saw smoking a joint as no different to being a raving junkie.

Dennis Budd came out on the balcony with a half-empty bottle of Olde English cider clutched in his mitt and a half-cut look on his face. I liked Dennis. He had been one of the up-and-coming youngsters when I had gone away and now he was a fully-fledged rebel Ted. He offered me a cigarette and a swig from his bottle, the latter of which I declined, and tried to speak seriously. 'What was it like in prison?' he asked. I looked at him standing there with the bottle cradled in his arms and a cigarette dangling from his lips, eyes screwed up to avoid the spiralling smoke, and I wondered if I should tell him the truth: how I had been beaten, forcibly drugged and put in a straitjacket; how I had spent months in solitary confinement in an underground cell slowly sinking into a trough of despair and near madness until I tried to kill myself; how I had opened the face of a kid from North London with a razor and had bitten off part of another kid's ear because extreme violence was the only way to survive the system; or how I had helped another kid attempt to commit suicide by cutting his wrist for him with a broken light bulb, and how his skin had split like paper under the glass and then gushed blood and nearly killed him. I knew that Dennis would probably never spend a day in prison and that the truth would only sicken him. I flicked my butt over the balcony and watched it hit the road with a shower of sparks. 'It was just like 'Jailhouse Rock',' I said. 'Only without the singing and dancing.' Dennis nodded his head wisely. 'That's what I thought,' he said.

There was a bit of a commotion coming from inside the flat and Jenny poked her head out of the front door and said, 'Mick's here!' I had been hoping to see my little brother all day. The last time I had seen him had been in 1978 when he, Harry, Samantha and my mum had come down to Kent to visit me in Rochester borstal. I remember how proud I had been when Mick and Harry had both turned up in drape suits, even though Harry's had been bright yellow! Even Samantha had been wearing a Teddy Girl drape jacket. I was eager to see Mick again but, apparently, not as eager as some of the girls in the flat. I wondered at their obvious excitement as word spread through the flat. 'Rocky Mick's here! Rocky Mick's here!' I was almost knocked over as a couple of Teddy Girls rushed to the window of the front room and I grabbed Harry by the arm. 'What the fuck?' I asked. Harry smiled and shrugged. 'It's Mick, ain't it. The birds love him cos he's such a flash fucker. Thinks he's fucking Elvis.' There was now a crowd gathered at the open front-room windows, with girls at the front, and I pushed my way through until I could see what was going on outside. Though darkness had fallen, there were pools of bright light on the grass outside coming from the windows of the flats and Mick, along with two others, was standing in one of these pools. He had certainly matured in the years I had been away. He still had a bit of a babyish face, a bit like Fabian, but it suited him. He was wearing a black box suit with pegged pants and a pair of two-tone black and white loafers. His hair was jet black and greased into an Elvis quiff circa 1957 with a couple of loose strands artfully arranged to hang over his forehead. I had to look closely, and I hoped I was mistaken, but it looked as though he was wearing black eyeliner! He had a guitar on a strap and looked ready to play. I then recognised the two cats with him. One was a black Teddy boy from Streatham Common, named Olly who, looking for all the world like a young Chuck Berry, was wearing a black drape suit with leopard-skin trim and holding up a double bass. The other cat was Adrian Street, dressed in rebel Ted gear comprising jeans and a red Harrington jacket, and he was also clutching a guitar. Mick put up a hand and waited until everyone at the window went quiet. Then he strummed the guitar strings once and began to sing 'Treat me like a fool … treat me mean and cruel … but love me …' It was a passable impression of the young Elvis and sounded pretty cool when Olly and Ade played along and joined in as backing singers. I shook my head in wonder. I could see how Mick was such a big hit with the girls, as he definitely had a bit of style about him. He was the full teen heart-throb package: he looked good, dressed well, could sing and dance and was always the life and soul of the party. It was no wonder the girls got all girlish when he was around! I could barely believe it.

When I had gone away Mick had been a monkey-faced little kid who used to wear my cast-offs and walked like Jimmy Cagney. Now he was a cross between Elvis and The Fonz! His song came to an end and the girls were squealing for another, but Mick flipped the guitar onto his back and saluted before jumping onto the window ledge and pulling himself in. He was immediately surrounded by girls and I shook my head again. Olly was having trouble passing his double bass through the window. I leant out and asked him why he didn't walk around and come through the front door. 'The door is for squares, man,' he replied, and then he looked at me more closely. 'Razor?' he asked. I nodded and he burst into a smile and stuck his hand through the window to shake mine. Ade, standing next to him, began to laugh out loud when he saw me. 'Fucking hell! You look different, man!' he said. 'Has Mick seen you yet?' I shook my head. 'He's too busy with the skirts.' Olly decided that his bass was a square and headed around the block to come in through the front door and Ade jumped in through the window and gave me a bear hug that nearly broke my ribs. 'Mick!' he shouted across the room. 'Mick! It's your brother!' Mick looked up at the shout and his face broke into a smile. He came across the room and hugged me. 'Good to have you back, bruv.'

Once the music was blaring again and people were jiving in the middle of the room, Mick and I went to one of the smaller bedrooms to have a little chat. He said he was doing okay at the hostel, it wasn't a bad gaff and he pretty much had plenty of time to himself. By rights he was on a 10 o'clock curfew but it was hardly ever enforced and most nights he didn't bother going back if he was staying with a girl or just dossing down in the flat. He, Olly and Ade had formed a band but they were still in the practising stage and had yet to get any gigs. He couldn't really play much guitar, but Ade was better than Buddy Holly on lead guitar and Olly was mustard on any kind of bass. After a while a few of the lads wandered in and conversation turned to what had been going on with the gangs. I was told that there was a firm of skinheads not too far away on an estate across the road from Poynders and that there was often a bit of skirmishing with them. There were also a lot of punk rockers up at Clapham Common who all gathered there to sniff glue and drink cider whenever the sun came out. I asked about the Balham Boot Boys and was told that they were now mostly punk rockers and they were being led by an old schoolfriend of ours called Henry, only now Henry was sporting a two-foot orange Mohican and wore a nappy over his bondage trousers, which earned him the nickname of 'Junior'. Junior was six foot one and about 17 stone, and he was a fearsome fighter. I found this hard to take in, as I remembered hitting Henry/Junior with a lovely right-hander that had knocked all the fight out of him in the school playground when we were kids.

As the lads spoke it became clear to me that we were surrounded by enemies and that we were getting the worst of it. The punks at Clapham Common were strong in numbers and had already attacked several of the rockabilly crowd. Little Roy had been stabbed in the leg by punks a couple of months before I got out and any rockers who came out of Clapham South tube station had to run a gauntlet of punks. There was a soul boy gang in Brixton Hill who had started a craze for carrying scissors, which they would use to cut the quiff off any Ted or rockabilly who came through their turf. We all agreed that was a dire fucking liberty as our hair was a big part of our identity. A Teddy boy without a quiff might as well be a skinhead. The Mitcham skinheads were also stronging it and had taken to attacking Teds and rockabillies who had to pass through their turf on the way home from the Chick-A-Boom club. And as if all this wasn't bad enough, there were now several mod and scooter-boy gangs starting up around South London.

The film *Quadrophenia*, about the fighting between the mods and rockers at the seaside resorts in 1964, had led to the rise in the neo-mod movement, and rockers also seemed to be making a bit of a comeback. The trouble for us was that there weren't really enough of the neo-rockers compared with the neo-mods, and the mods seemed to target anyone who greased their hair and wore a leather jacket so the rebel Teds and the rockabillies were high on their shit list. We didn't really sweat it. We were already fighting the war on so many fronts that a few mods weren't going to scare us off.

By 1979 the streets of South London had become dangerous for young people because of the number of subculture gangs that had formed. It had got so you couldn't walk to the shops without some other teenager, with a different hairstyle and different clothes, wanting to stab you or bash you up on sight. There had always been fighting among the youth of the inner city, but never before had the lines been so visible and clearly drawn. In the early 1970s kids could slip by in a crowd and fade into the background if need be, as there was nothing in their dress to mark them out from everyone else, with a few exceptions obviously, but now we were advertising our loyalties for everyone to see. With our hairstyles and dress we were nailing our colours to the mast and, to the young of that era that was a blatant invitation to fight.

Looking back, it seems as though every teen subculture that had existed since the end of the Second World War had suddenly come back to life on the streets of South London – Teds, skinheads, mods, rockers, bikers, scooter-boys and even some kids who were into the hippy thing. It was as if there had been a glitch in the matrix and all the teenagers of the post-war times had popped back up in new bodies. And, to add to the conflict, there were the relatively new subcultures evolving almost on the spot: '70s kids evolving into punk rockers, Teddy boys morphing into rebel Teds and rockabillies, skinheads splitting into Nazi, anti-Nazi, oi and ska skins, and soul boys turning disco freaks. It was like a big bubbling pot of volatile chemicals with the flames under it turned up high. Sooner or later there was going to be an explosion. Mick introduced me to a rockabilly from Battersea named Joe. He was an amateur boxer and you could see it in the way he moved, rolling his shoulders and swiping his nose with this thumb as he talked. I liked Joe straight away. He was relaxed and funny in any company and not afraid to say what he was feeling. He and Mick had a regular banter going about who was the better looking, combing their hair every five minutes and asking if there were any girls watching them – it was very funny. Joe was also up for a ruck and spoke vehemently about the punks and the skins taking liberties with us. I knew right away that Joe would be an asset in any gang of fighters, as not only could he fight himself but also he was good at getting others fired up.

By midnight a lot of people had left the flat and there were only incapable drunks left scattered throughout sleeping and a few couples slow-dancing in the darkness of the front room. I was lagging drunk but feeling great as I sat on the window ledge and listened to the sweet doo-wop from the speakers. Peter hadn't shown up for a couple of days and I was disappointed at not seeing him, but Harry said he had a habit of staying away from the flat, sometimes for a week at a time, and he thought he had a bird tucked up somewhere. Mick walked into the front room looking pleased with himself and sidled up to me. 'There's someone who wants to see you in the back bedroom,' he said, smiling. I asked who it was but all Mick would say was that it was a surprise. The bedroom was in darkness but I could make out a figure lying on one of the beds. 'Welcome home,' I heard, and I realised that it was a blonde rockabilly girl I had met earlier, who had been dancing with Mick. It wasn't until I sat down on the bed that I realised she was naked except for a pair of black stockings. My first day out had started quietly but it ended with quite a bang.

Getting My Colours

The morning after my coming-out party I had a bit of a sore head but I didn't feel that rough for someone who'd had his first piss-up in 27 months. The flat was pretty quiet and there were sleeping bodies everywhere as I picked my way through to the bathroom. I made a cup of tea and sat out on the balcony to drink it. The time was around 7 a.m. but I was well used to being up early after my time in borstal. It was sunny again and I felt full of the joys of spring as I watched some of the occupants of the estate marching off to work. I had six more days of freedom before I had to go back to Rochester borstal and serve the remaining three weeks of my sentence, so I was glad it wasn't raining. I thought about what I wanted from life. Before I had gone away I had been making a name and reputation for myself on the Ted scene and I wanted that back. I wanted to be someone more than anything. Sure, I loved the music, the fashions and the dancing, but I also needed the fighting. Since late 1976 I had immersed myself in a culture of violence, both inside and out, and now I couldn't live without it; it was my drug. I can see now, looking back, that I was living out a fantasy, but I wasn't the only one. Some of us didn't just see ourselves as kids having a punch-up with other kids; we were proper armies, warriors wanting to prove our burgeoning manhood against other warriors. We were the working class of the inner-city, factory and building-site fodder with little to take us out of our mundane existence except carving a name for ourselves amongst our own. We had this short period of time to ourselves, as deep down we all knew that soon would come a time when we would have to grow up and settle down to the realities of life. This would be our last party and I, for one, was going to enjoy it.

After a while Harry came out of the flat, bare-chested and with his hair all over the place like a ginger hedge. He stretched and yawned, then lit a cigarette and sat down next to me. He smiled. 'It's great to be out, ain't it?' he asked. Harry had done his share of prison and borstal and he was still only 18, so he knew what I was feeling. 'You know what the sweetest moment is after you've got out?' he asked me. I shook my head. 'The first morning you wake up on the outside. The moment just before you open your eyes and it comes to you that you are really out. That's the dog's bollocks, mate!' I had to agree. 'How was Tina?' he asked, with a lewd smile on his features. I gave him a wink and a smile. 'I've had better,' I said. 'Though not lately.'

Mick had gone home with a girl he had met at the party, but he had left a message with Harry that he would be back that afternoon. I decided I would go home and check in with my parents to let them know everything was okay and then come back to the flat. I spoke to Joe and Gordon for a while. Gordon was a very funny guy, likeable and very into the lifestyle. He was one of the few rebel Teds in Mitcham, as it was a big skinhead stronghold, and he travelled by tube to Clapham South in order to get to the flat and see Jenny. He told me that he got chased by the skinheads in Mitcham and then chased by the punks when he came out of the tube station at the other end. The only time he relaxed was when he was at the flat, but he was bang in love and a pretty fast runner. Joe was a proper fighter, one of those geezers who just love a punch-up and will start a fight in an empty house. By rights Joe should have been part of the south Battersea crew as he lived on an estate off Battersea High Street, but he had a tendency to fall out with people, including his cousin Psycho Joe, who led the north Battersea, so he went anywhere that birds, booze and fighting were available.

Battersea was split into two factions at that time. In the south, on the Patmore Estate, you had the old Battersea Ted contingent. The Hogans and a few other originals, including a few rockers, all lived on the estate and kept the rock'n'roll flag flying. But the youngsters on the Patmore, including Tommy Hogan Jnr, who had now come of age, were into rockabilly, much to the disgust of the originals who called them 'Billies'. Tommy, Tin-Tin and Rockabilly Steve, along with Little Bopper, Little Roy, Steve the Spiv and a few others, were the real fighting core of the north Battersea crowd. Tony 'Bopper' Hogan was also an on/off member of the gang, but most of the time he was in prison and only made infrequent appearances.

The north Battersea, who were all rockabillies, were led by Psycho Joe, a mean fighter who took no prisoners and had a formidable reputation for violence. Also in Psycho Joe's crew were his younger brother, Steve, Battersea Bob, Toothless Terry (who only had one missing tooth despite his nickname) and a handful of other rocking cats who were game for a kick-off. So the Teds and the rockabillies had Battersea and Clapham Junction pretty much sewn up between them and it was a brave punk rocker who would enter their turf.

I still classed Balham as Wild Cat turf, but since the flat at Poynders was really in Clapham South I realised, even at this early stage, that if I wanted to shape a decent gang I would first have to make an impact from Poynders and radiate outwards. I had missed all the fighting in the King's Road and I had a real longing to take up where I had left off in 1977. The first priority would be to see who among us could fight, but, more importantly, who had the bottle for what I was going to kick off. I had been told that a few of the original Wild Cats had drifted away and that The Wanderers had all but disbanded. But there were still a few hard-core members of the old gang and the juniors were now battle-hardened veterans after all the fighting of the previous two years. Then there were the new crowd, like Joe, Perry and Gordon, whom I got the impression would be willing to do almost anything so long as it was a laugh and they got to break a few heads. So I began to think seriously about putting together another gang.

After I had checked in at my parents' flat, said hello to Samantha and had a meal and a change of shirt, I went back to the flat at Poynders. Harry told me that we were going rocking that evening at a pub on Balham Hill called The George. The George was close to Clapham South tube station and had a mixed clientele of rockers,

Road Rats, Teds, rockabillies and rebel Teds on rocking nights. The music was supplied by a band called CSA, who used to play at The Fountain, and they could rock it up with the best of them.

Everyone in the flat was up and about by midday and once again the music was on. I asked Harry what the neighbours thought about having this madhouse in their midst and he shrugged. 'What can they say?' he replied. 'If anyone dares complain we just tell them to fuck off out of it.' I couldn't argue with that and I don't suppose anyone else could either. Poynders Gardens was what the council referred to as a 'problem estate', the sort of run-down gaff where they would place young homeless families and people who had fucked up in other council properties. I have no doubt that at some stage Poynders had been a lovely place to live, but by 1979 it was the kind of estate where the kids could burn down the community centre and then stone the firemen who were trying to put out the blaze. There were more stolen cars parked up on Poynders than there were in the police compound, and at every turn there were gangs of kids stripping them for parts and working with a speed and dexterity that would dazzle most Formula One pit mechanics.

Mick showed up at the flat with a couple of girls in tow and another present for me. It was an original 1950s Bronx black leather biker's jacket. The back panel had been painted in acrylics by a well-known gang artist and rocker named Johnny Cobra. It featured a pair of crossed revolvers over a Confederate flag and the words 'Quantrill's Raiders Raid Again'. The leather had a bit of history, like all good leathers do. It turned out that it had been taken in a battle between the Streatham Teds and a punk rocker gang. The fight had occurred in the car park behind the ABC cinema on Streatham High Road and as the punks, being outfought, had legged it one of them had been grabbed by the collar and in order to escape he had slipped out of the jacket and left it behind. The jacket became a trophy until Peter Mayne took a fancy to it and swapped one of his old drape jackets for it. He had cleaned the punk paint, 'Anarchy', 'UK Subs', 'The Crass', etc. off it with meths and pulled out most of the studs and all the badges and then handed it over to Johnny Cobra to paint. This was just before Pete started up The Mohican Warriors and he was thinking of calling his gang Quantrill's Raiders, after an old black and white film he had seen about Jessie James. Pete had left the jacket with Johnny Cobra and never went back to pay for the work, so Mick had gone and got it as a present for me. I tried on the leather and it fit like it was made for me. I had never worn a leather jacket before, as I had been more of a suit man due to the Teddy boy penchant for sartorial elegance, and it's hard to describe the feeling I got when I put on that leather. It was like armour and it creaked and jangled with every movement; it was tough and yet at the same time sleek. There seemed to be something intrinsically dangerous and rebellious in putting on a couple of yards of black cowhide studded with metal and adorned with zips and buckles. I looked in the full-length mirror that the girls had in the corner of the front room and thought I looked as slick as a used johnny in a rainstorm. I thanked Mick. 'You can always get the paint changed if you like,' he said. But for now I was happy to wear the leather even though it had the name of a non-existent gang on the back.

I had noticed that there seemed to be a lot of Confederate flags in evidence, sewn onto jeans as patches, painted onto jackets and pinned on shirts in the shape of enamel badges, and I asked the lads about this. It seemed that the Confederate flag had become the flag of the rockabilly rebels and the reasons for this were slightly convoluted though nothing to do with racism as some people now think. Rockabilly music was, on the whole, played by white southern boys from America's Deep South and the flag was evident on some of the obscure record labels that put out the rockabilly bootlegs and in the background of photos of the artists. It seemed as though the flag hung from every municipal building in the south. To us kids in South London, who knew next to nothing about the reasons for the American Civil War of the 1860s, the flag was known only as the 'rebel flag' and as we classed ourselves as rebels it became our flag. It wasn't until the mid-1980s that I became aware of the racial connotations of the flag. The strange thing was that I was never once pulled by any black person for wearing the flag and I was a regular around Brixton market.

Joe turned up at the flat that evening with a couple of rockabillies, half-caste Gary from Battersea and a fella called Paul from Pimlico. By the time we left the estate in the early evening sunlight we were mob-handed for our short walk through the backstreets to The George. There was me, Mick, Harry, Alan, Dennis, Eamon, Perry, Gordon, Little Roy, and Joe and his pals. The girls walked about ten feet behind us because they loved to rabbit about girlie things, but every now and then there would be a bit of banter shouted back and forth. I walked at the front of the group, stopping every now and again to check my hair in the reflection from the windows of parked cars, but we all did; it was one of those things that we hardly noticed anymore, but it seemed that the most important possession most of us had was our comb. As The Fonz once said: 'Live fast, live clean, and don't let nobody else use your comb.' Our hair was a big part of our outward identity and it had to be perfect at all times. I once saw Mick stop in the middle of a punch-up to comb his hair; that's how important it was. I was starting to pick up on things that were new to me. Before I had gone away we had described things with the word 'Ted' to denote its 1950s connotations, so, for example, a club where rock'n'roll music was played was called a 'Ted club', or those who were into the 1950s were 'Teds'. Now it was 'rockin'. There were rockin' clubs, rockin' bands, rockin' clothes, and we ourselves were rockin'. If you hadn't seen someone for a while you might ask if they were still rockin'. The word seemed to cover everything to do with our world as we were no longer Teds. The actual Teds themselves were being left behind and were being considered old-fashioned by the newer, younger, rockabilly crowd, and so the word 'Ted' had become half an insult. It was ironic really, since the 1950s and all through the dark years of the '60s and early '70s the Teds had kept the flame of rock'n'roll alive and dreamed of a day when their clubs and pubs would be filled with the new generation of 1950s-loving youngsters who would take the mantle. But, instead of the hoped-for revival, they ended up with a revolution. Rockabillies now out-numbered the Teds by about 20 to 1 and there was little the former could do except shake their heads in disgust and watch as the new breed took over and changed the scene forever.

The rockabillies didn't give a fuck about the Queen, weren't really that interested in racism as a hobby and bought most of their clothes second-hand. In 1976 you would often hear Teds boasting about how much they had paid for their suits, but by '79 the rocka-billies were boasting about how little they had paid. Whereas the Teds could only get their clothes made by a handful of original tai-lors in order to be authentic, the rockabillies could pick up their gear in charity shops and jumble sales and still be accepted anywhere. It all became too much for some of the originals and they took the retirement that had eluded them at the start of the 1960s. Some of the Ted DJs saw which way the wind was blowing and changed their sets to include more rockabilly, thus ensuring their clubs were packed, but a handful did not. By 1980 the original Teds, or what remained of them, had been pushed into little enclaves of Teddy boy-dom, out-of-the-way pubs where they could parade their hand-made suits, dance to the 1954 version of 'Rock Around The Clock' and grumble about the 'fucking billies'. Some of the Teds still turned up at the mainly rockabilly clubs but they had become anomalies, worthy of comment.

Tommy Hogan Snr was one of the originals who moved with the times. Though he was never less than a fully-fledged Teddy boy and wore his drape with pride, he allowed Tommy Jnr up onto his decks to spin the wax that attracted the rockabilly crowd. Tommy's residency at The Clarence attracted the south Battersea mob who'd always be found either there or at another pub up the road called The Tower. At The Clarence it was something for everybody when it came to the music. It was probably the only rockin' pub in London where you could hear Warren Smith's seminal rockabilly classic 'I've Got Love If You Want It' being played straight after the frothy novelty rock'n'roll of Dodi Stevens' 'Pink Shoelaces', as senior and junior took turns on the decks. It was a good place to go on a Tuesday night and most nights ended in a fight. Either the north Battersea would start something with the locals, or the crowd of rockers who got in there would take a liberty with someone and the gaff would turn into a Wild West saloon.

So the scene I came back to in May 1979 was different to the one I had left, and I had the feeling that all the changes were not over yet. The scene was still evolving and I was going to be part of it. In the meantime I was going to The George for my first live gig in a long time and I was wondering how I could make my mark. Little did I know that I was about to commence building my reputation that very evening by starting an internecine war that would simmer for years and eventually destroy the whole rockabilly scene.

Kicking off at The George

The George pub is situated at the top of Balham Hill, opposite a petrol garage and a Chinese restaurant, and less than 300 yards from Clapham South tube station and Clapham Common. The pub itself is a big old gaff with an open tarmac space in front where there are usually wooden tables and benches for drinking outside during good weather. To get to the function hall at the back you have to pass through the long front bar and then through a set of double doors. The function room contains a fair-sized hardwood dance floor with a small stage at the far end and tables and chairs arranged around the outside of the dance floor. There is no bar inside the function room and drinkers would have to go into the front bar to get served and then carry their drinks in. On rockin' nights the double doors were kept wedged open for easy access. It was still light when we came out of the side street opposite the pub and I caught my first sight of it. There was a white transit van, which I rightly guessed belonged to the band, parked up on the tarmac along with several large British motorbikes. A couple of rockers were standing over one of the bikes smoking and talking, but other than that there was nothing that might suggest that the gaff was rockin'. I looked down the road on my right and I could see the big blue and red sign of the tube station and just beyond it a patch of green that was the start of Clapham Common. The Common's usual bunch of glue-sniffing, cider-drinking punk rockers, like beat bobbies, seemed to disappear in the evenings. I knew that if we wanted to take this manor we would have to take on the punks, who usually gathered in great numbers, and if not beat them then at least run them and drive them out of Clapham South. I was already planning military-style moves.

As we came through the front door of the pub I was surprised to see that it was already fairly packed with a rockin' crowd. There were a lot of rockers, mainly dressed in black leathers with white silk aviator scarves around their necks, motorbike boots and greased-up quiffs, and a couple of the Road Rats MC and their prospects. A 'prospect' is someone who has applied to join a biker gang, or motorcycle club as they call them, but has yet to prove themselves worthy. The biker gangs take their shit very seriously indeed and when you join you become a member for life. Being a prospect for any MC is like serving an apprenticeship, and how you shape up will decide whether you will be accepted into the gang or not. I believe the whole process is based on rules laid down by the original Hell's Angels of America. Prospects can be fucking dangerous to non-MC members simply because they are always out to impress. One of the ways they can show their future gang that they have 'class' is by impacting over-the-top violence on anyone who happens to be around, so I've always avoided a prospect whenever I could, but that was not always possible. The biker gangs made us look like a bunch of immature kids playing at soldiers – which I suppose is what we really were.

There were a few Teddy boys in the pub and a lot of rockabillies and rebel Teds. We got our drinks from the bar and made our way into the function room. The band had set up their instruments on the stage but had yet to start their first set. There was no disco at The George, but CSA always brought a tape system on which they would play a selection of rockin' music between sets so that their gigs were never quiet. We found a couple of tables down near the front of the stage and sat down. The girls had spotted some of their mates on the other side of the dance floor and joined them at their table. I just sat back and soaked up the atmosphere and every now and again someone would come over to our tables and I would be introduced, usually as Rocky Mick's brother who's just got out of borstal. Ahmet, a Turkish kid who used to hang around Sinclair in '76, came and sat with us. Ahmet wasn't rockin' but was liked by the whole crowd and was given the tongue-in-cheek nickname of The Rockin' Smoothie. Ahmet was so into the whole scene and ended up going everywhere with us that I often wondered why he didn't just go the whole hog and get a haircut and a leather jacket. Sometimes he would come down to Poynders when we were getting ready to go out for the night and get someone to grease his hair and comb it into a quiff and then borrow items of rockin' clothing so that he wouldn't look out of place. But he always washed the Dax out of his hair and changed back into his square clothes before going home. It wasn't until some years later that I found out that Ahmet's family were strict Turkish Muslims and his older brothers threatened to beat him up seriously if he brought shame on the family by becoming a Teddy boy. They didn't even want him hanging around with us and he had to keep it all secret.

Mick introduced me to two good-looking sisters called Geraldine and Josephine, who looked like biker chicks, but I was still a bit rusty with talking to girls, especially gorgeous ones, so I wandered out to the bar for another drink. I was waiting to be served at the bar when I overheard some geezer talking to a couple of tough-looking rockabillies. The bloke who was talking was big but running to fat and he had a bald head, though naturally bald and not shaved into a skinhead. He was wearing a donkey jacket with the words 'Elvis' and 'Bill' painted on the back shoulder panel and a load of enamel Confederate badges on the front. He was holding a large penknife in his hand and I heard him say, 'If they start, Bill is going to cut them up good!' and then he chuckled. He sounded like a bit of a halfwit to me, but I was alert enough to know that there was trouble brewing. I went back to the table, pointed the bloke out to Harry and asked if he knew him. Harry laughed. 'Yeah, that's Nutty Bill. He's harmless. Comes from Tooting and I think he's a dustman. He's about 40 and still lives with his mum!' I told Harry that he had a knife and Harry just laughed again. 'A penknife,' he said. 'He'd shit himself if anyone ever fronted him. He just likes to act tough.' I accepted what Harry said, but in the borstal system I had found out that even the most inadequate fuckwit can be a danger with a tool in his hand. Maybe it was this incident that set me on edge for what happened next, but I was ready.

Around 9.30 CSA were in full swing on the stage and the dance floor was packed with dancers, CSA being one of the few bands that people would dance to rather than just stand staring at. Harry came over to the table and told me that we might have a bit of trouble. It seemed that Mick, Harry and Peter had had some sort of run-in with a couple of members of the north Battersea gang at some stage and there had been rumours flying around that Psycho Joe was looking to carry it on. I didn't know Psycho Joe from a hole in the ground, having only heard his name and reputation for the first time the day before, so I didn't see what all the fuss was about. I told Harry to point this fella out to me and I would go and have a chat with him. However, it turned out that he wasn't actually at the pub yet, although a few members of his gang were and they were giving it the big 'un. Harry pointed out four rockabillies who were standing at the edge of the dance floor with mean looks on their faces. I noticed that they were all wearing donkey jackets, but the full-length ones with leather back patches that railway men and coalmen usually wore. One of them, a big blond fella, turned around to talk to someone behind him and I saw he had a Confederate flag painted on the leather patch with the words 'Battersea Bob' in gothic script. I sized them up but didn't think they would give us too much trouble. Harry said he was going to talk to them and I told him I'd watch his back. I couldn't hear what Harry said to the north Battersea crew because the music was so loud, but I could see by the hardness of their faces that they weren't interested in talking. I got out of my chair and walked over to stick my nose in, but Harry was walking away by this time. 'What's up?' I asked. Harry shook his head. 'They're just mugs,' he said. 'They reckon Psycho Joe is coming down later on and there'll be trouble.' Harry shrugged. 'Forget about it.' I knew from experience that sometimes Harry could be too laid back for his own good. He was one of those sort of geezers who would deal with things as they came up and not before. I wasn't happy and I told him so. Harry just smiled. 'Relax,' he said. 'They won't start nothing, and this thing with Joe is nothing serious. Joe's all right, I'll just buy him a pint.' With that, the band launched into a Gene Vincent song and Harry legged it onto the dance floor along with about 30 others. I went and sat back down.

In those days I used to drink light and bitter, which is a pint glass half filled with bitter and a separate bottle of light ale to top it up. People had been buying me drinks all evening and I had about six light ale bottles and pint glasses on the table in front of me. I was fairly drunk but not so drunk as to be incapable, and I was keeping a close eye on Battersea Bob and his companions. So I sat up when I saw him walk over to the table on the other side of the dance floor where the girls were sitting and lean over to talk to Jenny. I couldn't hear what he was saying but it was pretty obvious that he was asking her to dance, and I saw Jenny shake her head. She was smiling up at him in a friendly way and I saw her pointing at Gordon, who was deep in conversation with Mick and Perry near the entrance to the room. I guessed that she was telling him that Gordon was her boyfriend. I could hardly believe my eyes when Battersea Bob grabbed her by the arms, pulled her to her feet and began to hustle her out onto the dance floor. He wasn't being overly rough, just one of those geezers who wasn't used to taking no for an answer and he was going to have a dance with her whether she wanted to or not. Jenny was looking a bit distressed and that was enough for me.

Before I had really had time to think about it, I was out of my seat, snatching a light ale bottle from the table, and striding out onto the dance floor. Battersea Bob had his back to me and was struggling with Jenny. I didn't even slow down, I just swung the bottle at shoulder height and stepped into the swing as I brought it down onto Battersea Bob's head. The bottle shattered and I felt the force of the blow right up to my shoulder. Battersea Bob went over like a felled tree, straight out on his face. I heard a girl screaming somewhere on the other side of the dance floor. I looked at Jenny and she looked shocked and shit scared. The dancers cleared the floor in a panic and the band, realising something had gone wrong, came to a ragged stop in mid-flow. 'Out of the way!' I shouted at Jenny, and then I launched three swift, hard kicks into the ribs of the prostrate Battersea Bob and a couple more times for luck. 'What the fuck?' Harry shouted at me. 'He grabbed hold of Jenny!' I shouted back. I saw Harry's face change from shock to anger. 'Cheeky cunt!' he snarled, and he turned away, probably to launch a few kicks at Battersea Bob himself, but Mick grabbed his arm. By now Battersea Bob, all credit to his toughness, was climbing to his feet. There was a rivulet of blood flowing from the back of his head and down his neck into his collar and he was groaning and holding his head with one hand and his ribs with the other. Someone shouted 'You're fucking dead!' and I heard the sound of breaking glass.

Battersea Bob's companions had obviously taken exception to his treatment and fancied the odds, because they were shaping up on the edge of the now deserted dance floor. One of them held a lead pipe cosh and the other two had the jagged ends of broken bottles. Battersea Bob limped over to join them. At a quick glance I could see Dennis, Alan, Ahmet and Big Nose Eamon hovering not too far from them and I didn't fancy the north Battersea crew's chances in a rumble. From smashing the bottle into Battersea Bob's head until his pals making their intentions plain was only about a minute and a half, though it seemed like a lifetime. Some people had legged it into the front bar but they were now drifting back to see what was going on. Tony, the lead guitarist and singer of the band, got on his microphone and his voice boomed around the pub. 'All right, lads. You've all proved how tough you are. We've got a good place here, but if you keep it up you'll get us closed down. So if you want to fight, please take it outside. There's a fucking Common just up the road. Come on now.' A few of the rockers who followed CSA everywhere got between us and the north Battersea and began to usher them out through the front bar. Harry was looking daggers at Battersea Bob for daring to manhandle his little sister. He turned to me as the other crew disappeared out of the pub. 'We gonna let them get away?' I was still fired up and ready to rumble. 'Fuck it,' I said. 'Let's finish it.' And I grabbed a couple of beer bottles from a nearby table and strode through the pub followed by the rest of the lads. The band struck the first notes of an instrumental called 'Sleepwalk' as we left the premises. By the time we got out onto the street, the north Battersea crew were walking up towards Clapham South tube station but keeping an eye out behind them for us. Harry threw a beer bottle up the street at them and it shattered at their feet. They still had their weapons in their hands and they stopped and turned to face us, but they hadn't realised how many of us there were until now. We charged them and they legged it, but Battersea Bob was left behind, unable to move too fast because of the beating he had already received. The main bulk of our mob chased the other three up past the tube station and onto the Common and Mick gave Battersea Bob a slap in the face in passing. Me, Harry and Ahmet cornered Battersea Bob in a shop doorway and Harry dragged Ahmet away when he tried to attack him. 'He's mine,' he snarled. I stood back and watched as Harry laid into the unfortunate Battersea Bob, throwing lefts and rights at his head and body. He really took a beating that night and ended up in a bleeding heap in the doorway. Harry leant over him and waved a finger in his battered face. 'You ever lay a hand on my family again and I'll fucking kill you. Understand?' Battersea Bob nodded. Harry lifted him to his feet. 'Now, fuck off,' he said and pointed him in the direction his pals had gone.

Mick and the rest of the boys chased the north Battersea halfway across Clapham Common before giving up and walking back. They passed Battersea Bob, staggering along with his head in his hands, on their way back and verbally abused him until he was out of sight. Back in the pub we discussed the incident and I saw the fearful looks I got from a few people when my bottling of Battersea Bob was relived. I had made my mark and proved myself in the only way I knew how, by swift and extreme violence. I knew that when I talked people would listen and that was exactly what I was after: a little bit of fear and a little bit of respect. Razor Smith was back and firing on all cylinders. Psycho Joe never did turn up at The George that night, but what goes around in this world tends to come around and there was no way the north Battersea crew were going to swallow a very public humiliation. They would be back. But I wouldn't be around to see it.

The Wildkatz at The Chick-A-Boom

The fight between us and the north Battersea crew at The George was certainly the first time I had ever made violent moves against members of my own subculture. There had always been rivalries between the old Ted gangs, but if they did spill into violence it was normally a straightener between individual members, never a gang fight. And it wasn't as if we didn't have enough enemies already who were outside of our subculture. What happened at The George had been, on the whole, spontaneous, but the repercussions would be long-lasting. I take most of the blame for what happened. I was like a sore-headed bear looking for someone to unload my pain on. Violence was normal to me and I had grown used to doing my arguing with my fists or whatever item came to hand. I wanted to fight anyone and everyone and I wanted everybody to know who I was. Incarceration had changed me for the worse and whatever humanity I had once had was lying on the cold stone floors of underground punishment cells along with my blood and tears. The system had won in the end because it had the biggest gang, but now I was out and I was going to win by having the biggest gang and giving back some of the pain I had suffered.

The day after The George a few more rockabillies turned up at the flat at Poynders and brought word that Psycho Joe's crew were planning a comeback. I shrugged it off and put on a tough face for everyone to see. 'Let 'em come,' I said. 'They're only mugs.' In truth I really didn't give a fuck. I wanted a fight. I noticed that the lads were very deferential to me and took notice of what I had to say. At the time I convinced myself that this was through respect, but I now realise that a lot of it was fear. We had always been a pretty violent bunch of kids, but our violence had been mostly heat of the moment. What I had done to Battersea Bob had not only been over the top but also, as Harry later remarked, seemed machine-like. There are always people who will flock to a strong camp and want to be associated with someone who is gaining a reputation. Some of them do it out of fear for their own safety and others because they want to be on what they perceive as the winning side and catch some of the notoriety that inevitably builds up. I didn't care what these people wanted but I would accept them all with open arms, as I knew that when it came to having a gang around you, numbers were crucial. The more of us there were the more we could intimidate other gangs.

That afternoon a rockabilly called Lloyd and a couple of his pals turned up at the flat. Mick told me that they were from north Battersea but he wasn't sure if they were part of Psycho Joe's crew or if they were independents, of which there were quite a few around. I figured that if they were enemies then they wouldn't have turned up on our turf empty-handed, especially after what had happened at The George. Lloyd and his pals were in one of the bedrooms with Joe K and Perry when Jenny called me into one of the other bedrooms, where I found a worried-looking Elaine. She said that she used to go out with one of Lloyd's pals and that Lloyd and the other two who were with him had beaten her up one night because she'd split up with his pal. She said she was afraid to come out of the bedroom in case they started on her again. I told her not to worry and left her, Jenny and Kim in the bedroom. I walked into the kitchen, picked up a big carving knife from the draining board and walked into the bedroom where Lloyd and his pals were. They all looked up as I came in. I swung the knife in Lloyd's face, intending to open him up, but missed as he dragged his head back in shock. Joe K jumped up and got in front of me. 'What's going on?' he shouted. I struggled to get past Joe. 'Out of the way, Joe,' I snarled. 'These cunts are getting it.' It was lucky that we were on the ground floor, as Lloyd and his chums made for the only unblocked exit and dived out of the open window. I knocked Joe out of the way and went out of the window after them. I chased them to the boundary of the estate, but fear must have lent them wings because they left me in their dust.

Joe, Perry and Harry caught up with me just as I turned back onto the estate and crowded around. They wanted to know what it was all about and I told them the story Elaine had told me. Joe shook his head. 'All right. Fair play,' he said. 'But if I hadn't stopped you, you could have killed one of them.' I stopped walking and stared at him. 'So what?' I asked. Harry smiled. 'You're fucking off your head!' he said. And this incident only added to my fast-growing reputation for swift and merciless violence. Inside I was laughing. I wouldn't have stuck the knife into anyone – that would have been too much even for me – but nobody else knew that and I just let them keep guessing. Certainly Lloyd and his pals thought I would have killed them and that's how the story went the rounds. I wanted to hurt people, but not actually kill anyone if I could help it. I was mad, bad and dangerous but not completely evil. I would draw the line some way before cold-blooded murder. But, of course, nobody else knew that.

Peter Mayne had been on the missing list for a couple of days before I got out and I had really wanted to see my old crime partner. Then word reached the flat that he had been nicked, along with his Mohican Warriors cohort, Johnny Virgo, for a string of shop and warehouse burglaries. He was due up in court the next day, having already been remanded in custody the previous week, and we decided to turn up and show him a bit of support. Peter looked fucking terrible sitting in the dock of Lavender Hill Magistrates Court. His hair, which had been cut into a Mohican with shaved sides, was all over the gaff after a week in custody with no hairspray and he had stubble on his face, but he smiled at me and winked. I was sitting in the public gallery with Harry, Jenny, Marina, Mick and Joe K and we all listened as a seemingly endless list of charges were read out. The lads' solicitor made a passionate plea for bail on their behalf, but anyone could tell that the magistrate wasn't going to wear it; he looked as though he'd been up all night sucking on fresh-cut lemons. The boys stood to hear the decision and I noticed that they were both wearing sleeveless denim jackets with a grinning Mohican skull motif and the words 'Mohican Warriors – London'. They were both remanded back into custody for three weeks and gave us defiant salutes as they were led out of the dock.

That was the only time I was to see Peter for quite a while. I was gutted; not only because Peter was my pal but also because he had a reputation as a fucking good fighter and he would have been an asset to the gang. Peter had the nickname 'Potty Pete' because everyone thought he was half a lunatic. He didn't give a fuck about anybody and reputations did not impress him, but he was always loyal to me personally and would back me up in the most dangerous of situations. So I was sorry to see him go back inside for the foreseeable future as it was odds-on that he and Johnny Virgo were going to end up with custodial sentences. But I took a bit of consolation from the fact that there was still plenty of raw material left in the gang to work with.

That evening when we were all gathered at the flat I put forward the idea that we should form a proper gang. I laid out my thoughts about how too many people were taking liberties and how we should start fighting back. Gordon shouldn't have to get chased from Clapham South tube station by punk rockers; this was our fucking turf! The Cubbitt House skins should be walking in fear, not strutting onto the estate when they felt like it. And we should be sending out the message that if you fucked with us then you were likely to cop an unfortunate one. There was safety in numbers, and belonging to a gang was the best way to make sure of that safety. Everyone became enthusiastic about the idea and pretty soon we were discussing what to call ourselves. We kicked a few ideas around for a while and I suggested 'The Wildcats'. Most people liked the name because it was close to our old Ted gang name, but there were already a couple of gangs with similar names, The White City Wild Cats and The Woolwich Wildcats to name but two. Harry got a magic marker out of a drawer and wrote on the wall in gothic script. 'What about this?' he asked. He had written 'The Wildkats'. Marina punched him in the shoulder. 'Don't write on the fucking walls. This ain't a fucking squat!' But I liked the spelling. Mick was smooching with Tina on one of the armchairs but took a moment to say, 'Harry, cross out the 's' at the end and put in a 'z' instead, it'll look better.' We all agreed that it was different, so we took a vote on it. That night we became The Wildkatz.

In May 1979 the core of The Wildkatz consisted of me, Mick, Harry, Dennis, Alan, Gordon, Perry, Joe K, Big Nose Eamon, Ahmet, and a bunch of independents who could be called on in order to make up the numbers, including Adrian and Vince, Olly, Roy, Ronnie and Eddie. The real fighters were the core, but I knew that as soon as we started becoming known others would be attracted to the gang. Big Dave Wall, who had been one of the original Wild Cats, and his brother Bernie had pulled out of the rockin' life while I had been away. Dave was now the lead singer in a new-wave band called Roadrunner, and Bernie had gone a bit soul-boyish and hung around with what was left of the original members of the Sinclair Mob. They were all into soul, funk and disco, wearing Farah slacks and stripy shirts and going on the pull at The Cat's Whiskers club in Streatham every Saturday night. Johnny Boyd was now a rocker and could be seen at the tea stall on Chelsea Bridge every Friday night pulling wheelies on his Triumph 650. I asked about Blue, the mad Teddy boy from The Wanderers, and was told that he had fallen out with Bopper Hogan one night outside the Fountain in '78. Bopper had smashed a portable tape recorder over his head several times and fractured his skull. He had been in hospital for a while and when he came out he had put away his sky-blue drape suit and got a job as a runner for a small-time Balham villain called Belfast Joe. Blue, despite his beating by Bopper and failure to exact revenge for it, still had a reputation as a fighter and it was rumoured that he had been involved in more than a few stabbings since he had put his drape away. I thought I might see if I could talk him into making a comeback, as he would be a big plus to have in the gang.

The rest of the week seemed to fly by in a haze of birds, booze and bass, but I had one more night out before going back behind bars to finish my time. The Chick-A-Boom at The St Helier Arms pub in Carshalton, Surrey, was now the premiere club for those with a penchant for the music and fashions of the 1950s. The pub was massive and set in the centre of a pre-war housing estate of neat maisonettes with front and back gardens. Set back from a roundabout, called The Circle, The St Helier Arms had a large tarmac car park at the front, surrounded by a two-foot brick wall, with access at both sides. The front bar was the watering hole for all the residents of the large estate and had a reputation for clannishness and violence. The locals didn't take too well to strangers on their turf and it was the kind of pub where the lack of a facial scar would make you highly suspect.

There had always been fights at The Arms, as it was known, and the local police stationed a patrol car on The Circle most Friday and Saturday nights. The Chick-A-Boom club was situated up a wide bit of road that ran along the side of the pub and into another large car park. The club was, in fact, a large function hall tacked onto the back of the pub and it had its own bar and entrance as well as its own car park. The Chick-A-Boom ran on Wednesday night from 7.00 till midnight and on Saturday nights from 8.00 p.m. till 1.00 a.m. Not only did they have the best DJs on the rockin' scene but also they had great bands every Saturday, including headliners from the '50s like Ray Campi, Bill Haley, Buddy Knox, Del Shannon and Wanda Jackson.

In order to get to the Chick-A-Boom we had to walk up to Clapham South tube station and get a Northern Line tube to Morden, at the southern-most end of the line, and then catch an M1 bus to The Circle. It was a long journey and sometimes fraught with danger, especially on the tube as we had to pass through seven stations, most of which were in enemy territory, and occasionally enemies would either be waiting in ambush or there would be chance meetings with gangs of punks or skinheads also on a Saturday night out. But it was on the journey home that most of the trouble took place. The club served last orders at 12.45 but the last tube left Morden heading north at 12.30. Catching the last tube would mean catching the last M1 bus at 11.55 and that would mean missing out on valuable drinking time, not to mention the slow dances. The last 20 minutes at any rockin' venue were crucial if you wanted to pull a bird, because that would be when the DJ put on the slow dance records like 'In The Still of the Night' by The 5 Satins, or 'Angel Baby' by Rosie and The Originals or 'Maybe Tomorrow' by Billy Fury. You could spend all evening eyeing up a girl in the club, but it was usually only when the slow records came on that you had drunk enough courage to make your move. So, for most of us, it was essential to stay in the Chick-A-Boom until the last minute.

To get home from the Chick-A-Boom club meant a walk of around six miles for most of us and all through what was, in effect, enemy turf. The streets of South London could be a dangerous place, particularly after dark. But first we had to get there. I had been told by everyone that the Chick-A-Boom was the best club ever, so I was looking forward to it as we left the flat. I was in my jeans, boots, white T-shirt and leather jacket and had already decided that I was not going to have another drape suit made. The rebel Ted look suited me and I felt comfortable in it. It had always been a bit of a pain in the arse trying to keep my suit clean whenever there was agro, but it seemed as though the new style was functional as well as stylish. We marched up to the tube station in a loose group, chewing gum, cracking jokes and stopping to comb our hair in every reflective surface. There was no way we would pay our fare on the tube, we never had, so it was just a matter of walking through the exit barrier. A ticket collector tried a half-hearted shout after us, but Harry turned around and gave him the finger and he just looked away. Down on the platform we milled about waiting for our train. Mick took out a thick felt-tip pen and wrote on the wall: 'Mick Smith A.K.A. Rocky rebelted'. I shook my head and laughed. 'That ain't how you spell 'rebelled',' I said. Mick gave me a look. 'It says 'rebel Ted', not fucking rebelled.' I shrugged. Harry and Eamon were trying to force open the chocolate machine with Eamon's cheap French flick knife but the tip of the blade snapped off and we all started laughing at the gutted look on Eamon's face as he surveyed the damage.

When the train pulled in we got on board with hard looks on our faces and sat with our feet on the seats under the sign that said 'Please Do Not Put Feet On Seats'. The few citizens who were on the train gave us a wide berth and we ignored them. Every time the train slowed down to pull into a station we all stood and got ready just in case there were any enemy troops on the platforms, but it was a quiet journey. We walked through the ticket barrier at Morden and no one said a word to us. Outside at the M1 bus stop there was a crowd of rockabillies waiting for the bus. Some of our gang knew a few of them and I was introduced to Mitch and Snapper, formerly of the Streatham Teds but now independents, and also a fella named Roy Sears from Tooting Broadway. The crowd at the bus stop were in high spirits and bottles of booze were being passed around freely. I noticed several good-looking girls in the crowd and once again I was just buzzing to be out of jail.

The Chick-A-Boom club was everything I had been promised it was. The car park was full of classic 1950s cars and motorbikes and inside the gaff were wall-to-wall birds, booze and rockin' music. You could almost eat the atmosphere like candy floss and it would have tasted of Brylcreem, Brut, chewing gum, perfume and hair lacquer, snakebite and Pernod. I loved it and felt at home from the moment I paid my three quid and stepped through the big double doors and into a crowded barn of a room with a packed hardwood dance floor at its centre. I had never seen so many people bopping at the same time and it would have sounded like heavy gunfire if the music had not been so loud. The two DJs, Martin and Jerry, were behind the decks on a small stage at one side of the dance floor and there was another larger stage at the far end for the live bands. The music played by the DJs at the Chick-A-Boom was cutting edge as far as the rockin' scene went and it was here that I first heard such classics as 'Roll Hot Rod Roll' by Oscar McLollie, 'Drugstore Rock' And Roll' by Janis Martin and 'Sixteen Chicks' by Joe Clay. I can still remember the record that was playing when I walked into the club for the first time – 'Skinny Jim' by Eddie Cochran – and just hearing a snatch of it takes me back.

There were many gang colours on display at the Chick-A-Boom and you could find yourself between leathers proclaiming 'Deptford Alley Cats' and 'The Cool Daddio Club – Pimlico' just standing at the bar waiting to be served. I hadn't realised that there were so many different rockin' gangs until that night. There were even cats and kits who had come over from France, Belgium and Holland for the weekend to take in a Saturday night at the Chick-A-Boom and then a Sunday night at The Greyhound in Croydon. It was fucking wild. I was to find out that the Chick-A-Boom was classed as neutral territory and that there was little animosity between the different gangs inside the club. The head bouncer, a huge hippy-looking man with a big nose and long hair named Barney, was the brother of Jerry the DJ and, despite his penchant for love beads and Afghan coats, he didn't take no shit from anyone. At the first sign of aggro Barney and his team were in like Flynn and breaking heads. There was also a rub-down search on the door before you were allowed entry, though the easiest way to get a weapon into the club was to let the girls carry it as they couldn't be searched. I liked the Chick-A-Boom club – a lot. And that would turn out to be very ironic seeing as how I was to be involved in most of the violence that eventually got it closed down. But on that first night I just relaxed and took in the atmosphere, meeting a few faces who would become part of my life for the next few years. To me at that time the Chick- A-Boom club was a rock'n'roll heaven; there was plenty of time for me to turn it into hell.

Doing the Clapham Common Punks

After my home leave was up I returned to Rochester to serve my remaining weeks. I had left in an ill-fitting Teddy boy suit with a head full of rock'n'roll, but I returned to borstal seven days later in my gang leather as a rebel Ted. To the casual observer this change may have seemed subtle, but it marked a major shift in my subculture: different clothes and different music. Where Teddy boys had always been a thing of the past, the rebel Teds and rockabillies were of the now. I was part of a fast-growing movement again, but this time it really belonged to me and others like me. In this game we were now the 'originals' and it was up to us to make the rules. We had broken away from the patriarchal influence of the original Teddy boy movement and were now running free. I was impatient to get back to the gang, and my remaining three weeks of porridge seemed like a lifetime but I managed to get through it.

While I was away the north Battersea crew had made their comeback. Led by Psycho Joe they had stormed The George and laid into the Wildkatz with real venom. Harry's head was split open by a lead cosh and the fighting spilled out onto the pavement. Ahmet had his nose broken and Mick took a bit of a kicking. One of the old Sinclair Mob, a guy called Andy, had arrived as the fight spread out across Balham Hill. He jumped out of his car, a second-hand Mini Cooper that he had just bought, to lend a hand and he ended up getting his face kicked in and his car turned over on its roof by six of the north Battersea. A rocker girl got pushed over in the melee and when her boyfriend objected someone threw a lump of paving slab at him, which he dodged, and it hit his girl in the leg, snapping the bone. The Wildkatz were forced to beat a hasty retreat down the side streets towards Poynders, but Mick was cornered by Psycho Joe himself who, according to Mick, pulled out a small revolver and put it to his head. He told Mick, 'Tell your brother I'm looking for him.' That was all he needed to say and I got the message. At this time it was unusual for firearms to be brandished on the rockin' scene, though not unheard of, but it didn't bother me. I had already served a sentence for possession of firearms and armed robbery and I knew where to get my hands on a gun if I needed one, but I was so full of arrogance I didn't think that I did need one. I laughed off Psycho Joe's message and went about building up the gang again. They would get courage from my confidence and I was supremely confident.

The first order of business when I got out was to find Blue and see if he still had a taste for the scene. So Harry and I went down to Balham one afternoon and had a mooch about. I had heard he was working for Belfast Joe and that when he wasn't on a mission he could be found either hanging around the indoor market or in Effy's cafe on Bedford Hill. I had always had a strange affinity for violent lunatics, maybe because I was only half a step from being one myself, and Blue and I had got on well in the old days. I knew that he had really been into the music and I was hoping that there was still enough rock'n'roll in his soul to tempt him back. The beating that Blue had taken from Bopper Hogan had been pretty severe, but it wasn't this that had made him hang up his blue suede shoes; I think it was more the sense of betrayal and disappointment. Bopper and Blue had been the best of pals before their disagreement, and falling out with a good friend in such a violent way always tends to leave a bad taste in the mouth. I thought that Blue had probably left the scene because of that.

After asking around for a while without success, we were about to give up when I spotted Blue standing in the doorway of the record shop. I had to look twice to be sure, but it was definitely him. He was wearing a checked lumberjack coat with the collar turned up and a flat cap with clumps of wild hair sticking out from under it and he was unshaven. I walked over. 'Blue!' I said. 'How's it hanging, mate?' He looked at me and Harry, sharply at first, and I noticed the furtive movement as his hand slipped into his back pocket. 'It's me,' I said. 'Razor!' Blue visibly relaxed and broke into a grin that showed a gap where one of his lower front teeth was missing, knocked out by Bopper Hogan it was said. Blue seemed genuinely glad to see us and after a bit of hand shaking and back slapping we took a walk down to Effy's for a cup of tea and a sausage sandwich.

In the steamy interior of the cafe we sat around a scarred wooden table and filled each other in on what had been happening in our lives. I told Blue a bit about my time inside and how I was now out and forming a gang, just like the old days. He seemed interested but told us that his Teddy boy days were over. We explained to him that we were no longer Teds as such and he asked a lot about the latest music and the fashions we were now into. 'What about the old gang?' he asked, and I told him that a lot of them were still around and up for it. 'How about the Bopper?' he asked. 'He still around?' I shook my head. 'Nah,' I replied. 'He's doing 21 months in the Scrubs. Attempted theft and assaulting old bill.' Blue nodded. 'Rockabilly, eh?' he said. 'Is that the stuff they used to play over at Bobbysox?' It was my turn to nod. Blue drained his tea and looked up at the clock. 'I've gotta shoot,' he announced. I got a pencil from behind the counter and wrote the address of the flat at Poynders on his fag packet. 'Listen,' I said. 'If you fancy seeing a few of the old faces and having a good night out, get down to this gaff on Saturday night before about 7.30. It'll be a great laugh.' We shook hands and he was gone. As we left the cafe I asked Harry if he thought Blue would turn up. Harry shook his head. 'And if he does,' he said, 'I hope he has a fucking haircut first.'

Barry Louvane was the top gang tattooist in South London and had a little shop at the bottom end of Garratt Lane near Wandsworth Arndale Centre. Barry kept his own hours, sometimes not opening the shop until 2 in the afternoon, but he was never short of customers and there was usually a queue outside his shop. Most days Barry could be found in the bar of the snooker club across the road and one of his customers would have to go over and ask him to come and open up the shop. He had tattooed every South London gang in existence since the early 1970s and, despite his prodigious alcoholic intake, he was fast and good with the tattoo gun. I had quite a few homemade and jailhouse tattoos, including S.T.U.D. on my left wrist, which had been my first, but now I wanted my first professional gang tattoo so I came to Barry Louvane's. Barry's tattoo parlour was another one of those places that was classed as neutral territory and it wasn't unusual to see Teds, skinheads, punks and rockabillies hanging around outside the shop and giving each other no more than dirty looks. I decided to get the words 'Balham Katz' on my neck and hardly felt a thing as Barry inked me up. Harry got 'Made In Balham' on one arm and a skull with a quiff and the words

'Forever Rockin' on the other. Mick got 'Made In Balham' around his navel, and Alan and Perry both got Confederate flags and the words 'Balham Katz' on their arms. We met up with young Tommy Hogan and Tin-Tin as well. Tin-Tin was having 'Gene Vincent & The Blue Caps' around his neck and Tommy was having a Confederate flag and 'Battersea Rebels' on his chest.

Getting inked was a strange kind of bonding ritual among gang members. Nowadays it seems as if everyone, even the most middle-class and respectable of people, have at least one tattoo, and they have become a fashion statement among young girls. But back in the day it was only Maoris, sailors and the criminal classes who sported tattoos. A teenage boy with a tattoo was considered thuggish by 'nice' people, and that was the whole point of it for us. We wanted to be outsiders, to be thought of as different and somehow dangerous, and tattoos, along with our hairstyles and clothing, achieved that effect. We were like walking advertising hoardings for our chosen lifestyle. And tattooing was popular among all the teenage subcultures of the time.

After getting our ink done we all plotted up in a cafe a few doors away from Barry Louvane's and compared results. It was the first time I had really got to talk to Tommy and Tin-Tin, though I had been on nodding acquaintance with them around the clubs. I knew Tommy's brother, Bopper, very well and in the Teddy boy days we had always got on well with the south Battersea Teds. Tommy told us that there had been a lot of speculation about whether we would be making a comeback against Psycho Joe's crew. I assured him that the trouble was far from over, though, as yet, we had no firm plans for our revenge. The south Battersea cats had never really got on with Psycho Joe's crew and Tommy intimated that his mob might be interested in lending us a hand in any future trouble. I knew this offer would depend entirely on how we shaped up as a gang in the near future. If we took another defeat from anyone we would lose all credibility and no one would be interested in helping us out. We parted on good terms with Tommy and Tin-Tin.

While I had been away for my final three weeks, Peter and Johnny Virgo had appeared in court again and been jailed for 18 months apiece. Without any parole they would have to serve a minimum of 12 months before release, so I could count Peter out of any action for a while. We still had a pretty formidable bunch of fighters though and I decided that we needed a victory of some kind in order to boost our confidence. And I knew just where that victory would come from. Nobody had elected me leader of our gang, or had even spoken about it out loud, I just seemed to fall into the role because I was the most violent and aggressive amongst us. Some of the gang looked up to me because of my criminal past and time spent in jail and others remembered the reputation I had been building as a Teddy boy before I was jailed. I would like to think that I had a certain charisma and leadership qualities that made others follow me, but I think my real talent lay in enticing other immature young men into my fantasy world and making them believe it. I could inspire people to take it all seriously because I believed it myself and we were all looking for something, anything, that was better than real life. Our petty violence and macho posturing were our rite of passage into manhood. We didn't have the option of going out into the bush to kill a lion, or even of striding a foreign battlefield with a gun in our hands; our generation had no war in which we could prove ourselves or die trying. So we divided ourselves into armies and beat the shit out of each other on the streets – until we grew up.

The punk rockers who hung around on the south end of Clapham Common were hard-core fighters who had had it all their own way for long enough as far as I was concerned. Just opposite the entrance of Clapham South tube station, at the start of the Common, there was a small brick building that housed the public toilets and it was at the back of this building that the punks would hang around, sniffing glue, drinking cider from the bottle and verbally abusing passers-by. On sunny days there would be as many as 20 of them lying about on the grass and comparing rips and safety pins. Quite a few of the rockin' crowd had been chased or had aggro from these punks, so I suggested that we should take a march up to Clapham Common and tell them that their reign was over. I was in the front room of the flat at Poynders when I suggested it and my suggestion was greeted with much enthusiasm. Joe K and LOB were there, along with a few of the regulars, and we were soon on our way up to the Common mob-handed, with fire in our eyes and righteousness in our hearts. It seemed as if a party atmosphere prevailed as we made our way there. We were off to bash our most hated enemies, the punks, and it was just what we needed to do. This was what being in a gang was all about: the camaraderie that we craved and the unity in having a mission that bonded us. Even the least violent members of the gang, like Dennis and Little Roy, were all fired up and enjoying the moment. In a gang-fight situation it's not always the biggest gang that wins but rather the gang with the element of surprise on their side. A sudden unexpected attack can, most times, be better than superior numbers. Also, doing things on the spur of the moment means that people don't really have time to be scared about what's going to happen, so there's less chance of analysing what can go wrong. And we were caught up in the moment.

We came out of a side street opposite the Common and should have been in full view of the punks, but they had become so used to having it all their own way on their turf that none of them even noticed us. We charged across Clapham Common Road, forcing traffic to a halt, screaming like banshees and waving our weapons about our heads. We were all armed with coshes of various kinds, from chair legs to lead pipes. I had a two-foot length of lead pipe pinched and taped at both ends and filled with sand for extra weight. It was a massacre. There were ten or so punk rockers in their usual spot, most of them lying in the sun or just sitting on the grass, and we were in among them before they had fully realised what was happening. I bounced my cosh off the spiky-haired cranium of one individual who was wearing a pair of tartan bondage trousers and felt the thud of lead on skull up to my elbow. I kicked another punk who was scrambling to his feet and started beating him about the arms and legs as he fell back to the ground. There were screams, squeals and shouts of anger all around me as the punks tried to get away, but they were being coshed all over the place. I gave the fella on the floor a proper doing and left him rolling in agony and screeching at the top of his voice. 'Shut up, you cunt!' I shouted at him. 'You sound like Johnny Rotten on stage!' I was feeling great and invincible with the excitement and adrenalin rush of the violence coursing through me. I saw that Joe K had a big punk up against the back wall of the toilets and was giving him a pasting, throwing a fast flurry of punches to his head and body. Joe had thrown his cosh down as he preferred to use his hands. Mick was rolling around on the floor with a geezer with blue hair, but seemed to be getting the upper hand. Harry and Gordon had chased after a guy who had been quicker than his pals and was legging it across the Common, but as I watched they caught up with the fleeing punk and set about him. I didn't want it to end, I was enjoying myself so much, and I wanted the punks to put up more of a fight but they had been slaughtered. The punk in the tartan trousers whom I had initially coshed was getting shakily to his feet, so I took a couple of quick steps in his direction and gave him another whack across the canister and he hit the ground again.

It was all over, bar the groans of pain from the punks, in a couple of minutes and I shouted to Harry who was still beating his victim with the thick end of a sawn-off pool cue. 'Let's go!' We walked away from the scene of carnage, patting each other on the back for a job well done and ignoring the looks of terror and disgust on the faces of some of the passers-by who had stopped to watch. They were civilians as far as we were concerned and we treated them almost as though they didn't exist, unless they were silly enough to try to get involved. Harry was the last one off the Common and he launched a hard kick into the ribs of the fallen tartan-trousers as a final farewell.

Back in the flat there was a great atmosphere as we all relived the violence. We had done the Clapham Common punks on their own turf and it was gratifying to get a bit of payback for all the times they had attacked one of ours. We were really starting to bond as a gang – there's nothing like a good victory for that – and I was happy. Throughout the rest of the day and that evening as people turned up at the flat, the battle was talked up and exaggerated and I knew how quickly word of our exploits would now spread through the scene. It had been a good day's work.

Some time after this we were to receive a visit from one of the most high-profile punk rockers in South London at the time – Punky Pat Marc, a dyed-in-the-wool punk rocker who was very much a part of the Kings Road scene. Punky Pat turned up at our HQ in Poynders Gardens one summer's morning on a Suzuki 50. There were several of the gang kicking back on the balcony when we saw him pull up bold as brass. I had to admire his chutzpah, parking his bike and casually walking up onto the balcony to greet us with a smile. Punky Pat was around 6-foot tall, with short hair dyed in a kind of blond leopard skin pattern and was wearing a blue leather and what looked like a pair of red vinyl trousers. We all stood up and watched this cheeky interloper walk straight onto our turf. I came forward to meet him. 'Are you Razor?' was his opener. I nodded. I could see no fear in him at all, even though he was facing six tough greasers with murder in their eyes.

'What do you want?' I asked. I was genuinely interested. Punky Pat put his crash helmet on the ground and leant against the balcony railings, perfectly relaxed despite the dangerous situation he was in. 'I've come in peace.' He said. 'I want to try and sort out all this bollocks.' I grinned and lit up a butt. 'What 'bollocks' might that be?' I asked, and blew smoke in his direction. He smiled thinly. 'You know what I'm talking about,' he said, 'the attack on my mates up at Clapham Common was out of order, for a start. Why the fuck are we fighting each other anyway?' I shrugged. I liked the fact that he had the bottle to walk into the lion's den on his own. I invited him into the flat for a cup of tea and we spent about an hour together, chatting about the situation.

When Punky Pat left we shook hands. We had brokered a truce between us and the Clapham punks, though both of us knew it was fragile and would only take one incident from either side for it to collapse. But Pat was the first punk rocker that I had a bit of respect for. Meanwhile we had other heads that needed breaking.

We Fought the Law ... and the Law Won

Doing the Clapham Common punks was a great move for us, both on a confidence level and also as a message to everyone else. We had taken our lumps from the north Battersea crew but had come back stronger on another front. People were talking about the Balham Wildkatz as an emerging force who were not to be fucked with, and that was just what I wanted. The punks had definitely got the message, as they moved their meeting spot further north to the small seating area at the rear of Clapham Common tube station; this was one of the concessions I had won during my chat with Punky Pat. When we found out about this it gave us a further boost, as we had managed to throw them off what was now our turf. In the weeks following our attack we would regularly go up to Clapham South and look for any sign that they might still be around, but they never came back. Dennis spray-painted 'Balham Wildkatz 1979' on the wall at the back of the toilets, straight over all the anarchy signs, and this was our proof that we ruled this particular patch of empty ground. From such small and pointless victories legends are built.

My next idea was to sort out the small gang of skinheads who hung out on the estate across the road from Poynders, the Cubbitt House skins. Only about three skinheads actually lived on the estate, but on some evenings seven or eight skins would gather on the perimeter wall of the flats and shout threats and abuse at any of the rockin' crowd who came by. They were a nuisance more than anything, but I realised that we couldn't be seen to tolerate any threat, no matter how insignificant, especially on our own doorstep. I was given a good excuse one evening when Jenny and Elaine came into the flat and told us that when they had been using the phone box outside the estate a couple of the skinheads had crossed the road and given them a load of verbal and then held them in the phone box by blocking the door for about ten minutes. It was kids' stuff really, but I grabbed a cosh from the pile we kept behind the settee in the front room and said I was going to sort them out. As usual, everyone followed my lead and soon we were crossing into Cubbitt House on a skinhead hunt.

The Cubbitt House skins legged it when they saw us coming, and though we went through every inch of their estate there was no sign of them other than their graffiti. Dennis did the honors with the spray can and laid our moniker on a couple of walls. Our honour satisfied by their cowardice, we headed back to Poynders. After that we hardly ever saw a Cubbitt House skinhead again, though every now and again we heard a rumour that they were going to mob up and attack us, but it always came to nothing. We were now the top gang in north Balham and Clapham South and getting well known on the rockin' scene. On Wednesdays and Saturdays we would be regulars at the Chick-A-Boom club, Sundays we were rockin' at The Greyhound in Croydon, Thursdays it was The King's Head in

Collier's Wood and Fridays we were at The Squire in Catford. There was now no shortage of rockin' pubs and clubs in South London and we tried to get to all of them.

Things were going well, but I kept hearing how the north Battersea were going to be coming for us and it seemed that the more high-profile we got on the scene the more I was hearing these rumours. One night, after hearing once again how Psycho Joe was going to get me, I decided to get in first and end the rumours once and for all. Together with Harry, who was a pretty good car thief and driver, I went out on a mission. My idea was for us to steal a car big enough to pack four or five of our best fighters and then drive around north Battersea until we found the other mob and jump out and do them on their own turf. It sounded like a good plan to everyone, so Harry and I headed out to get the transport. I don't know what it is but there are certain times when, no matter what you do to prepare, things can only go wrong, and this was one of those nights. In the '70s all you really needed in order to nick most cars was a car key known as a 'double FS', which was basically a double-edged Ford key, and you could open and start nearly every Ford car on the road and some other makes as well. Harry always had a couple of double FS keys hanging around in case of an emergency, so all we had to do was find a car that fitted our needs and drive off in it. It was starting to rain as we left Poynders on foot and headed up to Streatham and we should have taken the rain as a bad omen and just gone back into the warm, dry flat, but we zipped up our leather jackets and trudged on. We couldn't nick a motor too close to Poynders, as we wanted to park it up on the estate for a couple of days and we couldn't take the chance that somebody would recognise it, so the further away we went the better.

An hour after leaving the flat we were up past Streatham hill and looking like a pair of drowned rats from the incessant rain. We had tried around ten cars, but either the key wouldn't do the ignition for some reason or the cars were alarmed and had steering locks. We found a perfect big old Humber Super Snipe on one of the back-streets and got in and got the engine started, but when we pulled away we realised that one of the tires was completely flat. We left the Humber and headed for the car park opposite the *South London Press* building on Leigham Court Road, which was a favourite hot spot for car thieves. There were only two cars in the entire car park, a Morris Minor and one of those little blue three wheel disabled buggies, which we insensitively called 'cripple cars'. Cold and wet, Harry suggested that we give up for the night, but I was impatient to find a car now and I wasn't going home until we had one.

Ranging out from Streatham we came back down the back-streets and across the dark and rain-lashed Common until we reached Bedford Hill and followed it back into Balham. We must have tried another dozen cars and been walking in the rain for over two hours when Harry had an idea. We were pretty close to an off-road garage where he had stolen cars in the past and Harry said it was the last place he was going to try. 'If we don't get a motor here, I'm off home.' I had to agree. The garage was at the end of a long roofed passage between our old alma mater Henry Cavendish Junior School and a row of houses. There were lights on in some of the houses, so we had to creep up the alley to avoid alerting anyone and keep very quiet in the courtyard. As we came to the end of the alley, Harry tugged the sleeve of my leather and whispered, 'Bingo!' The car parked outside the locked double doors of the garage met our requirement perfectly. It was a big old Austin Cambridge estate, which would hold at least six people in comfort – the perfect battle wagon. The driver's door was unlocked and I felt relief and excite-ment as I got into the passenger side. It was dry and relatively warm inside the dark interior of the car and I unzipped my leather and shook the rain off my head, running my fingers through my hair and then reaching for the rear-view mirror and my comb. The rain was making a lot of noise as it bounced off the exterior of the car and the sound of the engine seemed muted as Harry jiggled the key in the ignition and made contact. Harry flipped a switch and the dashboard and exterior lights came to life, the headlamps' powerful beams cutting through the dark of the yard and highlighting the falling rain. Harry grinned at me. 'We have lift off,' he said happily and released the handbrake and shifted the column lever into first gear. I whipped my comb back into my pocket and punched him lightly on the shoulder. 'Let 'er roll!' I said, and we crept smoothly down the passage and out onto the street.

The car was a beauty and seemed to glide through the wet streets like a stately liner on a calm sea. Both Harry and I were happy now that we were out of the rain and heading home with the prize. I switched on the radio and went through the stations until I found one that was playing something decent. Then I relaxed into the big leather bench seat and watched the rain in the headlights. We had driven up Radbourne Road and were waiting to turn onto Thornton Road, which would bring us to the roundabout opposite Agnes Riley park and about five minutes' driving from the back entrance to Poynders Gardens and safety, when Harry uttered the words that can chill the heart of any ne'er-do-well who's committing a bit of skullduggery, such as being in a stolen car. 'Shit. Old Bill, right behind us!' It took all my willpower not to spin around and take a look, but I managed to keep looking ahead. 'Are they on us?' I asked. Harry leant over and casually turned off the radio, also keeping his eyes on the road ahead. 'I don't know,' he replied. 'It can't be the motor. We've only had it five minutes.' He risked a glance in the rear-view mirror and my heart sank as he spoke again. 'They're waving us to park up.' My mouth went dry and I could clearly hear the ticking of our indicator light and the swoosh-bump of the windscreen wipers on our windscreen. Harry had been indicating to turn left when the police, in an unmarked maroon Hillman Hunter, had rolled up behind us. I risked a glance behind and saw the two uni-formed coppers putting on their hats in anticipation of an arrest. Harry looked at me. 'Chase?' he asked. I nodded.

'Fucking go!' I shouted.

Harry slammed the gearstick into second and stamped on the accelerator. The front of the big old car seemed to rear like a wild stallion for a second, and then we were off, speeding out into the near empty street and fishtailing around to the right, heading up Thornton Road. I looked out of the back window and saw the police Hunter sitting there for a second before the blue flashes of the dash-mounted light lit up the street and the bell-clapper siren began to ring out. The police driver was no novice, that was for sure. He came around the corner without even a skid and was right behind us as Harry pushed the old Austin up to 70 mph. The reflection of the police car's blue flashers seemed to fill my field of vision and light up the whole interior of our car and the street beyond. I risked another look back and they were stuck to us like shit on a blanket. 'Get ready!' Harry shouted above the siren, and I knew he was about to pull his favourite car-chase manoeuvre. I put my arms straight out and braced myself against the dashboard. With one quick glance in the rear-view mirror, Harry slammed the stick into first gear and jammed his foot on the brake. If the road had been dry he might have pulled it off. The idea was to bring our car to a sudden stop so that the following police car would smash into the back of us, hope-fully damaging his engine or radiator and bringing the chase to an end. Front-end damage could incapacitate the police car but getting hit in the rear would not be enough to stop us pulling away again. It was a common manoeuvre amongst South London car thieves and Harry had used this tactic before with some success – but never on a wet road. As the brakes bit in, the Austin began to aquaplane across the road out of control and the police Hunter, instead of crashing head first into our back bumper, clipped our rear wing and sent us into a wild spin. I was jolted forward by the impact of the Hunter and then sideways as our car hit the kerb side-on. The car lifted up onto two wheels with a terrifying ease and seemed to hang there for a long second before crashing back onto the road with a jolt of the suspension. My head cracked against the side window and I felt dizzy and sort of seasick. For a moment there was only the sound of the rain crashing off the roof like a spray of pellets from a sawn-off shotgun and then I was aware of Harry twisting the key in the ignition and the engine stuttering into life again. I looked out of my window and saw that the coppers were out of their car and running over to where we had stopped. 'Go! Fucking go!' I shouted, and at the same time I pressed down on the button that would lock my door from the inside. Harry revved the engine again and threw the stick into gear, fishtailing away just as one of the coppers reached my door and yanked on the handle. I looked back and saw the coppers run back to their car. The chase was still on.

I often think that at any other time we would have got clean away, but that night the fates seemed to be conspiring seriously against us. Harry spun the car onto a long, quiet road with a dog-leg curve halfway up it and gunned the engine up to top speed. We knew the area like a cat knows its own vomit, as this was the turf we had grown up on. Sinclair Estate was only two streets away, so if we reached the end of Parkthorne Road we would be out onto King's Avenue and away down the straight. But as we approached the curve in the road at close to 75 mph we found out why the car had been sitting outside a garage when we nicked it. I was facing the back window watching the Old Bill car trying to sail up our arse when I realised that we were going to overshoot the curve in the road by quite some way. 'Steer the car! Steer the fucking car!' I yelled in panic. And I heard Harry shout 'Here! You fucking steer it!' and something bounced off my thigh. It was the steering wheel. I looked at Harry and realised that he was trying to twist the steering column with his bare hands and that the half-chrome Bakelite steering wheel was on the seat between us.

For a split second I thought Harry was playing some sort of unfunny joke on me, and then I saw the sheer panic on his face as he struggled to get some sort of grip on the column and I knew it was definitely no joke. I found out later that the mechanic who had been working on the car's steering problems had only made the nut hand-tight before leaving work, as he had intended to take the steering wheel back off for a full overhaul. If Harry hadn't been such an experienced driver we might both have died in that car. As it was, he managed to slow us down with a swift and instinctive combination of gear changes and brake-pumping whilst getting enough of a grip on the steering column to steer us away from the brick garden walls on either side of the street. I braced myself for the crash, but when it came there was little I could do.

We ran into the back of a parked Ford Granada, ironically just the make and model we had been searching for when we had set out earlier that evening, and I was thrown through the windscreen and across the bonnet of our Austin. I was fully aware of what was happening, but I felt no pain and was unable to stop myself as I slid off the bonnet and up the boot and back windscreen of the Ford, ending up on the roof for a second before falling sideways onto the wet tarmac. I lay there for a second, rain splashing directly into my face, and looked up at the black sky. Fuck this for a game of soldiers, I remember thinking before hearing the sound of running feet. Without stopping to check how seriously I'd been injured, I rolled under the Ford and out on the pavement side. I got to my feet and glanced about. The police Hunter was parked with the front wheels up on the pavement and with both doors open.

The front of our stolen Austin was a mess, all crumpled metal and shattered glass and with clouds of steam belching from the broken radiator. And the back of the Ford wasn't going to be winning any beauty prizes either. I looked down the road in the direction we had come from and saw Harry being chased by one of the coppers from the Hunter. I just had the time to wonder where the other copper was when he grabbed me by the collar of my leather jacket and swung a punch at my face. I jerked out of the way and the wet leather slipped out of his fingers, and I was off up the road. I ran in the opposite direction to Harry, up towards King's Avenue, and the copper was right on my tail. I was young and fit and I could run for fun. Not only was I fast but I also had endurance and had twice won the 3,000-metre race in borstal against some very stiff opposition. So when it came to a foot race I was confident that there could only be one winner and this is what my head told me.

Unfortunately my body was a different matter and very early on in the race it started to remind me that I had just been thrown through a windscreen at 30 mph. I had almost reached King's Avenue before I was caught. I had a pain in my side and I was growing dizzier by the second and slowing down when the copper rugby-tackled me and brought me down hard on the pavement, my face falling right into a puddle. He gave me a few digs in his excitement, but I was quite beyond feeling by then. I had concussion and a cracked rib from the crash. Harry had also been caught and we both appeared at Lavender Hill magistrates court the next morning looking like two sorry scarecrows. Harry, being the driver, was charged with 'Taking and Driving Away' and I was charged with allowing myself to be carried in a stolen car. We were both remanded in custody to Wormwood Scrubs for three weeks.

Jailhouse Rockers

B-wing of Wormwood Scrubs held 120 young men on remand and serving sentences for a variety of crimes, but mainly violence. Just as on the outside, the subcultures stuck to their own and didn't mix. It was like our own brand of self-imposed segregation and if anyone broke it there would be violence. Harry and I were celled up together and we joined the rockabilly crowd on exercise and association. Kidd, the black Brixton rockabilly, was there, doing six months for ABH (actual bodily harm) on a mod at Margate during a bank holiday bust-up, as were a couple of rebel Teds from Colliers Wood, Colin the Blade and his best pal Eddie. Stud of the Shepherds Bush Rebels was there, awaiting transfer to Camp Hill to start his ten-year sentence, and a rocker from Islington named Ton-up Tony. We held the southernmost corner of the caged-in exercise yard as our prison turf. The skinheads, of whom there were around a dozen, held the north end of the yard, and the punks, looking slightly ridiculous now that they had no access to hairspray for their Mohicans, plotted up on one side opposite the handful of mods. The rest of the prisoners were soul boys, sticksmen, squares and smoothies and they spread out over the rest of the yard. You could have cut the atmosphere with a spoon.

The toughest reputation on the yard went to a handful of a gang called the New Park Dreads who were all on remand for a murder that had happened in a wine bar at Streatham Hill. We had grown up on an estate just half a mile away from the NP Dreads' turf, so you could say we were neighbours of a sort, but there was no love lost between us and we gave each other a wide berth. There was the occasional bit of trouble on the yard, usually when the PE instructor tried to sort us into teams for a game of football, but the most dangerous time of the day was when exercise finished and we were milling about waiting to get back onto the wing. End of exercise was when the screws took their eyes off us in order to open the doors and count us in, and a few people took this opportunity to settle old grudges or start new ones. Colin the Blade had exchanged words across the yard with one of the punk crowd who he said was 'screwing him out' and on the way back into the wing he popped the punk a right-hander on the jaw and knocked him spark out. Nobody saw him do it, but after the screws had us all locked down the air outside the windows was blue with threats.

Apart from the physical violence in the Scrubs there were also the nightly verbal assaults as 120 rowdy teenagers with little else to do would climb up to their cell windows and let loose a torrent of abuse and threats at each other. Sometimes it could be hilariously funny and very entertaining trying to outdo each other with the cracks and insults flying about, but it was not for the fainthearted or anyone with a stutter. The most disgusting filth and the most extreme forms of racist insult were acceptable and the only no-go area was if you mentioned someone's mother. If you did bring mothers into the argument you could be ostracised even by your own mob. There we were, young criminal scum willing and able to stick knives in each other and anyone else who got in the way, but we were all mummy's boys at heart.

Harry and I stuck with our crowd and spent three long weeks living in a tense and violent atmosphere while keeping a don't-give-a-fuck mask firmly in place. We had both done more than our fair share of bird and knew the dance steps we had to follow in order to survive, but it was still no walk in the park. I was glad to get back into the dock of Lavender Hill magistrates court and enter a formal plea of guilty to the charge. Harry also pleaded guilty, but his charge was a bit more serious than mine and he had quite a few previous ones for car theft. What also went in my favour was the fact that according to court records my last conviction had been in May 1977. They didn't work out that my record had only been clean so long because I had spent the previous two years in jail. The magistrate gave me a stern talking to and then gave me a six-month sentence suspended for 12 months. I was free, but Harry was not so fortunate. The magistrate remanded Harry in custody for sentence at the Crown Court, which normally meant a borstal sentence. I was fucking gutted for him. He had already served 17 months of a previous borstal sentence and I knew he would now serve another nine months minimum. My heart went out to Harry as I saw the screws lead him out of the dock to the cells below and then back to the Scrubs. I had lost a good mate and an invaluable member of the gang.

Most of the gang had turned up in the public gallery of the court to offer us support and I was greeted with handshakes and slaps on the back as I walked out of custody, although the obvious joy at my homecoming was tempered by what had happened to Harry. Both Jenny and Marina shed a few tears for their brother and I felt like doing so myself. Back in the flat at Poynders I caught up on the news of what had been happening since I'd been away. It turned out that Psycho Joe's crew were having a bit of trouble of their own. When they had run us at The George and broken the leg of a rocker's girl-friend they made themselves the target of a gang of rockers who were gunning for a bit of revenge. The punks and skins on the manor had been keeping a low profile, but there was a new gang starting to large it at the rockin' clubs, particularly at the Chick-A-Boom. The Crawley Cats were from Crawley, obviously, and were a gang of young rockabillies who trained at ex-middleweight champion Alan Minter's gym. Most of the gang were amateur boxers and were led by a couple of pugnacious brothers named Shamus and Lenny. Along with us, the Crawley Cats were getting a reputation. And I wanted to see what they had. I quickly slipped back into the lifestyle I'd been leading before getting nicked, spending most of my time in the flat at Poynders or going out rockin' at the pubs and clubs.

Perry and Elaine had split up and I started seeing Elaine for a while. She was a great girl but just a bit scatty and sometimes her Sicilian temper could be a bit too much. One day she went off to visit her mum and the next thing I knew she was on remand in a girls' prison called Cumberlow Lodge. She had argued with her mother and ended up trying to strangle her again. Perry, Gordon, Joe K and I decided to go and visit her. I had some mad idea about breaking her out and the boys were up for it. Cumberlow Lodge, as far as I could figure, was like a females' version of Standford House, where I had spent much of the summer of 1976, and held girls between the ages of 14 and 18 who had been remanded by the courts without bail. It was in Norwood, halfway between Crystal Palace and Gypsy Hill, and consisted of a modern-looking house block surrounded by a 12-foot wire fence. We got there around 7 in the evening, long after visiting hours were over, and strolled right up to the house block. There was a glass door, which was firmly locked and bolted, so I rang the bell. Some geezer who was obviously the night-patrol screw came to the door and asked us what we wanted. Perry told him we'd come to visit our sister and gave Elaine's name.

The screw shook his head. 'Visiting hours are over for the day, lads,' he said. 'Come back tomorrow.' I stepped forward and spoke in what I thought was an Australian accent. 'Come on, mate,' I said. 'We've just flown in from Australia to see our sister. Just give us five minutes to say hello to her.' The screw wasn't fooled. 'You ain't got much of a tan for Australians,' he responded. I was starting to lose my temper. 'It's the fucking rainy season,' I said impatiently, forgetting to use the accent. The screw smiled. 'Yeah, come back during visiting hours,' he said and turned away. I kicked the door. 'Let us in or I'll just smash this fucking door down,' I shouted. The screw pulled a personal radio from his belt. 'Go ahead and try,' he said. 'The glass is bulletproof and I'm directly through to the police on this radio.' There was fuck all we could do except retire ungracefully. We shouted a few threats in the screw's direction, gave him the wanker sign and told him we'd be waiting for him one morning when he came off duty. Then we headed back down the drive.

Our shouting had attracted a few girls up to the windows of the house block and they started calling to us. I thought blokes could be pretty near the knuckle, but these birds were shouting the sort of filth that you'd expect from a bunch of drunken merchant seamen! I was quite flattered by some of the things they said they'd like to do to me and I'd have been up for it at any other time. When I managed to get a word in edgeways I asked them to tell Elaine we had called. She was obviously in a cell on the other side of the building or she would have been up at the window as well. I didn't see Elaine again until 1987.

My cousins, Ronnie and Eddie, and the remnants of the old Wanderers gang were now drinking in a pub on Bedford Hill called The Bedford and they sent me word that the Rocking Devils now had a regular gig there on Tuesday nights. So I decided to go down one Tuesday for a visit, as I hadn't seen the lads for a while. Although they had 'gone smoothie', the lads were still into the music for old times' sake so long as they didn't have to leave their local to hear it. So the Wildkatz went down there in force. We weren't expecting any trouble in the pub itself, but is was bang in the heart of what was disputed territory.

The old skinhead gang, the Balham Boot Boys, were now a mixed gang of punks, skins and mods and they had formed this unusual and unholy alliance under the leadership of the big nappy-wearing punk rocker, Junior. The Wildkatz had claims on the whole of Balham, but the revamped BBBs also laid claim to that particular turf and so it would go to whoever was the stronger gang. To add a further complication, a gang of Asian disco freaks who called themselves The Flash Pakis also had designs on Balham. The Flash Pakis were second-generation Asian youths who, unlike their parents, were willing and able to fight at the drop of a hat. Tooting Bec, the next station along from Balham, was known locally as Little India because of the number of Asians living and working there, and the Flash Pakis had a very large gang to call on in times of trouble. The Flash Pakis dressed in suits with black and white pointy Jam shoes and carried red neckerchiefs either hanging from a pocket or tied around their wrists. They had moved in on Balham High Street and made the Wimpy bar their HQ, hanging around outside in large groups or inside drinking tea. They had never really fought anyone that we knew of, but they had the attitude that made you believe they would if anyone tried to push them, and if you walked past them on the high street they weren't shy about screwing you out. I knew the Flash Pakis would bear watching. There was too many of them to ignore.

The Bedford turned out to be a great night out. There was a circular revolving stage where the Rocking Devils belted out some great rock'n'roll, a half-decent dance floor around the stage, and a DJ who knew his music. The pub was crowded, but as it was my cousins' local we never got any trouble at all. In one corner of the front bar, away from the music, sat a small group of pimps who made Huggy Bear look like a very conservative dresser. Bedford Hill was a big red-light district and The Bedford was the watering hole for the working girls before they headed up the hill to look for punters. The pimps made me laugh, as they were proper caricatures of what a pimp should look like and I wondered if there was some sort of pimp handbook of instructions that they all had to read. They were all black and wore sunglasses, even at midnight, and the most outrageous clothes and headgear outside of a Slade concert: berets, purple velvet homburgs and fire-engine-red fedoras, silk scarves, check suits so loud your eardrums might be damaged if you stood too close, and multi-coloured platform boots with everything except goldfish swimming in the heels. Most of them carried canes and Ronnie informed me that they were actually swordsticks concealing 18-inch blades. The girls were a rough-looking lot with more scabs than a leper colony and make-up so thick you could have laid breeze blocks with it. I actually found them quite fascinating to look at. But the pimps and their pros kept to their own end of the pub and the locals had become so used to seeing them that they no longer even noticed their garish raiments and ludicrous headwear.

The old Wanderers gang and even a couple of the now disbanded Pharos, such as Gerry Suggers, were regulars in The Bedford, and when CSA played there the Road Rats MC and the Deptford Alley Cats turned up in force, the latter pair being biker gangs. I had a good chat with Ronnie and Eddie and met their birds. Ronnie was with a good-looking bird called Gaynor, who seemed very shy, and Eddie was with one of a long line of Barbie doll types whose name he couldn't remember when he tried to introduce us. He was a bit of a ladies' man our Eddie. I had a bit of a chat with my old pal Gerry, the ex-Pharos, and I had a bit of a bop on the dance floor, a few pints and a look about. I was leaning up against the wall at the back of the pub just watching the dancers when I saw this gorgeous little bird come in and walk up to my cousins' table. She seemed to know everyone and I watched her closely. She was about 5 foot 5 inches tall with curly blonde hair and curves in all the right places. She was dressed like a smoothie in a grey three-quarter-length skirt and pink blouse with a flyaway collar and I noticed that when she smiled the whole room seemed to light up. She must have felt my beady eye on her as she looked directly at me for a moment and then looked away, but I saw the hint of a smile in her eyes and that was invitation enough for me. I flicked up the collar of my leather jacket, ran the comb through my hair and sauntered across to say hello.

Alison, for that was her name, looked even better close up than she did from a distance. She had flawless skin, pretty blue eyes and a mouth that looked made for kissing. I stood at the table with my thumbs hooked in my belt and looked down at her. Ronnie introduced her and she smiled at me full on, and I was gone. Of course, when you're young and as full of yourself as I was it wasn't cool to let your feelings show, so I nodded and gave her my best Elvis sneer. But I made up my mind then and there that I was going to ask her out before the night was over. I pulled Eddie aside. 'Is that Alison going out with anybody?' I asked, trying to sound casual. Eddie told me she was single and asked if I fancied her. 'Me?' I said. 'Nah. I was just wondering, that's all.' Eddie nodded. 'Okay,' he said. 'But I think she likes you.' I dismissed it, straightened my shoulders and walked away feeling pretty good.

Throughout the night I kept looking over at Alison and on a couple of occasions I caught her looking at me. Then it was time for the DJ to play the slow songs, so I went over to the decks and asked for 'There's a Moon Out Tonight' by The Capris, one of my favourite slow doo-wop songs at the time. As the lights went low and the first beautiful notes of the record rang out I got to Alison's table. I rolled my shoulders and flicked my quiff out of my eyes.

'Fancy a dance?' I asked nonchalantly. Alison smiled and stood up and the next thing I knew I was out on the dance floor with this gorgeous creature in my arms. She smelled like a mixture of rose-scented shampoo and Juicy Fruit chewing gum and before the dance was over I was seriously in love for the first time. We stayed on the dance floor through the entire slow dance set, just holding each other and swaying around in time to the music, and I forgot all about prison, gang fights and looking cool. When the music ended we sat at a table together and talked about nothing in particular until closing time and then I walked her home. Our first kiss on her doorstep lit me up like a two-bob rocket and saying goodbye took nearly an hour. I just didn't want to leave and if her mother had not called her in I would probably still be standing there now.

Alison worked on the cosmetics counter at Woolworths in Tooting Broadway and I promised to pick her up from work at 5 the next day. Being in love was all new to me but I liked it. I had a kind of good feeling all the time and found myself laughing out loud for no particular reason at odd moments during my long walk back to Clapham South. Things were going pretty well, but if I had learned one thing in my life it was that when things were looking this good there was some cunt waiting around the corner to fuck it all up.

Part Three

The Rockabilly Rebels

Rockabilly – slang, a form of rock'n'roll with elements of hillbilly music.

Enter Popeye

It used to be said that you weren't a real rockabilly until you'd had your first Mac Curtis haircut, as it was the only way to tell the rocka- billies from the rebel Teds. And I suppose there's some truth in that, as we all wore the same clothes eventually. But the first wave of rockabilly kids, known as 'rockabilly rebels', had a pretty distinc- tive style of dress from their predecessors, the Teds. When the first rockabilly compilation LPs were released in the late 1970s they fea- tured pictures of the artists and the bands, which, in most cases, had never been seen before by a British audience. We had all assumed that rockabilly singers must look pretty similar in dress and hairstyle to their rock'n'roll contemporaries. You had Elvis in his gold lamé drape suit and Bill Haley in his shawl-collared red and black check drape coat, which all bore at least a passing resemblance to clothes that were worn by the Teds. But the LP photos of rockabilly artists showed them in jeans, cowboy shirts and neckerchiefs or in sharp pegged pants and baggy box jackets. They were dirt-poor Southern boys from the backwoods in most cases, enticed into the inde- pendent recording studios by the phenomenal success of the orig- inal Hillbilly Cat, Elvis Aaron Presley. But they had their own style, and it was plainly different. As rockabilly, a mix of rock'n'roll and hillbilly music, was performed by a bunch of rural farm labourers and truck drivers, it was kind of a working-class rock'n'roll and the style of dress reflected this. In England the first kids who took it se- riously adopted a British working-class style of dress and turned out at the pubs and clubs in donkey jackets, jeans and boots, usually with a neckerchief knotted around their necks. Donkey jackets were cheap, around £5 a throw, and this was a strange concept to the Teds in their expensive hand-tailored suits. They chose to take it as an insult, when in actual fact it was an inexpensive gateway onto their scene for thousands of youngsters who could now afford to be part of it. The Teds, steeped in arrogance and elitism for so long, chose to reject rockabilly and then tried to ignore it instead of embracing the new movement and reaping the benefit of young blood. The result was that the Teds began slowly to fade away and the rockabilly army grew stronger.

The early rockabilly look was functional and warm in the winter, but not much cop if you wanted to impress someone with your sartorial elegance. I once went to pick up a bird for a night out, resplendent in my donkey jacket, jeans and boots, and was a bit disappointed when her dad opened the door and thought I'd come from the council to fix the drains. But the rockabilly look soon evolved. By 1979 the rockabilly rebels were a dying breed and the new style was known as 'hepcat' or 'cat' for short. The typical rockabilly cat would have in his wardrobe at least one box suit – a box-backed jacket with no vents and single-breasted lapels, and pegged pants – trousers with pleats at the waist and narrow bottoms with a turn-up. Box suits were normally worn with either an open-necked polo shirt, always with the collar of the shirt out on the lapels of the jacket, or with a normal dress shirt and slim-jim tie. In summer it was garishly coloured Hawaiian shirts, faded Levi jeans and chukka boots. A leather biker jacket could be worn at any time and some cats, like Mitcham Roy and Joe K, would even wear their leathers over a shirt and tie with a pair of pegged pants, although you usually had to have a bit of panache to carry off this look. The favoured footwear of the cat was chukka or commando boots for casual wear and wingtip brogues or penny loafers with a suit.

By the summer of 1979 the WildKatz had put the rebel Ted phase behind them and evolved into fully fledged rockabilly cats. Mick, Joe K, Gordon and I went down to Water Lane in Brixton to have our first Mac Curtis cut. Andy, the barber, was a Greek fella who cut the hair of almost everyone on the rockin' scene of South London at one time or another. He was mustard with the clippers and could turn a quiff and DA into a flat-top Mac Curtis in minutes. The Mac Curtis was actually a flat-top but with certain modifications. It had a bit of hair at the front that was longer than the rest and could still be shaped as a quiff of sorts. The back and sides of the hair would be shaved into a number one cut and the top would be left as a number three and shaped flat. Andy actually featured in a London Weekend Television documentary about rockabillies in 1980 and as far as I know he's still down in his shop at Water Lane giving rockabilly haircuts. On that day Mick didn't get a Mac Curtis, but a G.I, which is shaved back and sides like the American Marines. To this day Mick, who still has all his hair, swears that it is the Mac Curtis cut that led to a lot of us losing our hair in the later years!

The Wildkatz were now a rockabilly gang, but things had been pretty quiet since Harry went away. The lads didn't mind the occasional tear-up, attacking the odd punk or skinhead we came across on our daily travels, and Joe K was always guaranteed to start something. But I was starting to lose a bit of my edge. I was in love and that kind of mellowed me out. I would be outside Woolworths almost every evening to pick up Alison and most times we went to Olly's house in Streatham and spent the evening listening to records, getting drunk and generally annoying the band with our starry-eyed love talk as they tried to practice. Alison had dropped the smoothie look and was now a rockabilly chick and wore tight pencil skirts and pointed stilettos. We went to The Bedford together and up to the Chick-A-Boom on Saturday nights and we couldn't keep our hands off each other for more than five minutes. I was doing the occasional bit of work on building sites and the odd bit of thieving, but mostly I was just hanging about with the gang.

One Wednesday night Buddy Knox, a headliner from the 1950s who had a top-10 hit with a song called 'Party Doll', was due to play at the Chick-A-Boom and a load of us decided to go. Alison had to stay in that night for some reason, so we decided to make it a boys' night out. We didn't have tickets for the gig but all turned up flying our colours anyway, and in the end we couldn't get in as the club was packed out. There was me, Mick, Gordon, Perry, Adrian, Dennis and Alan, Ahmet and Olly and we all fancied a piss-up, so we decided to go to a pub on Streatham Common, near Olly's gaff, called The Railway Arms. I think it was Olly who picked the pub because it was near his house and it would be easy for him to get home. But what we didn't take into account was the fact that the pub was just up the road from the headquarters of the South London branch of the National Front and that they were having a meeting that night. We were soon to find out, though.

The Railway Arms was a clean and quiet little pub across the road from Streatham Common train station. There was a decent-ish jukebox and we basically had the pub to ourselves for the evening except for a few locals. We had a good laugh and downed a few pints and then at closing time we decided to get a takeaway from the Chinese chip shop a few doors away and then go round to Olly's gaff to carry on the evening. I had my bag of chips and was standing outside the shop talking to Olly and waiting for the rest of the gang when I heard a car horn sounding on the road in front of us. The traffic was pretty steady and I glanced at the road and noticed that a car had pulled up at the kerb and the passenger windows were being wound down. The car was full of skinheads and they must have thought all their Christmases had come at once when they saw a couple of lone rockabillies standing on the pavement, especially as Olly was also black. 'What you doing with the wog?' one of them called. 'Do you want to sell him?' There was laughter from inside the car. I smiled at them, walked over to the car and bent down to look inside. There were five of them, all proper skins with big bald heads and more tattoos than the crew of a pirate ship. 'All right, lads?' I asked, friendly as you like. 'Fancy a chip?' And I slammed the bag of hot chips into the face of the skin who had spoken first.

His scream as I smeared the wrap of hot salted chips over his ugly mug was music to my ears. And then it was all off. As I had been walking towards the car Olly had pushed open the door of the chip shop and alerted the rest of the gang and they came straight out, ready to kick off.

The skins came out of every door of their car like clowns out of a circus jalopy and, to give them a bit of credit, our numbers and willingness to fight didn't make them falter. In seconds we were all rolling around the pavement punching the shit out of each other. It was a great fight. I had hold of the fella to whom I'd fed my chips by his braces and ran him head first into the door of his own car. He left a dent in the bodywork but it didn't slow him down and he caught me with a hard punch under the ribs. I fell to the ground, winded, but I wasn't letting go of his braces and he fell on top of me. Olly smashed a beer bottle on chip-face's head when he managed to get the upper hand and we generally gave the skins a good kicking. We left them nursing their wounds and shouting that we were dead, and walked through the backstreets to Olly's house. About five minutes later we heard the screeching of tyres and were surprised to see the skinheads' car, followed by a Bedford van, speeding up the road towards us. It seemed as though they now had reinforcements and wanted a second go. When we saw the skins coming we all did the street fighters' dance, which we were well versed in by now and which consisted of ducking into the gardens of the nearest houses. You'd be amazed at the weapons you can find in some people's front gardens and unless you're very unlucky there are always empty milk bottles waiting on most doorsteps. I grabbed a couple of milk bottles, the long-necked sterilised sort, and flew out onto the pavement ready for battle. Mick had a length of wooden fence and Ahmet had found a couple of big kidney stones. Everyone else had bottles, except for Perry, who'd had the foresight to be carrying a lead cosh. This time we didn't have the advantage of surprise and from the number of skins who piled out of the back of the van the interior must have had the dimensions of Dr Who's Tardis. The fight was swift and bloody and we were getting the worst of it when the police suddenly turned up all lights flashing and sirens wailing. It turned out, lucky for us, that someone had phoned the police during the first fight outside the chip shop and so they had arrived in time for the second fight. At the sound of the sirens we all scattered and began to leg it in different directions.

We all met up some time later at Olly's house and compared our wounds and stories. I'd had my nose broken again in the melee and had no idea who or what had hit me. Ahmet had a cut above his eye that looked as though it might need stitches and Mick had a broken knuckle, but apart from the usual cuts and bruises we were all okay and none of us had been nicked. We classed the evening as a result and no one was really that disappointed at missing Buddy Knox. We found out later that his performance had left a lot to be desired and that he had turned up with an outrageous perm on his head. Perhaps it was for the best that we hadn't been at the Chick-A-Boom that night, as it would have been painful to have to bottle a genuine '50s legend off the stage, but that's probably what we would have done.

The story about The Wildkatz's battle with the NF skins soon made the rounds and went down in rockin' myth as a major victory. The way we told it, if the police had not turned up when they did we might have done the skins and then stormed their headquarters. We lapped it up. The next Saturday night there were around 15 of us on our way to the Chick-A-Boom when the tube pulled into Balham station. We always got into the first carriage so that we could spot any undesirables and be ready to ruck or defend ourselves as the train entered and slowed down through the length of the station. When the doors of the front carriage opened I was surprised to see a fella standing there who looked vaguely familiar. He was wearing a light grey box suit, snow white shirt and maroon slim-jim tie, with highly polished penny loafers on his feet. The hair was in a greased-up and squared-off Mac Curtis and his whole demeanour was one of cockiness. I only had a second to place him before he smiled and I noticed the missing lower tooth, and then it all dropped into place. 'Blue?' I said. He stepped onto the tube train and nodded. 'I'm back,' he said. 'Let's go rockin'!'

Bopping with the Crawley Cats

To go with his change of fashion and direction, Blue had also given himself a new nickname and from now on he told us he would be known as 'Popeye'. Popeye was a strange cat and I don't suppose anyone really understood what was going on in his head. He was flash, but he had the minerals to back it up. He was just average in a fist fight but the reason he was such an asset to the gang was because he was a known and feared tool merchant. His favourite weapon was a flick knife or lock knife, but he was equally adept with a cosh or a bottle. A lot of people, even violent fighters, would hesitate to stab or cosh someone and it takes a certain lack of empathy to be able to do it. It's not as easy as you might think to cold-bloodedly attack another human being with a weapon with the express intention of doing them serious harm. A lot of our gang fighting involved bottles and coshes, but only the real mad fighters would aim for the head, and they were pretty rare. A lot of injuries received in gang fights were to the body, legs and arms. Popeye, however, was the real deal. He would plunge a knife into anyone and not think twice about it. He had a certain coldness about him that could be distinctly sub-zero if you were in his line of fire, but at the same time he was a very funny and likeable character.

With Popeye in our gang the stakes were raised considerably. I knew from experience that a fighter with a reputation would attract more challenges from like-minded people who want to enhance their own rep on the back of destroying yours. It was the way of the world. The north Battersea had Psycho Joe, south Battersea had Bopper Hogan, the Crawley Cats had a guy named Snake, and we had both me and now Popeye. Every gang had at least one rep fighter who loved to talk about, and build into a legend, their own personal bogeyman whom they could use to instill fear into the enemy and maybe win a bit of the fight before it had even started. So the more of these bogeymen you had on your team the better. But it was actually me who kicked off on that night at the Chick-A-Boom when Popeye made his first appearance.

By now we had our own corner staked out and this is where we all headed every Saturday as soon as we got into the club. Everything was going fine and late in the evening I was sitting at our table with Mitcham Roy and Snapper just drinking snakebites and shooting the shit when I felt eyes on me. I looked over the back of the alcove and saw five or six rockabillies and one of them was proper staring at me. I stared back until he slowly looked away and out onto the dance floor. I leant close to Snapper's ear. 'Who's the mug in the Buddy Holly T-shirt?' I asked, and indicated the next alcove. Snapper took a quick look. 'His name's Jimmy, I think. He's one of the Crawley Cats.' I knew some of the Crawley were in the club that night, but they were hard to spot in the crowd as they weren't flying their colours. I looked around the club and noticed Mick and Adrian talking to a couple of girls over by the entrance, and Popeye was out on the dance floor where he had been for at least half an hour. He could certainly dance, the geezer, and it was like he was catching up on lost time. I don't really know why I decided to give Jimmy a clump; maybe I was bored, or maybe I wanted to get it on with the Crawley Cats or maybe I just didn't like the way he was looking at me. Or maybe all three.

I stood up and walked out of our alcove and round to where Jimmy was sitting. He saw me coming but stayed in his seat, though he never took his eyes off me. He had a cocky look on his face as I stood in front of him. There was a small round table between us, with drinks, bottles and glasses on it. 'Had a good look?' I asked. 'Do you want a fucking photo of me or something?' He smiled, reached over to the table, picked up a half-pint mug by the handle and took a sip of his drink. 'Fancy yourself then?' he asked cockily. 'That why you think I was looking at you?' I tipped the table up so that everything on it went flying in his direction and then I jumped on him. He was no pushover and the next thing I knew I was on my hands and knees and my head was ringing. As I had leapt forward he had swung the heavy glass into the side of my head. It gave me a good belt, but fortunately the glass didn't break or he might have had my ear off. I barely had time to look up before I got a real hard kick in the ribs that hurt like fuck. I rolled across the floor a couple of times to get a bit of distance between us and got quickly to my feet. At this stage in my life I was fitter than a butcher's dog and battle wise and hardened from the borstal system where I'd fought almost every day. I rushed at him and managed to get my head under his chin and force him back onto the seating, and once I had him down I launched a head butt into his face. I knew it had hurt him because it had certainly hurt my head. I had him by the throat and started throwing wild right-handers at his face.

This whole episode had only taken a couple of minutes at most, but it was long enough for the commotion to be noticed and for people to come running. The first I knew that Mick was beside me was when I saw his fist fly past my line of vision and whack the now senseless Jimmy in the mouth. I didn't need any help, but it was nice to know that it was there. Barney, the bouncer, and one of his pals grabbed me and dragged me away. Jimmy had a bloody nose and mouth, and probably a couple of loose teeth, but he got shakily to his feet. 'You fucking wanker!' he shouted at me. And Mick stepped forward and punched him in the face again. For a second it seemed as if the fight might kick off again, but more bouncers turned up and I was marched outside into the foyer, followed by Mick and a few of the boys. The Crawley mob had also started coming out of the woodwork and there was a slanging match in the foyer, with Barney and his bouncers in the middle trying to calm everyone down. It was the usual mayhem after a fight in a club, but after a bit of shouting and a few threats were bandied about people started to drift back inside. Jimmy and a couple of his pals called a cab and fucked off, probably down to St Helier Hospital to get his nose straightened, and I classed the evening as a job well done. The Crawley Cats would have got the message loud and clear. I was feeling pretty good and the amount of alcohol I'd consumed was keeping at bay any pain from the clumps I'd taken, although I would feel it the next day.

Barney didn't want to let me back inside the club, but a couple of girls named Lesley and Jeanette, who I knew from around the scene, talked him into it. Barney was a bit of a sucker for a pretty face. But he told me I was on my last warning and that if I started anything inside again he would bar me. I liked Barney; he was a funny bloke but well able to handle himself in a ruck. So I promised to behave and went back inside. I found Popeye just coming off the dance floor, no jacket on and his shirt wet from his non-stop bop marathon. 'Cheers for your help with that bit of bother,' I said sarcastically. Popeye downed his pint of snakebite in three gulps, belched and then shrugged. 'I was watching,' he said. 'You had it covered. And if it'd looked as though you didn't,' he patted his trouser pocket significantly, 'I'd have been over to finish it.' From this I guessed he was tooled up, but then I'd never heard of a time when he wasn't. Later on in the evening we were all sitting around in our alcove fairly drunk and I spoke to Popeye. 'So, you fancy joining the gang then?' Popeye looked around and shrugged. 'Why not?' he replied.

'Birds, booze, bass and plenty of tear-ups, you wouldn't fucking think so!' We clasped thumbs in the rebel handshake. 'Welcome to the Wildkatz,' I said.

Just before the slow records started, Joe K came up to our table to introduce us to a girl he fancied. Her name was Debbie and I have to say she was hot, even for Joe who only pulled gorgeous birds. Debbie had curves in all the right directions and was very feminine looking, but she also had an air of toughness about her. Her jet-black hair was cut in a boy's style, near enough a flat-top but a bit longer in the front, and it looked good with her heart shaped face and sparkling green eyes. When she smiled I didn't know whether to kiss her or challenge her to an arm wrestle. 'All right?' she said when Joe introduced her to me and she gave me a bloke-like hand-shake. If Joe hadn't been there I might have made a move on her myself despite the fact that I was going out with Alison. Debbie just had this kind of a sex-on-legs quality, like a raven-haired Marilyn Monroe, but I also got the impression that she could throw a decent right-hander if the need arose. A Mac Curtis record came on, one that had everyone running for the dancefloor, and Debbie said, 'See ya,' and was off. I looked at Joe. 'Where'd you meet her?' I asked. Joe grinned. 'Gorgeous, ain't she? She's going out with a geezer I know, Derek. You know, the cat with the Yamaha 650. He ain't here tonight, though. I think I'm in love.' I shook my head. 'You don't want to be moving in on other geezers' birds, it's always trouble,' I warned. Joe winked. 'I'm up for a tear-up,' he said. 'Especially for her.' I shrugged. 'It's your funeral, mate.'

Alison and I had been getting on great and were talking about getting engaged. We were just a couple of kids really and had no intention of getting married, but getting engaged sounded good to us. I was very immature for my age, and I blamed that on the life I had led. I had never worked for any more than a couple of days at a time and though I was what is now called 'street smart' I was irresponsible and very impulsive. I had already spent a lot of my life locked up, a large portion of it in solitary confinement, and I hadn't really had the chance to develop in the conventional manner. When my friends were leaving school and getting their first jobs, making their start on real life, I was drugged up and in a straitjacket in an underground solitary cell. And, although Alison was the first girl I had stayed with for more than six weeks in my life, I still wasn't able to stop myself looking at other girls. I just didn't have the self-discipline or commitment to keep a relationship going for too long.

In the week after my tear-up with Jimmy I was hearing word that the Crawley Cats were gathering like storm clouds and that I was on the list of the people they were planning to rain on. Joe K also made the list after he got into a punch-swapping contest with a minor member of the gang at The Greyhound. By all accounts, the Crawley Cats were 'screwing' over these minor setbacks to their growing reputation and were looking for swift and merciless retribution. I couldn't have cared less. My arrogance had not yet reached its peak, but it was climbing higher and faster than Sherpa Tensing, so I shrugged off these threats and went about my business.

Popeye brought new dimensions to the Wildkatz. Not only was he a boost in the violent reputation department, but also he had picked up some moneymakers during his time as a runner for Belfast Joe. He could get hold of very good fake jewellery known as 'snides'. Snides looked and felt like the real thing and they were ramped up with genuine hallmarks, but they were usually made from base metals and dipped to add the sparkle. We could get rings and chains of all description, including the 1oz 'gold' ingot on a chain that was very popular in those days, and all the top watches from Piaget to Rolex. So some of the gang, including me and Popeye, earned a nice few quid by selling this gear around south-west London. Our favourite sales ploy was to pretend that the gear was stolen and so hot that you could get second-degree burns on your eyeballs just by looking at it, and the suckers ate it up. With more cash on the hip we could now afford to buy second-hand motors instead of nicking them and Popeye and I went halves on a 1957 Ford Consul. We did plenty of work on the car and it became invaluable for getting us to the more out-of the-way clubs. The Wildkatz were now mobile.

Influences

The music we were now listening to was an eclectic mixture of what can be lumped together under the heading of 'rock'n'roll', although it ranged from 1940s pop and swing, Glenn Miller's 'In The Mood' and 'Boogie Woogie Bugle Boy' by The Andrews Sisters, to 1970s-re-corded British rockabilly, 'Rockabilly Guy' by The Polecats and 'Hot Dog' by Shakin' Stevens. Every now and again some innovative DJ would kick-start a record in the clubs that, though not strictly rock'n'roll or rockabilly, would be adopted by the rockin' crowd so long as they could dance to it. A couple that spring to mind are that old mod classic 'Green Onions' by Booker T and The MGs, and 'My Baby Just Cares For Me' by Nina Simone. Both of these records became massive at the time because they were perfect for dancing 'the stroll' to. Some rockabilly recordings had become instant clas-sics, even the Rollin' Rock revival singles that had been recorded in Ronny Weiser's sitting room in his house in Van Nuys California in the late 1970s. Ronny Weiser had set up the Rollin' Rock label and brought a few of the original rockabilly artists out of retirement to redo some of the classics and knock up some new stuff. Mac Curtis, Ray Campi and Sleepy La Beef particularly benefited from this and all had excellent records released on Rollin' Rock. The label took off in the clubs and the artists soon found themselves getting bookings for European gigs on the back of these records. Ray Campi played at the Chick-A-Boom club on one of his first English tours and a lot of his records became dance floor classics with the rockabilly crowd.

Ray Campi had the biggest audience-participation record in the clubs with a recording called 'How Low Do Ya Feel?' At various stages in the song there is just a bass drum counting down the chorus with four beats, and whenever this song was played everyone in the club would stamp on the floor four times along with the beat. It was great at the Chick-A-Boom, which had a solid floor, but the record was banned at The King's Head in Colliers Wood because the club was upstairs in a function room located above the main bar and the first time everyone stamped along chunks of plaster fell on to the drinkers below. Campi stompers like 'Caterpillar', 'Tore Up' and 'Quit Your Trifling' were guaranteed to fire up the crowd, as were records by his label mate and originator of the standard rockabilly haircut, Mac Curtis. 'Half Hearted Love' and 'How Come It' by Mac Curtis both reached number 1 on the *Sounds* rock'n'roll chart. *Sounds* was a music paper that came out every week and printed a rock'n'roll top 20 compiled by club DJs.

Looking at *Sounds* now, it's strange to see the chart from the rockin' clubs next to the British national chart. On 4 March 1978, for example, Abba were number 1 in the national chart with 'Take A Chance On Me', while number 1 in the rockin' chart was a double A side single, 'Train Kept A Rollin'/Honey Hush', by The Johnny Burnette Trio. If you listen to Abba and The Johnny Burnette Trio you could fall straight into the huge yawning gulf between the two styles. It's not so much chalk and cheese as chalk and vomit.

The main style of music being played was tough, raw rockabilly from such artists as Charlie Feathers, 'One Hand Loose' and 'Bottle To The Baby'; Marvin Rainwater, 'Boo Hoo' and 'I Dig You Baby'; Sonny Fisher, 'Pink and Black' and 'I Can't Lose'; and a host of other early rockabilly artists and recordings. But the rockabilly crowd, not content with largely taking over the Teddy boy clubs and pushing them into the background, also began to plunder the lockers of the original rock'n'roll musicians and dust off their earlier recordings. Such Teddy boy stalwarts as Buddy Holly and Elvis were given a new welcome by the rockabilly crowd, but not for their commercial rock'n'roll recordings. Both Buddy and Elvis had recorded some fine rockabilly at the start of their careers. You only have to listen to Buddy's 'Blue Days, Black Nights' or 'Rock Around With Olly Vee', and Elvis stuttering his way through the echoey 'Baby Let's Play House' or 'Good Rockin' Tonite', to find the gems among the commercial dross. How the original Teddy boys must have rent asunder their £300 suits and gnashed their teeth at the audacity of these youngsters raiding their musical archives and 'discovering' such recordings. Not only that, but the rockabilly crowd barefacedly claimed the likes of Gene Vincent And His Blue Caps, Eddie Cochran and Johnny Burnette as their own. For the Teds it must have been a bit like the Native American Indians seeing the white man 'discover' their land.

Two other styles of music that were big on the rockin' scene and deserve a mention were doo-wop and hillbilly. Slow doo-wop, like 'Daddy's Home' by Shep and the Limelites, 'Goodnight, Sweetheart, Goodnight' by The Spaniels or 'A Thousand Stars' by Kathy Young And The Innocents, were standard for the end of the night slow dance, but there was also a lot of fast or mid-tempo doo-wop that was perfect for jiving to. Stuff like 'Oh Gee' by The Crows and 'Why Oh Why?' by The Cues could fill the floor in a hot second. In 1979 hillbilly music was just starting to kick in, but as it was part of the roots of rockabilly more kids wanted to hear what it was like. Hillbilly in the clubs would reach its peak around the end of 1980, after it had spawned a short-lived mutation of the rockabilly subculture, but in '79 you could hear such classics as 'The Blues Keep Knocking' by Buck Trail and 'Wore To A Frazzle' by The Lamie Bros.

The big rockin' film of 1979 was called *The Wanderers*. Based on a novel by Richard Price and set in New York in 1963, it told the story of the rivalry between the various gangs of that era, and featured a fantastic soundtrack of early '60s rock'n'roll. I'd guess that most of our gang had seen *The Wanderers* at least twice, and once we all went to Streatham ABC cinema to see it together and ended up in a fight with a gang of Mitcham skinheads who were also in the cinema at the time. *The Wanderers* featured a skinhead gang called the Fordham Baldies. We lapped up what we saw on the screen and then went out and lived it on the street, and so did others. Another big teen film doing the rounds and influencing kids in 1979 was *Quadrophenia*, the story of a group of young mods set in the early '60s when mod was at its peak. Some people think that the release of *Quadrophenia* started the mod revival, but in actual fact it was a band that had ridden to shore on the crest of the punk movement. The Jam were sporting mohair suits and playing an aggressive blend of mod R&B as far back as 1977, and a lot of teens became attracted to the mod movement through The Jam.

There is no doubt that *Quadrophenia* was responsible for flooding the mod ranks, in much the same way that *Grease* did for the rock'n'roll scene, but there was already a hard core of mods around London even before the film came out. Over in Shepherds Bush there was an early movement towards neo-mod in 1978 directly due to The Jam, and the Shepherds Bush Mods started to get known as a gang. Shepherds Bush had always been a big Teddy boy area, but with Stud and the Duke, the leading lights of the Bush Rebels, away in borstal and others turning into rockers, the turf was wide open and the mods filled the vacuum. There were other well-known mod gangs around the London area, including a firm from West Ham known as The Glory Boys and another gang from Sutton called the Big Faces.

At first the mods and the skinheads were very pally, as they usually went to the same gigs and shared the same venues, but it didn't last for long and soon they were punching the shit out of each other. It all kicked off in a big way when the Ladbroke Grove skins attacked a crowd of mods who were attending a gig at The Acklam Hall on their manor. After that the gloves were truly off and whatever fragile alliance there had been between the two sub-cultures was shattered. While the mod scene was growing, the skin-head movement also received an infusion of new blood on the back of the Two-Tone phenomenon. Two-Tone was a Coventry-based record label that had such bands as The Specials and Madness on their roster. The bands played a sort of modern version of the ska sound, which had originally attracted the first skinheads in the 1960s and was now attracting a younger skinhead element. The NF tried to adopt Madness as their own and this led to a lot of violence from skinheads at their gigs. Most of the Two-Tone followers were into tonic suits and porkpie hats, some were skinheads and some were suede heads, but to all other subcultures they were clearly another enemy.

Along with the regular skinheads there was also a small group of fanatics who called themselves Sieg Heil. It was rumoured that they all came from different areas and only met up for gigs and rallies. They dressed in SS uniforms, including jackboots and with death's head badges on their jackets and, like the old Millwall FC hooligans, their motto was 'Kick to Kill'. I did not believe that they actually existed and thought they were just a horror story that the skinheads told in order to frighten people. I first heard about them after we had run the Cubbitt House skins, when a message came across to the estate that a gang called Sieg Heil would be paying us a visit. The rumours about them persisted, but most people just laughed them off as a myth. Then one night I met them.

Joe K and I had been to The King's Head in Colliers Wood and caused ructions. We had started a fight downstairs in the smoothies bar and it had ended up outside in the car park. Joe, as usual, had stripped to the waist and offered to fight everyone in the pub, but they shut the doors on us. We were both steaming drunk and, as there was a bus garage right next door to the pub, we had the brilliant idea of stealing a bus and driving it through the front of the pub. Getting into the driver's seat of the bus was no problem as they don't even lock the fucking things, but there were no keys so we decided to bump-start it. Just then around six of the Clapham Junction Rebels were passing on their way into the King's Head and I asked them to give me a hand pushing the double-decker. The lads were very obliging, and with seven of us pushing and Joe at the wheel we soon had the bus rolling out of the garage at a fair old trot. Unfortunately, or fortunately if you were one of the customers in the pub, Joe had never driven anything – other than people to distraction. Instead of dropping the bus into gear and then clutching it, he just sat in the driver's seat giving rebel yells and steering straight ahead. Just opposite the bus garage was an iron fence and beyond that a steep embankment that led down to the River Wandle. The Wandle is a pretty narrow and shallow strip of water at that point in its meander, but still no place to park a Routemaster. We stopped pushing when we realised that Joe was steering right at the river, and it was lucky that mounting the kerb slowed the bus down enough to stop it crashing through the fence by weight and momentum alone. As it was, the iron fence bent inwards at the point where the bus met it but did not break and the vehicle crunched to a stop. Joe jumped down from the cab with a happy smile on his drunken face. 'I drove a bus!' he was shouting excitedly. 'I drove a fucking bus!' The CJ Rebels legged it into the car park of the pub and I grabbed Joe and dragged him over to Colliers Wood tube station. We left the bus sitting there, straddling the road and holding up traffic on both sides, and made our way down into the tube.

Once on the tube we met up with a couple of smoothie girls and started chatting them up, so we stayed on past our stop and ended up in Victoria. The girls were going to a club in Kensington, so we walked them over to their platform and waited with them for their train, as even at night the place was busy. After the girls had got onto the tube safely, Joe and I made our way back to the Northern Line platform and we walked around a corner and straight into a gang of five or six skinheads. It all happened very quickly, but we just had time to take in the fact that they were wearing leather trench coats over Nazi army uniforms and highly polished jackboots. We all stopped and stared at each other for a second, and then I yelled 'Leg it!' and started running off down the corridor with Joe close behind me. I heard a shout and then the sound of boots echoing off the tiled floor and walls, but I didn't look back. We ran up a 'down' escalator and through a few more corridors, pushing people out of the way in our panic to get away. We found ourselves on a platform where there was a stationary train with its doors already open, so we jumped on. We could hear the echo of boot steps running towards us from the corridor we had just exited and I was willing the doors of the train to shut. We ran further into the train and threw ourselves flat on the floor, much to the bemusement of the rest of the passengers, and then I heard the most welcome sound of the doors swishing shut. I poked my head up, looked out of the window and saw the Nazi skins milling about on the platform with murder on their faces. The train began to pull away and I stood up and knocked on the window. When the skins turned towards me I smiled and gave them the wanker sign with both hands and so did Joe. The train began to pick up speed and one of the skinheads ran alongside it shouting something at us and making cut-throat gestures, but we just laughed at him. I did notice that he was wearing an iron cross on a ribbon around his neck and I wondered what he had done to merit that award. That was our one brush with Sieg Heil, and we knew it was them as there would hardly be another gang walking around London in full Nazi dress and regalia, and they may have been evil bastards in a ruck but they couldn't run worth a shit in their jackboots.

The Balham Baldies

A perfect example of how the big teen flicks of the time could influence our actions can be seen with the Balham Boot Boys. In 1976 they had been a pure skinhead gang led by the football hooligan element of the Zennor Road Mob, but by 1979 Zennor Road itself no longer existed as the houses had been demolished to make way for an industrial estate and most of the skinheads were now in jobs and living in other areas. So the Boot Boys were now a mixed gang of punks, skins and smoothies, led by the orange-haired punk, Junior. But soon after *The Wanderers* had been shown in the cinemas of South London most of the Boot Boys began sporting completely shaved heads just like the Fordham Baldies gang in the film. I might have thought this was just a coincidence, but I was sitting on an old car seat outside the breaker's yard on Balham High Street drinking cider and enjoying the sunshine with Popeye and a Tooting cat named Andy when we saw the Boot Boys, en masse, coming down Bedford Hill Road with their new baldie look and one of them was carrying a tape deck that was playing loudly 'Walk Like A Man' by The Four Seasons, which is actually the song featured on *The Wanderers* when the Fordham Baldies make their entrance. Their penchant for imitating art was further evidenced after *Quadrophenia* had been shown in our local cinemas later in the year and the Boot Boys turned up on the manor in fishtail parkas and pork-pie hats, though with not a scooter between them.

Bank holidays were big fighting days for all the subcultures and the place for doing this fighting was on the seafront of some small coastal town. Back in the early 1960s the original mods and rockers had started the tradition of the bank holiday punch-up and it had been revived in 1976 as part of the gang social calendar. On the south coast it was Southend, Brighton or Margate for us, although Southend also had The Minerva, which had always been a Ted pub, and the Kursaal amusement park which was always good for a laugh, particularly the midget motorbikes. In 1978 most of the sea-side towns on the south coast were invaded by hordes of London Teds, punks and skinheads and battle ensued, much to the consternation of the locals and the delight of the media. But in August 1979 a new dimension was added with the rise of the neo-mods. And the Wildkatz were going to be there to make sure it all kicked off.

I had been looking forward to the punch-up at Southend for weeks and it was just my luck that on the Thursday before the bank holiday I was nicked for possession of an offensive weapon and held in Tooting police station over the weekend. My arrest had come about after a fight in The Bedford pub. A couple of leery soul boys from Streatham had been drunk and giving it the big 'un and got into an argument with my cousin Eddie. I got involved and ended up head butting one of the Streatham boys into the jukebox and then threatened them both with a cut-throat razor. The fight was over after that and the Streatham boys left, but somebody must have phoned the police as they came into the pub and they pulled me outside for a 'chat'. They searched me and found the razor, so I was nicked on the spot. I was a bit drunk, so I gave them a lot of lip and put up a bit of a struggle, but they eventually got me into the back of the panda car. Seeing me struggling with the police, and being fairly inebriated themselves, my cousin Eddie and a Mullingar street fighter known as Big Pat came out of the pub and started remonstrating with the police. Next thing I knew there was another struggle and several more police vehicles arrived, lights flashing and sirens wailing, and both Eddie and Big Pat were nicked too, for obstruction. We all ended up in the police cells for the weekend and were bailed on bank holiday Monday. Which meant that I missed the big tear up in Southend.

According to the newspapers, the police at Southend had called in a 'crack Essex police unit' called the Special Support Unit (SSU) to deal with the expected outbreak of violence. In the event, the SSU had to work hard for their overtime payments that weekend, making 75 arrests for public order offences as around 1,500 teenagers descended on the Golden Mile and began kicking the shit out of each other and anyone else who got in their way. The biggest mob were the skinheads, closely followed by the mods and then the Teds and rockabillies. Gangs had come from all over London, and the South London rockin' scene was well represented. Mick, Eamon, Gordon and Joe K were slightly injured in an early clash with a gang of skinheads at Southend railway station as they were getting off the train, but there was plenty more fighting outside The Minerva and along the seafront. None of our mob was arrested, but the police did confiscate their footwear and march them out of town in their socks before returning it. I also missed the next bank holiday kick-off, at Margate, when Joe and the boys were featured in a photo on the front page of the local paper. I've yet to see that newspaper's front page, but it has gone down in rockin' legend.

Meanwhile, back in South London things were also hotting up. I was still going strong with Hollywood, which was what Mickey A had nicknamed Alison because he said she looked like a film star, and I was picking her up most days after work, but the first flush of love had worn off and I had returned to fighting again. Popeye was now working and living in a breaker's yard on Balham High Street facing the entrance to Bedford Hill Road. The site used to be the old RACS co-op building but it had been demolished in 1974 and the land had lain empty until some enterprising villain began squatting there and opened it up as a breaker's yard. Popeye lived in a small caravan on the site along with two vicious dogs, an Alsatian and a Great Dane, who guarded the yard at night. It was terrific for Popeye, as not only did he get paid and live there rent-free but there was also plenty of scope for fiddles. There were around 150 vehicles in the yard and people would come from miles around to buy spare parts. The owner never knew exactly how much stock he had, as there were cars coming in and out all the time and he was rarely there, so Popeye could charge whatever he thought he could get away with – and that was usually plenty. Popeye was the sort of geezer who would sell a rat's arse to a blind man and swear it was a diamond ring.

Of course, with Popeye living in the yard it became our new hangout. With both Peter and Harry in jail, the flat at Poynders was being reclaimed by the council and Marina and Jenny had to find alternative accommodation. Marina went to live with her new boyfriend, some soul boy, in Tulse Hill, and we decided to find a squat for Jenny. We found a two-storey house on Ferndale Road in Balham just a short walk from The Bedford pub and changed the locks before moving Jenny in. We now divided our time between the breakers and Jenny's squat, both firmly in the heart of our turf, Balham. I spent most of my days mooching around South London with my cousin Eddie, selling snide jewellery and nicking any-thing that wasn't nailed down as well as some things that were. Or I would help Popeye out in the yard and earn a few quid stitching up his boss. Most days we'd start drinking strong cider early in the morning and be steaming drunk by lunchtime, and so the days seemed to fly by.

It was on one of the days that I was working with Popeye at the yard that we spotted the new-look Boot Boys doing their impression of the Fordham Baldies. We laughed so much that I nearly dropped my cider bottle. But, while the Boot Boys were going downhill fast, the Flash Pakis were living up to their name. One evening Popeye and I were suited and booted and on our way to the Chick-A-Boom club for a Wednesday night session, featuring a new young rocka-billy band called The Blue Cat Trio who everyone was raving about. As we headed to Balham tube station we were sharing a bottle of Olde English cider to fortify us for the journey. Outside the Wimpy bar, which was about 100 yards from the station, stood a group of four Asian youths wearing sharp suits and black and white shoes. As we walked past, one of them, the tallest of the group, gave us a proper screwing. Popeye, not one for refusing a challenge, stopped and scowled back. 'Who you fucking looking at, you stinking paki?' Popeye asked. The Asian youth smiled. 'I'm looking at you, you fucking white greaser dog,' he replied. I noticed one of the Asians slip into the Wimpy bar. Popeye's head nearly exploded at the tall kid's reply. 'You what?' he shouted. 'You fucking what?' And with that he launched himself at the Asian kid and stuck the nut on him. Not slow on the uptake myself, I gripped the neck of my cider bottle and whacked one of the other Asians in the head with it. In my haste to get into the action I had momentarily forgotten that the bottle was half full, and cold cider flooded over my hand and down the sleeve of my best light grey box suit, drenching me and spreading a dark stain as it immediately soaked into the material of my jacket. This pissed me off even more, so I whacked the other Asian in the face with the bottle as well.

Popeye was fumbling in his pocket for his flick knife when the double doors of the Wimpy bar burst open and what seemed like a wide and angry river of Asian youths flowed out onto the street. I couldn't believe how many of them there were and I noticed that a few of them were waving knives and sticks in our direction. Neither Popeye nor I needed to be told that we were neck deep in shit here and we both started running at the same time. Running is great for getting away from trouble, but in cases like this the enemy cannot resist chasing, like greyhounds after a mechanical hare. We legged it towards the tube station and got a bit of distance between us and the Flash Pakis and then Popeye reached over and snatched the cider bottle from my hand. I hadn't even realised that I was still carrying it. Popeye slowed down and turned towards the gang and I, against my better judgment, slowed and turned with him. Popeye pulled his arm back over his shoulder and threw the cider bottle with all his might into the crowd of Asians. About 15 yards separated us and it was a good throw. I watched the bottle tumble end over end through the air and, just a second before impact, it was snatched, one-handed, from its trajectory by a hard-faced Asian kid who, judging by the skill of the catch, should have been playing test cricket for his country instead of hanging around in a Wimpy bar. He held the bottle above his head and shouted in triumph, 'Flash Pakis rule!' And then they charged at us. Popeye and I legged it into the station, leapt the ticket barrier like a pair of Olympic athletes and slid down the rail of the escalator. There was a train on the platform destined to head in completely the wrong direction to where we wanted to go, but we got on just as the automatic doors were closing.

Once again the tube system had saved us from a beating. The London Underground system in the late '70s was a lot different to how it is today. There was no CCTV and once you were down in the bowels of the city anything could happen. You would never see an Underground worker or a copper and the tunnels and walkways offered plenty of space for gang graffiti. You could usually tell what sort of welcome awaited you above ground by the spray-painted gang names and messages you would find in the station. Up at Clapham Common tube station the remnants of the Clapham punks would sometimes come down onto the station platform to sniff glue and drink cider when the weather was too inclement to do it outside, and this is where we made our next attack on them.

A Visit to Mad Harry

Travelling across London by tube could be dangerous after dark, but in the daylight hours it wasn't so bad, depending on which station you planned to emerge from. Sloane Square, for example, could be a bit iffy because the chance of running into a rival subculture, particularly the punks, was high. It was okay if you were mob-handed yourself, but in small groups or on your own it wasn't advisable. So for three of us to traverse London on the tube flying full colours was going to be a bit of a fantastic journey and took a bit of planning. We were going to visit Harry in Wormwood Scrubs and pride and protocol dictated that we would not go incognito but with our colours, and Harry's, on display for all to see. Taking Harry's colours with us was our way of showing a downed member of the gang that he was still one of us and being thought about on the outside. It is a great morale booster to get a visit when you are in jail, but even more so if there's a female visitor. In jail in those days, before the equal opportunities policy allowed women to work on the landings, you could go for months without smelling a hint of perfume or seeing a well-turned ankle. So it was a treat to see a girl on a visit and that is why I decided to take Hollywood along – after all, she was sex on legs.

There is a three-person limit to the number of prison visitors allowed, so I chose Popeye to come along with me and Hollywood. I figured that he would be handy if we ran into any trouble, as he was as game as a brace of rabid pit bulls. Flying our colours meant wearing our leather jackets with our gang name and sigil emblazoned on the back panel. Our sigil was a grinning cat's head with a quiff and with a smoking butt hanging from its mouth. Across the shoulder panel was the word 'Balham' and underneath the cat's head was the word 'Wildkatz', done in white paint and gothic script. My own leather had been repainted from the Quantrill's Raiders days and I also had my nickname painted in gold letters on the waistband of the jacket. Hollywood wore Harry's leather, which was too big for her but looked surprisingly sexy with her tight pencil skirt and white stilettos. I had a lead pipe cosh in the waistband of my jeans and Popeye had his favourite pearl-handled flick knife and a bicycle chain. We were leaving nothing to chance.

We walked straight past the ticket collector at Balham station and Popeye and I slid down the escalator rail at some speed, leaving Hollywood to come down the slower, girl's way. Down on the platform there were only about three or four people waiting for the train. I sat on one of the benches and got into a spit-swapping contest with Hollywood while Popeye made himself busy by trying to force the chocolate machine to spit out an extra Bar Six by shaking and slapping it. When the train came rushing into the station, pushing a tide of chip wrappers and fetid air before it, we stood, alert, to see if there were any undesirables in the front carriages. Satisfied by the emptiness of the carriages, we got into the last one and slouched into our seats as if we owned the train.

Popeye and I had a bit of a plan. If there were any punks loitering on the platform of Clapham Common station we were going to launch a surprise attack. Our fragile treaty, brokered by Punky Pat, had broken down when Joe K punched out a couple of punk rockers at a bus stop in Clapham South, so we were now back at war with the punks. And as it turned out there were four or five punks sitting on one of the benches as the doors of our carriage opened. Leaving Hollywood sitting in the carriage, chewing gum and watching us as though we were fascinating children, we had our coshes ready when the doors slid open. We jumped onto the platform, ran a few steps to where they were sitting and set about the unsuspecting punks. They didn't stand a chance and we were in amongst them before they even knew it was happening. I kicked one under the chin and knocked him straight off the bench and then swung my cosh at one who had been in the act of raising a cider bottle to his mouth. The bottle shattered in his face and I laid my cosh across his spiky head with some force. Popeye was like a wild animal, swinging his bike chain with gusto, but I had warned him not to stab anyone as that might be serious enough to get the train stopped and us nicked further along the line. 'Maybe on the way back?' he'd asked hopefully.

We slaughtered the punks and then hopped back into our carriage. I leant out before the doors closed. 'Meet the Wildkatz!' I shouted at the top of my voice. You get a really good echo in a tube station.

As the train pulled out we could see the punks just getting to their feet, a couple bleeding heavily, and we laughed all the way to Clapham North. Doing the punks was a good start to our journey, but it was a long way over to East Acton and we would have to keep our eyes open. We had to go through 22 stations before reaching our destination and every station could hold a nasty surprise. At Stockwell a couple of soul boys went to get into our carriage but moved further down the train when they spotted us. Popeye wanted to go and steam into them but I convinced him to leave it. I knew he was itching to stab someone, he always was, but I just wanted to get to the Scrubs now. We changed at Tottenham Court Road and got through to East Acton without another incident. It was a bit of a trek from the tube station, but we had soon reached the bottom of Du Cane Road. We knew we would receive at least a rub-down search in order to get into the prison, so we slipped into the public car park opposite the main gates and hid our weapons under a bush at the far end.

Harry looked well, considering he was rotting away in a prison cell 24/7, and he was delighted to see us. We filled him in on all the latest news and gossip and I slipped him a tenner to buy a bit of snout up on the wing. I sent Hollywood up to get us all a cup of tea and smiled when I saw Harry's face as he watched her slink up to the counter in his leather jacket. 'Wow!' he said. 'That is some tasty bird! Proper wanking material.' Popeye and I both laughed. 'Wipe your mouth, H,' I said.' 'You've started dribbling, mate.' The visit went really well and it seemed as though we'd only been there five minutes when it was time to say goodbye. We stood around the table giving Harry the rebel shake and a few pats on the back. Hollywood gave him a hug and a peck on the lips that I knew he'd be dreaming about for months, and then he was gone.

When we came out of the prison we picked up our weapons from the car park and set off back towards the tube station. I was feeling a bit depressed about leaving Harry in jail. I knew what it was like in those places and I knew Harry was strong enough to do his bit of bird with few problems, but it didn't feel great leaving him there. We were about two-thirds of the way to the station and I was deep in thought when I felt Popeye tug my arm. I looked up and saw a bright yellow Ford Capri parked half on the pavement ahead of us. The car was obviously customised, with a back spoiler and mag wheels and whiplash aerials. Leaning against the car were four flashily dressed Asians. I had heard about an Asian gang in West London called The Holy Smokes, who sometimes hung around in Acton, and I had the feeling that those boys could be part of that gang. They were in their late teens or early twenties and seemed to favour pencil moustaches and disco clobber: high-waist trousers, fake silk shirts and medallions. I gripped Hollywood by the arm and manoeuvred her so that she was on my inside, away from the kerb, and looked at Popeye. He smiled an evil smile and patted the pocket of his leather. He may have been happy to mix it up with a quartet of evil-looking fuckers miles from our own turf, but I wasn't so sure. We definitely didn't have the element of surprise here and we were a long way from home. 'Say nothing,' I said to Popeye. 'There's four of the cunts.' Popeye never lost his smile, he just shrugged. We carried on walking towards them and they were now watching us. I thought we were going to get past them and be on our way and I was hoping that Popeye could keep his mouth shut, but as we drew nearly level with them one of the gang made kissing noises at Hollywood. 'Hello darling,' one of them called. 'Want to come for a ride with some real men?' That was it. When I heard those words the white-hot rage just descended on me all at once. I felt my face burning. How dare these cunts talk to my bird like that? I reached into my waistband, pulled out my cosh and steamed straight in. I must have hit the first

171

bloke, the one who had spoken, at least ten times in the head and body before his mates had a chance to react. I was like a fucking Tasmanian devil, ripping into him with the cosh and punching him with my other hand. I was gone, my head screaming at me to kill him and my body doing its best to obey. The rest of the mob, seeing how things were going down, reached through the open windows of their car and armed themselves with rounders bats and a cricket bat. I guess they were sporty types. I only managed to piece all this together later, after speaking to Popeye and Hollywood, because I was caught up in a violent frenzy and began laying the cosh into anyone who moved. I remember my arm getting tired from beating someone and then Popeye was dragging me away and shouting, 'Let's go!' Hollywood was even more white-faced than usual and her eyes were bigger than Bambi's. Popeye was pulling me up the pavement, but I stopped and turned back. All four of the Asians were on the ground, one clutching his stomach with one hand and trying to pull himself up by gripping the bumper of the Capri with his other. The first one I had steamed into was sitting with his back against the car door and his feet stretched out on the pavement; his face looked like a bit of raw meat and he was unconscious. Another one was lying in the gutter and the fourth was rolling around on the pavement, screaming and covered in blood.

We made it to the station and onto a southbound train. Hollywood was very shaken and I was a bit light-headed, but Popeye was just his normal self, calm as fuck. When the train set off, Popeye pulled out his flick knife, opened the blade and began wiping it with a bit of tissue. I looked at the blood on the tissue. 'Did you stab one of them?' I asked. Hollywood swallowed hard. 'He fucking stabbed all of them!' she said, slightly hysterically. Popeye spat on the blade of his knife and polished it vigorously with the bloodstained tissue. 'Fucking mugs,' he said. 'If they didn't want to get plunged they should have kept their gobs shut.' What could I say? Popeye's eyes suddenly widened and he smiled. 'I hope there's a few more punks at Clapham Common station when we go through,' he commented, holding his blade up to the light for inspection. 'I've got a fucking buzz on now.' Hollywood burst into tears.

As it happened Clapham Common station was empty of punks when we passed through and we got home without further incident. At that time I had been involved in a hell of a lot of violence and I did sometimes fly into a rage, during which I could lose track of what I was doing and just let my emotions rule me. I had little fear of anyone, but that was youthful arrogance as I was yet to suffer the kind of severe beating I had been dishing out. It's true that I had been seriously beaten in borstal and detention centres but I accepted that, as they had the biggest gangs and I was always going to be on a loser by fighting them, and through it all I never for one moment thought that they were actually going to kill me. But fighting on the street was different and being around Popeye brought this fact home to me. He had stabbed four men as though it were nothing and he didn't really give a toss whether they lived or died, and there were plenty more like Popeye whom I might bump into. It made me think.

Taking Our Turf

By autumn 1979 the Wildkatz were a gang with a lot of unfinished business. We were at war with the north Battersea Rebels, the Crawley Cats, the Balham Baldies and the Flash Pakis and had had run-ins with the Holy Smokes and the Clapham punks. It seemed as though every day there was another violent incident or bit of aggro, and I, for one, was loving it. Most of the gang were just along for the ride and would fight if they had to, but Popeye, Joe K and I were the driving force behind the trouble. And, now that we were actually based in the centre of Balham, I decided it was time to sort out the enemies we had on our own doorstep: the Balham Baldies and the Flash Pakis.

First in my sights were the Baldies. At one time, when they were still known as the Balham Boot Boys, the Baldies were a formidable and feared gang, but they had lost a lot of their best fighters and were now more of a joke around the manor. Don't get me wrong, there were still enough of them to offer anyone a decent tear-up, but the only thing really holding them together as a gang was their leader, Junior. He was now the only punk rocker left in the gang and he looked out of place with his bright orange Mohican, checked bondage trousers and bum-flap among all the polished heads and green flight jackets. I kind of admired Junior, not only because we went back a long way, but also because he refused to follow the herd. He liked being a punk and no amount of screenings of *The Wanderers* or *Quadrophenia* would make him change his mind.

Unlike most gang members, Junior actually had a job, of sorts. He was the bouncer on the door of a well-known punk pub on Clapham High Street called The Two Brewers. I only found this out when Dave Wall's band, Roadrunner, played there one night and Dave invited me and Big Nose Eamon to go and see him. Of course, we turned up in full rockabilly mode and it wasn't until we got inside that we found out the place was full of punks. Once in, there was no way of backing out without completely losing face, so we strolled up to the bar and ordered a pint. Even the barman had a safety pin earring and a Sid Vicious T-shirt and he served our drinks with a growl. It was like being in a cage full of lions and I guessed that any sudden move on our part would end in our being ripped to pieces. Everyone was watching us.

Dave, who had been doing a sound check when we entered, bounded down off the small stage. 'All right, lads,' he said. 'I meant to tell you to keep a low profile. We're the support band for the UK Subs!' I tried a smile, but it felt a bit lopsided as my nerves were jangling. 'Nice one,' I said. 'I'm really pleased for you. Now how the fuck do we get out of here before these cunts eat us?' Dave looked disappointed. 'You're not staying to hear us play?' he asked. I was keeping my eyes on a big lump with bright yellow hair and a padlock around his throat, who was inching his way down the bar to where we were standing. I half-guessed he wasn't part of a welcoming committee by the studded leather band he was wrapping around his fist. I had my cutthroat in my pocket and I knew Eamon had a bike chain around his waist – in the present climate none of us went anywhere without being tooled up – but I didn't fancy our chances against a pub full of gob-merchants. I glanced at Dave incredulously and then looked back at old yellow. 'Are you fucking mental, or what?' I said to Dave. Just then Junior made an appearance and stood in front of us. 'Listen, boys,' he said, reasonably. 'I'm going to have to ask you to leave. You're upsetting the rest of the customers.' I've never been so glad to see a fella with an orange Mohican in my life. I still don't know if Junior gave us a squeeze that night because he knew us or if he genuinely just wanted to throw us out, but we were glad to go. He and another punk escorted us to the exit and told us politely not to come back.

Out on the street in the fading evening light I realised what a result we'd had by getting out of the pub in one piece, particularly as The Two Brewers was bang in the middle of Clapham Punk turf and there had probably been a good few of that gang in there. 'That was fucking close,' I said to Eamon after we had jumped an 88 bus heading towards Clapham South. Eamon shrugged. 'Bunch of wankers, mate. We'd have took 'em.' And we both laughed. So I felt I owed Junior a favour and as it turned out I classed that as paid when things finally came on top with his gang and he wasn't around. The way I saw it, if Junior didn't take a beating from the Wildkatz with the rest of his gang then that was us even.

One afternoon Popeye and I, along with a few of the boys, were in the yard working on our motor when Hollywood and Sharon came by and happened to mention that one of the baldies had tried to chat up Hollywood outside the arcade. That was all the excuse I needed to launch an attack on them. Nobody was going to try to pull my bird, least of all one of the Balham Baldies. That was a dire fucking liberty and tantamount to saying the Wildkatz were wankers. Or at least that's how I presented it to the gang. There were about ten of us there that afternoon, including Mick and Joe K, and we immediately got tooled up and headed for the arcade.

The arcade on Balham High Street was just a big shop front with loads of one-armed bandits and Space Invaders machines inside. It was classed as baldie HQ because that's where you could find them most of the time. They didn't really hang around in any pubs, as they were more into glue-sniffing than drinking, although they did have a club at the bottom of Bedford Hill called The Colditz Club. However, it was the arcade that we stormed that afternoon. By now we were so organised as a gang that we even had our own version of an army bugle boy, Dennis, whose job it was to carry a portable tape player around so that we could be stirred by the rhythms of our chosen music as we went into battle. Our 'gang song', the record that always announced our arrival, was 'Wild Cat' by Gene Vincent, which had an appropriate title and even more appropriate lyrics: 'Don't ever try to tame a wild cat, you'll just be wasting your time ...' It became so much associated with us that some DJs would automatically slip it onto their decks when we entered a club flying our colours.

There were around 20 baldies and hangers-on in the arcade that afternoon, and the couple of spotters, who hung around outside to warn those inside of impending trouble, were so taken by surprise when they saw us flowing out into the middle of the street, forcing traffic to a halt, and heading their way waving a variety of heavy implements that they legged it without warning their pals. We rushed through the open doors of the arcade like a horde of

Hun and began laying into anyone with a shaved head. The surprise and ferocity of our attack meant that it was all over in a couple of minutes, and from that day on the baldies were a spent force on the manor. I personally accounted for two of them with a sawn-off pool cue, cracking shins and heads, and not one of our gang sustained an injury. By the time we heard the first siren in the distance we were heading out of the wrecked arcade and back to the breaker's yard, leaving behind some very battered Baldies. The danger of launching such an attack on a crowded high street on a weekday afternoon was that there were plenty of witnesses and no shortage of concerned citizens willing to phone the police. If we did get into a situation where the police arrived when we were in the middle of a tear-up, it was down to individual choice how you handled it. Some people would leg it, some would drop their weapons and give up and others would fight with the police as well. One thing that worked in all our favours was that we all seemed to have the same loathing and mistrust of the police and they actually found it very difficult to find anyone to press charges for assault. So long as you weren't caught with a weapon in your possession there was little the police could do. Even when they did charge two opposing gangs with an affray or fighting in public we would all put on the old pals' act for the magistrates and juries and say we were just messing about – youthful high spirits, yer honour! Sometimes the police, devious bastards that they were, would pick up a few of the abandoned weapons at the scene and plant them on any youth they managed to round up. An offensive weapons charge was usually a sure conviction in a magistrate's court. But, on the whole, we were usually long gone before the Old Bill got there. Don't forget, there were no mobile phones in those days.

After doing the baldies we legged it back to the yard and hid our weapons in various vehicles among the piles. Then we all split up and went our separate ways to meet up in The Bedford that evening.

There was never any comeback from the Balham Baldies over that beating and within a month the gang had disbanded. Some of them saw *Quadrophenia* and turned up wearing fishtail parkas and desert boots, and another group went back to being proper boots-and-braces skinheads and started hanging around with the Cubbitt House mob. The rest got into tonic suits and pork-pie hats and going to Madness concerts. Junior, who had missed out on the beating because, as I heard later, he was getting his hair dyed, just carried on being the only real punk in Balham. We would often see him, striding down Bedford Hill in his bondage trousers and leather vest, but there was never any trouble with him. He tended to ignore us and we did the same. There's no kudos in attacking a lone punk rocker, and I suppose we did have some standards.

Next on my list for a good kicking were the Flash Pakis. Ever since Popeye and I had had our run-in with them outside the Wimpy bar I had been smarting to get back at them and so had he. We had heard that they had put up a good showing in a street fight when the NF tried to march through Tooting Bec, so we knew that they were no cunts in a row. I thought about storming the Wimpy bar in a surprise attack, the way we had with the arcade, but I knew that, unlike the baldies, they would only come back on the warpath from something like that. So it would have to be something more decisive and final with them. I decided to try the old-fashioned method, from our estate days.

One day we were sitting outside the yard when a lone Flash Paki walked by on the other side of the road. I dodged through the traffic and caught up with him. 'Oi, Abdul,' I said. 'You and your mob are stinking the fucking area out.' He stood there, not saying anything but looking as though he wanted to kill me. 'You know who I am. The Wildkatz own this turf and we want you lot out. Tell whoever runs your mob that we'll be on Tooting Bec Common, by the playground, next Friday at 8. Be there or be square.' I added the last bit because I'd heard it on the Stuart Colman radio show and thought it sounded cool. Old cod-eye didn't say a word, he just looked at me as if he wanted to spit and then walked off. Knowing my luck, I thought, he doesn't even speak English.

But it turned out that he had understood everything I'd said, as he was back an hour later with another Asian fella who was wearing a bandanna around his head and throwing shapes like a boxer. They came right up to where Popeye and I were lounging on an old lorry seat. 'Greaser,' he said, 'we want to know if it will be a fight with weapons or fists.' I looked at Popeye and he reached inside his leather, pulled out his nine-inch pearl-handled flick knife and pressed the button. The wicked-looking blade snicked out and he began to clean one of his fingernails with the pointed tip. I looked back up at the two Asians. 'What do you fucking think?' I asked. Cod-eye just nodded once and the two Flash Pakis walked away. The fight was on. But, in the meantime, word was reaching me that Psycho Joe of the north Battersea was interested in a straightener with me. Rumours and second-hand threats had been flying back and forth ever since I had started our bit of agg with the north Battersea, but now it looked as if it was all coming to a head. I sent word back that if Psycho Joe wanted a straightener he could find me at the Chick-A-Boom club that Wednesday. With a straightener on Wednesday and a gang fight on Friday, it looked as though I had a pretty full social calendar.

Meeting Psycho Joe

Wednesday nights at the Chick-A-Boom club were attended by the hard-core rockin' crowd or those who didn't have to get up for work on a Thursday morning, as closing time was 12.30. There was normally a turnout of at least 200 people there and some people preferred it because there was room to move and no live band, just plenty of good records played. On the night that I was due to have my straightener with Psycho Joe most of the Wildkatz turned up for support and, just in case, the north Battersea decided to use the occasion to turn up in force and get one over on us. I had heard that Psycho Joe was a devious and unpredictable fucker who was not to be trusted, so, although I was not armed myself, everyone was carrying weapons. Olly the Cat turned up unexpectedly. He was not really into the violent side of gang life but was a musician who loved everything else about it. We called him The Cat as a piss-take because he was still a fully-fledged Teddy boy and always immaculately turned out in a drape suit. On the way up from Morden station on the M1 bus Olly pulled me to one side. 'You know Psycho Joe pulled a gun on Mick?' he asked. I nodded. Olly reached inside his drape and pulled out a small black revolver. 'Here,' he said. 'This'll give him something to think about.' I took the gun from his hand and noticed the shiny brass cartridges showing in the chamber. I whistled. 'Where'd you get this?' I asked. Olly smiled. 'It's a starting pistol,' he said, and, noticing the disappointment on my face, added, 'He won't know the difference, It looks the part and makes a loud enough bang if you pull the trigger.' So as not to seem ungrateful, I slipped the gun into my waistband and thanked him.

By now the Wildkatz were well known at the Chick-A-Boom and we were given a bit of a wide berth by some people, particularly when we turned up mob-handed and flying our colours because that was a sure sign that there would be trouble. We sent Dennis in to request that the DJ play Gene Vincent's 'Wild Cat' and then waited in the foyer until the first note could be heard over the sound system before strutting into the club. Our entrance was all show, like boxers entering the arena to the strains of their favourite fighting music, and designed to impress and intimidate. I have no doubt that some people, mainly the older crowd of rockers and bikers, found our antics highly amusing, but we really believed in this sort of shit. We were really living the fantasy to the full. Once inside the club we gathered in our usual spot and concentrated on looking hip and cool. I was a bit nervous about the planned punch-up with Psycho Joe, although I would never have let on. To settle my nerves I decided to get drunk pretty quick and started straight on the gin. By around 10.30 I was pretty pissed, though not falling-over-drunk, just very confident. I started to convince myself that Psycho Joe was not going to turn up. Then Snapper came over to my table and whispered in my ear that Psycho Joe was in the car park on his own and ready to rumble and that I should come outside alone. By now I was full of Dutch courage and didn't even bother telling the rest of the gang. I just got up and walked through the club and out into the vestibule.

My first sight of Psycho Joe was not what I was expecting. He didn't look very psychotic, he was of average height and build, he was wearing a leather and jeans and was standing, empty-handed, in a pool of light at the edge of the darkened car park. There were just the two of us and he spoke first. 'Are you Razor?' he asked. I was about ten feet away from him, standing in the well-lit vestibule. 'Yeah,' I said. 'You Psycho Joe?' He nodded. I felt the weight of Olly's revolver in my waistband and remembered what we were here for. 'I hear you pulled a gun on my brother,' I said. He shrugged. I took a couple of steps forward and pulled the revolver from my waistband and pointed it at him in one quick movement. 'How'd you like to get shot yourself?' I asked. He smiled. 'What, with a starting pistol?' he asked lightly. Inwardly I cursed myself for pulling the gun and if I had been slightly less drunk I might have been embarrassed enough to wish the ground had swallowed me up. Instead I shrugged and spun the gun around my finger by the trigger guard a couple of times. 'Nah,' I said. 'I brought this for starting the fight with, just in case there wasn't a bell handy.' Psycho Joe chuckled, then we just stood there looking at each other for a minute. I'd only just met him but somehow I liked him. Maybe I recognised something in him that was also in me, a kind of reckless bottle and a willingness to go along with the fantasy. I tucked the gun back in my waistband. 'Fancy a drink?' I asked. I really didn't have any desire to fight him, although I would if he decided to force the issue, and I think he felt the same. He looked behind him at the shadow-filled car park and then smiled again. 'Why not?' he replied, and he walked up to me. I stuck my hand out and gave him the rebel shake. Violent youths tend to make impulsive judgments and we had made ours.

It was a buzz to see people's faces when Psycho Joe and I walked into the club and up to the bar together. Popeye and a few of the boys made aggressive movements towards Psycho Joe but I waved them off. We stood at the bar and chatted about the state of war between the various gangs in South London, and about music and clubs. He said he'd heard about the Wildkatz's trouble with the Crawley Cats and that one of his members had taken a beating from them at The Squire in Catford. We agreed that they were nothing but yokels who were starting to get a bit above themselves. He said that the north Battersea might be interested in joining us when we decided to get a bit of payback on the Crawley and I said I'd keep that in mind. After one drink Joe said he had to be going as he was due at a party. I walked out into the car park with him. We shook hands again. 'What would you have done if that gun was real?' I asked. Psycho Joe smiled again and up close I saw something of his nickname in the glitter of his eyes. He reached under his leather at the small of his back and pulled an 18-inch machete out of his jeans. 'I might have had to take a bullet,' he said, 'but you'd have lost your gun arm.' I laughed. 'And this mob would have finished you off.' He waved at the car park and suddenly several sets of headlights lit up the darkness. I counted four on motorbikes, an old Wolseley with at least another four leather-jacketed gang members and a battered old Bedford J4 van that could possibly hold another eight. I shook my head but I had to smile. 'I thought it was a straightener with no tools and no gangs?' I said. Joe pulled on a crash helmet and climbed onto the pillion of a motorbike that pulled up next to us. 'You know the rules,' Psycho Joe said. 'There fucking ain't none.' He winked and the bike took off, followed by the rest of the convoy. I watched them go and then walked back into the club. Our war with the north Battersea was over and we had gained another set of allies. This was the life!

As I've mentioned before, the locals at The St Helier Arms, which was the front bar of the Chick-A-Boom, were not enamoured with having a twice-weekly invasion of greasers and Teds on what they considered, and rightly so, to be their turf. There were some tough boys who used the front bar and there was always a bad atmosphere between the two camps. On summer evenings the locals would gather on the front porch of the pub and watch the rockin' crowd stream off the buses and drive up in their classic cars and motorbikes, and you could tell by their faces that they didn't like what they were seeing. Unfortunately for them, the owner of the pub was making a fortune from the club and had made it clear that anyone who tried to fuck it up for him would be barred, and as The St Helier Arms was the only pub on the estate the locals swallowed their bile and just threw dirty looks at us – that was until a few of the locals had the idea of waiting for us further along Green Wrythe Lane and jumping us well away from the pub. At first it was just the odd couple of locals picking up the late-night stragglers who were walking home from the club. But then it began to seem more organised and there were more of the locals involved. They would always pick the easy targets – never more than two blokes – and sometimes they would do it in front of the girls although they never actually touched any of them. None of our mob had actually been jumped by them but we were always on the alert for them. The walk home from the Chick-A-Boom also took us through Mitcham, which was more hostile territory because there was still a big skinhead presence there, and they would waylay anyone they thought they could hand out a kicking to. It seemed as if our whole lives were fraught with danger and just getting home from a night out without getting your face smashed in was an achievement. We were living in dangerous times and it was us and others like us who were making them dangerous.

The rest of the week we spent getting ready for the rumble with the Flash Pakis. By now we had recruited new members to the gang, mainly from Balham, some of whom were eager to prove themselves in battle. Popeye and I spent most of Thursday getting around and making sure everyone knew exactly how the rumble was going down and where we were to meet. We made it quite clear that anyone who didn't turn up had better not show their face ever again. We gathered together an armoury of weapons in the yard: all sorts of coshes from rounders bats and sand-filled lead pipes to sawn-off pool cues and iron stair rods. Popeye suggested that we take a couple of 16-gauge shotguns, as he knew someone he could borrow them from, but I knocked that idea on the head. We didn't want to kill anyone, just have a bit of a tear-up and decide who were the top dogs on the manor, that's all.

On Friday afternoon we all met up in the breaker's yard. People were drifting in right up until the moment we left for the Common. There were all the old members of the gang, including Mick, Joe K, Little Roy, Big Nose Eamon, Popeye, Dennis and Alan, Johnny Boy, Tooter, Ahmet, Perry, Gordon, and there were also Ronnie, Eddie, Gerry and Big Chris from the old Wanderers days, and the newer members, Tall Paul, Ricky the Fly, Dodgy Derek and his brother Dodgy Dave and a few others. We were drinking a mix of gin and cider and buzzing off each other with talk of what we were going to do to the Flash Pakis. It was a good atmosphere; confident but slightly nervous, as you'd expect from a bunch of youths who were going into battle.

Sitting on the steps of Popeye's caravan and watching the gang mooching about v for the off, I imagined that this was how it would have been for us if we'd been alive and eligible to fight in the Second World War. I could see us all in a forest in France awaiting the order to go in and kick some German heads in. This was my army. Popeye had sorted out the transport. We didn't have far to go – it was less than a mile to the Common – so he just put wheels and batteries on a few of the wrecks that would still run. We had a couple of Mark 2 Cortinas, one of which had been turned into a convertible with a chainsaw, a Mark 1 Consul that belched black smoke out of the exhaust every time you pressed the accelerator pedal, and also a bright yellow ex-GPO Commer van with no glass in any of the windows. Popeye and I had devised a plan. There were two ways to get to the playground on the Common: the first was to park up on Emmanuel Road and walk onto the Common and under the railway bridge; and the second, which we hoped would be our ace-in-the-hole, was through a narrow alleyway off one of the backstreets of Bedford Hill and then straight down the pathway and under the second railway bridge. We knew that if we could get the van up on the pavement, through the alley and then down the pedestrian path and under the bridge we could catch our opponents in a pincer movement. We didn't really know if the van would be able to squeeze through the alley, but at least we didn't have to worry about damaging the bodywork on it so we could afford to force it.

At 7.45 we loaded the vehicles with our weapons and headed out of the yard in a smoke-shrouded, metal-rattling convoy. Popeye, Mick, Ahmet and I were in the lead Cortina, and Joe K was in the passenger seat of the van as he was leading the alleyway assault. We drove along Bedford Hill Road until we got to the indoor market, then the three cars turned left and the van chugged straight up the hill. The only real danger we faced on the way to the common was getting a tug from the Old Bill, and if there were any about they could not fail to give us a pull when they saw the state of the vehicles we were in. Luckily for us, there was not a copper in sight.

We pulled up on the south end of the Common and disembarked, taking our tools with us. It would have been ideal if we could have driven right up to the playground, but there was a barrier across the path under the first railway bridge to stop vehicles driving onto the Common, so we had to walk the last part. The playground itself is out of sight of any roads or buildings and is situated on a bit of ground between the two railway lines, so the only people who might see us there were those on passing trains. As we came out from under the bridge we saw about 30 Flash Pakis milling about in the playground. We stopped. I still didn't know if Joe K would be able to get the van through, and if he didn't it looked as though we were in for a right kicking. I had expected around 20 Flash Pakis to turn up and without the boys on the van we were sorely outnumbered. Mick was the only one of us who had a watch, so I asked him the time – it was 7.55. I made the decision to move forward and we all walked out from under the cover of the bridge and let the enemy see us for the first time. They were all tooled up and I noticed that a few of them had hockey sticks. I didn't fancy getting a clump from one of them, but then, to be honest, I didn't really fancy getting a clump at all.

The Flash Pakis began to move towards us and I could pick out the good ruckers by the way they moved. In any gang fight there will only be a small minority of really dangerous fighters. Most of the mob will be there to make up the numbers and will flee at the first sign that things are not going their way, but the real fighters will come to the front and be eager for the fray. I noticed that a couple of them were wearing turbans and others had bandannas around their heads and the gang as a whole seemed to favour facial hair, as there were a lot of pencil moustaches and pointy beards. This was it. My heart was pounding and I picked out one of the front runners and got a good two-handed grip on my rounders bat. There was no exchange of unpleasantries or formality. One minute we were facing each other and the next we were charging into each other and breaking heads. I gave my target a good whack in the face with my bat and moved on to the next one as he went down, but we were heavily outnumbered and this made even the most cowardly members of their gang get stuck in. I got a terrible clump on the back of my head, probably from a fucking hockey stick, and then I was on the ground and surrounded by a mob. I tried to scramble away on all fours but I was being hit and kicked by too many people. I didn't feel much pain, but I knew I was getting a bad hiding when a boot smashed into my forehead and everything went grey around the edges. And then, just like in the old Westerns, the cavalry arrived. I was struggling to get to my feet and fend off blows when above the grunting and shouting of my attackers I heard an engine whining close by. The van had finally been forced through the alley, although it was now minus both front wings, and our second wave was piling out and into the battle. Though I was really too battered to know much about it at the time, this was the moment when the battle turned in our favour. Thinking they had us beaten, the Flash Pakis were severely demoralised at the arrival of yet more 'greasers', and those who had been happy to kick the shit out of an outnumbered enemy suddenly lost heart and decided that discretion was the better part of valour. Plus, Joe K and the boys, seeing us getting a beating when they arrived, flew into the Flash Pakis like a gang of berserkers and laid the cosh about like it was going out of fashion. Once the first few Flash Pakis began to leg it, it was like a receding tidal wave and they were all running. They were chased up the Common by those of us who still had the strength and, although a few of them were still skirmishing, it was all over bar the moans of pain.

By 8.30 we were back in the yard nursing our wounds and reliving the battle in verbal excitement. I had a sore head, sore ribs and sore legs; in fact I was one big pain, but nothing was broken. Mick had two broken fingers, which he later got splinted at St James's Hospital. Johnny Boy had a broken leg and had to spend six weeks in a cast. The rest of the gang shared out assorted bruises, black eyes and a couple of broken noses. Popeye, as usual, didn't have a scratch on him and was claiming to have stabbed at least six of the enemy, although only one of them was confirmed. How Popeye never killed anyone I'll never know.

We had taken a bit of a beating but had run the Flash Pakis, and that was what it was all about for us. We were now officially the top gang in Balham. We had done them fair and square and there would be no comebacks. It was time to kick back and chill out before taking on anyone else. Wounds would be given time to heal but then we would be back at it. We'd come too far to stop now. We were the Balham Wildkatz and the world was our lobster.

My Baby Done Gone

In November 1979, just as the Wildkatz, and me personally, were getting to the top of our game, the criminal justice system once again caught up with me. I had been living on borrowed time ever since I had been arrested with a cut-throat razor just before the August bank holiday and now it was time to pay. I had been on parole from my three-year sentence and now the Parole Board revoked my licence and I had to go back to jail to serve the remainder of my sentence. I had seven months left to do, but it might as well have been seven years as far as I was concerned. It seemed as if every time things were going to plan I got dragged back inside, but it was something that had to be done so I did my best to curb my impatience and sat out the rest of my sentence. I was kept in the loop by various gang members and received visits at which I was informed what was going on in the scene and I was able to make a few suggestions. Without me there to drive them on, most of the gang were happy to take it easy. There were still occasional punch-ups, but they were really too individual to inspire the rest of the lads. So I sat on my hands and counted the days.

Before I went back to jail, Hollywood and I had sworn our undying love for each other. To tell the truth, after our first couple of months together I had begun to take her for granted. I had pulled other birds behind her back and had generally acted the clown, but I never for one minute thought that she might do the same to me. At that age – she was 17 and I was 19 – any time apart seems like forever, but I was expecting her to sit at home every night and not talk to anyone. I was about as selfish as you can get and my jealousy was a very dangerous thing. So when rumours began to reach me that Hollywood was out on the town without me I flew into a rage. I managed to mooch a phone call from one of the senior screws who knew me from my previous sentence. Hollywood picked up the phone and I said, 'Guess who?' We hadn't spoken for almost three months, but I still expected her to recognise my voice at least – after all, we were engaged! But when she answered, 'Is that you, Steve?' my head almost exploded in rage. One of the rumours I had heard involved Rockabilly Steve of the south Battersea and this was a confirmation of my worst fears. 'You fucking little slag!' I shouted into the phone, and then I proceeded to threaten all sorts of dire futures for her and Steve. When she put the phone down on me in mid-flow I had to consider that our relationship was truly over. But my pride meant that I could not just forget about the matter. Hollywood was known as my girl and, apart from anything else, I saw Steve's actions as a direct challenge. It was one of the things I would have to deal with swiftly on my release.

One of the girls I had met whilst out and about was named Denise. I had gone to a party at the house of one of the Sutton gang after the Chick-A Boom one Wednesday night, a guy named Tex who I had been in borstal with, and had got into an argument with a couple of rockers but they refused to fight me. I was drunk, as usual, and spoiling for a fight but no one was having it. An argument developed between a crowd of girls and I stuck my nose in.

Two of the girls, Mel and Denise, were best friends and were regulars at the Chick-A-Boom. Someone had told me that Mel fancied me, but in those days I took that kind of thing as my due. After all, what girl wouldn't fancy me? I was tall and slim with thick dark hair and white teeth and I was the leader of one of the hardest gangs on the scene! Even though I say so myself, I was a ride. Mel was okay, but Denise was the one I really fancied. She was tall and had long brown hair, deep blue eyes and the huskiest voice I'd ever heard. I spent a long time talking to the girls and, although I didn't realise it then, when dawn broke over Surrey I was a little bit in love with Denise. I invited both Mel and Denise to the ABC cinema in Streatham on the Saturday afternoon, as a load of us were going to see *The Wanderers*, and they agreed.

Now that I was back in jail the two girls wrote and asked if they could come and visit me. Because Mel had this thing for me, she spent most of the visit slagging off Hollywood and telling me all the rumours that were going around about her and Steve, but I wasn't really listening. I was too busy watching Denise. When I got back to my cell after the visit I could think only of Denise and how gorgeous she had looked. The only trouble was that she had given no indication that she might feel the same way about me. I thought about her a lot over the next couple of months and looked forward to letters from Mel because Denise would always add a little hello at the end.

Hollywood must have been worried about the consequences of her infidelity, because two weeks before my release date she came to visit me for the first time. She arrived with a girl called Jeanette, a good-looking rockin' chick who I had also tried to get off with behind Hollywood's back one night. She obviously didn't know and neither Jeanette nor I ever mentioned it. Hollywood said that she was sorry for what had happened and that she now wanted us to get back together again. I acted cool towards this suggestion, but inside I was strutting. I said I'd think about it, but Steve was still going to get what was coming to him, no matter what. We parted on kissing terms and I was looking forward to my release.

On my first day out, 30 May 1980, I had to appear at Lavender Hill magistrate's court to answer the deferred sentence I had got for allowing myself to be carried in a stolen car with Harry. I knew it was only going to be a formality, so I arranged to meet a few of the gang there. Both Harry and Peter were now out and it was great to see them again. Harry had a jacked-up Vauxhall Cresta PB, which sounded like a tank and was almost as big as one, and Popeye had done a lot of work on our Ford Consul until it looked as though it had just come off the production line, so we all piled into the cars and cruised down to The Bedford for my welcome-home drink.

Things had been pretty quiet on the manor since I'd been away. Popeye had stabbed a couple of pimps outside The Bedford when he thought they had been looking at him funny, and Mick, Alan, Johnny Boy, Eamon and Harry had had a bit of a skirmish with a gang of casuals outside a pub in Thornton Heath, but that was about it. The news of the Crawley Cats was interesting, though. They had gone from strength to strength, fighting with various gangs on their own turf, and were giving it the big 'un at the Chick-A-Boom and not winning many friends. They had upset a couple of the rockin' gangs, including the Bermondsey Mob, who were led by a tough little James Cagney lookalike named Jimmy Harris. Jimmy would fight anybody at any time and for any reason and was known as a handy man with either fists or tools. A few of us once went back to

Jimmy's gaff for a drink after a night at one of the clubs, and when he thought the cab driver was trying to overcharge him Jimmy told him to wait whilst he went into the house to get the money. Jimmy emerged from the house with a couple of Zulu spears and launched one through the cabbie's windscreen at him. Luckily for him, the cabbie ducked in time and the spear embedded itself in his headrest instead of his head and he was able to take off at full speed before Jimmy could launch the spear's identical companion. It would seem that the Crawley Cats were definitely fucking with the wrong people.

Popeye had been having a long-running feud with a smoothie named Gary B over a girl they had both dated, and while we were at The Bedford word reached him that his enemy was up at Mick the barber's waiting for a haircut. Popeye downed his pint and said that he was going up to sort it out. Not wanting a bloodbath on the manor on my first day of freedom, I agreed to go with him and told him there was to be no knife play. I got Popeye to leave his flick knife with Harry and we set off on the short walk up to the barber's. Popeye was wearing a blue cheese-cutter cap, which was unusual for him as he loved to show off his hair, but I never really thought much about it. We stopped outside the barber's shop and looked in through the window. Sure enough, there was Gary B, along with three others, waiting for his turn in the chair.

Since they had fallen out, about a year earlier, Popeye and Gary B had attacked each other at every opportunity. Popeye had stabbed Gary B in both legs and Gary B had smashed a bottle over Popeye's head on one occasion and kicked him off the platform of a moving bus on another. The way they attacked each other I figured that sooner or later one of them was going to end up killing the other, so I pulled Popeye aside and spoke to him outside the shop. I told him that he should call Gary B out of the shop and have a straightener to get the trouble sorted once and for all. I told him that if it looked as though he were losing the fight I would step in and stop it. Popeye seemed thoughtful. 'You're right,' he said. 'This has got to stop. You wait here and I'll go in and call him out.' I patted him on the back to encourage him. Popeye took off his hat and, holding it rolled up in his right hand, went into the barber's. Then hell came to Balham.

I should have known Popeye would never have a straightener – he couldn't punch his way out of a wet paper bag. He was a blade man, a student of the slash, a connoisseur of the cut and the lord of liars. I should also have known that a dyed-in-the-wool card-carrying lunatic like Popeye would always carry more than one blade. He was only in the shop a second when the screaming started. By the time I kicked open the door he had already stabbed Gary B twice, Mick the barber once, the girl who swept the floor once and one of the other customers. The place was in uproar, as you might expect after a knife-wielding fruitcake had steamed in and started slashing, and everyone was trying to get out of the way. Popeye had concealed a small steak knife inside his hat and was now clambering over the customers to get to the already wounded and cowering Gary B. I jumped on Popeye and dragged him towards the door. 'I'll fucking kill you, you muggy cunt!' he was shouting, and I was glad it wasn't directed at me. I got my arm around his throat and pulled him out of the shop. He had blood splashed on his face and his eyes were even bigger than normal. I grabbed the now blood-soaked hat from his hand and felt the knife inside. 'You cunt!' I shouted. 'I thought you were going to sort it out?' Popeye shrugged. 'It's sorted now,' he said. I went back to the door of the shop and asked if everyone was okay, but I think that was a bit hopeful on my part.

Gary B was in a bad way. One of the knife wounds had punctured his liver we found out later, but the others only had superficial wounds from getting in the way of the swinging knife. The barber had a cut to his chin and the girl who swept up had a small wound to her elbow. We knew Mick the barber, as he had cut most of our hair at one time or another. He looked at me. 'Get that fucking nutter off the manor, Razor,' he said. 'I've got to phone an ambulance and that means the Old Bill will be here as well.' I nodded. When I went back onto the street Popeye was counting his loose change. 'I fancy a bag of chips,' he said, as though nothing had happened. On the way back to The Bedford I dropped the hat containing the knife down a drain. I gave the gang the news as Popeye washed up in the toilets. There was no question that if he needed an alibi there were a dozen of us willing to swear that he had not left the pub all afternoon.

As it turned out, nobody at the barber's shop was talking. The customers had already gone by the time the police got there and the story told by Mick, Gary B and the girl was that some unidentified lunatic ran into the shop and began cutting for no apparent reason. Gary B was in hospital for a couple of weeks and they reckon it was touch and go whether he'd live at one stage but he pulled through. The feud between him and Popeye was over. Gary B didn't have the heart to make a comeback and no one could blame him. So that was my first day out – straight back into the violence and madness. I now took it all for granted; it had become casual. I had come a long way from that kid who felt sick after his first cutting outside The Edwardian Club in the summer of '76. I knew that some of the gang weren't too happy with how things were going, but I didn't really care. I wanted the excitement of it all to continue and was nowhere near ready to settle down and live a normal life. There was something in me, driving me on. I wanted recognition and notoriety and I didn't care how many people we had to stab and cosh to get it. I loved the respect we got in the clubs from the other gangs, and the feeling of belonging and camaraderie in the gang, knowing that if I started anything they would all be there for me as I would for them. Don't get me wrong, I didn't want to kill anyone or even seriously wound them, I just wanted the buzz of fighting and the satisfaction of being known. The trouble was, the more we fought the more we became desensitised to the seriousness of the violence and the more serious the violence got. And, with people like Popeye on board, it wouldn't be long before someone got seriously injured, or even killed.

Revenge Served Hot

When I first got out of jail Hollywood and I tried to make a go of our relationship, but we both knew that it was never going to be the same. I didn't handle betrayal or public humiliation very well and I knew that, sooner rather than later, someone was going to have to suffer in order to make me feel better. I wasn't the brightest spark in the fuse box, but I had learned to work out how to put my own pain onto other people in order to lighten the load. Whenever I met up with Hollywood now, it was just for sex and out of spite. I threatened her a lot and treated her like a doormat, and I now know that the only reason she stayed with me was through fear of what I might do if she tried to move on. I was becoming an ogre, but I didn't give a fuck; I was going to have my revenge no matter what it cost.

One night I was up at The Greyhound in Croydon with Joe K, Popeye and Hollywood, and I went up to the bar to talk to someone. I decided to get a round in while I was there and turned back to my table to see if anyone wanted a drink, and I saw Joe and Hollywood deep in conversation with their faces almost touching. I felt a surge of molten jealousy rush through me and before I knew what I was doing I had my cut-throat razor open in my hand and I was on my way to where they were sitting. I stood looking down at them, the open blade held down by my thigh, and gave them my coldest smile. 'What you talking about?' I asked. They both looked surprised but not guilty surprised. Joe smiled. 'I was just asking Hollywood if she thinks Debbie will go out with me at any time soon,' he said easily. 'That bird is driving me fucking mad. I think she likes keeping me hanging on.' I looked closely at Hollywood, but I couldn't detect anything out of place. My face was starting to ache from keeping the smile on. 'Keep trying,' I managed to croak out, and then I gripped Hollywood's upper arm. 'Come and help me with the drinks,' I said, and almost pulled her up to the bar.

When we were away from the table I began to interrogate her. 'What's going on?' I growled. 'You were near enough kissing him when I looked over. Are you trying to take me for a mug? Right in front of my face?' Hollywood was frightened and she tried to break free of my grip. 'You're hurting me,' she cried, and I squeezed her arm harder. 'Fucking answer me you little slag. What's going on between you and him?' She denied that there was anything going on and pointed out that he was only interested in Debbie and never stopped talking about her. Gradually her denials and tears made me calm down a bit. I started thinking that it was highly unlikely that if they were guilty of anything they would be so obvious about it in front of me. It was silly, I told myself. Joe was my best pal, we had watched each other's backs in many fights and, besides, he was the only one in whom I had confided my love for Hollywood before I had gone away. It had happened one night when a crowd of us had been invited to a party after the Chick-A-Boom club by a couple of 1940s girls, Andrews Sisters clones. The party was out in the sticks at a place called Three Bridges and, though we didn't know it at the time, it was a couple of stops away from Crawley. We were all drunk and raucous as usual. Joe and I were wearing suits and everyone else was in leathers and jeans. I remember it because we had gathered about 20 girls around us at the club and got the in-house photographer to take pictures of us posing with them James Bond style for a laugh.

The journey by train to Three Bridges was chaos and some people started to wreck the train carriage, throwing seats and light bulbs out of the window of the speeding train. By the time the train pulled in at Three Bridges station the platform was full of police with dogs waiting for us. We gave the police a load of lip and, after searching us and taking our details, the last train back to London had gone and the two 1940s girls whose party we were supposed to be going to had disappeared. The police ejected us from the train station and told us it would be a good idea if we left their town. Just to make sure we did, they escorted us to the outskirts by following behind us at a walking pace in their vans. Just to add to our misery it then began to rain. It was okay for those in leather jackets – the rain just bounced off them – but Joe and I were soaked through in seconds and had a long, wet trudge back to London. As we marched through the darkness and pouring rain up ahead of the others, Joe and I talked seriously about our lives and what we wanted out of it all. We had been friends for over a year but had never had a conversation of any seriousness before. I think it was at that moment that we really bonded and became best friends. Of course, the conversation turned to girls and Joe told me of his deep burning love for Debbie and how it was killing him not to be making any progress with her. I was still at the lovey-dovey stage with Hollywood in those days and I too confessed how much I loved her. I told him how much she meant to me and I knew that he understood, as he felt the same about Debbie. It was a deep moment. Around 4.30 in the morning we reached a small town and found the train station open and deserted and so we sheltered in the waiting room and caught the first train to Clapham Junction. So there was no way that he would betray me and I started to feel bad for even suspecting him. But now that these feelings had been awakened in me again someone was going to have to pay the price for my confusion. I carried on drinking and got into a very mean mood, just looking for someone to say something out of place or give me a funny look so that I could tear into them. Towards the end of the night I had fixed my attention on a couple of bikers who were standing at the bar and had convinced myself that every time they laughed they were laughing at me. It was nonsense of course, but they were a perfect target for my not so latent rage. I was wearing a jean jacket that night, and as the club was preparing to close I took it off and buttoned up the cuff before slipping an empty pint glass into the sleeve and hanging the jacket casually over my shoulder. I made sure we got out of the club before the bikers and told Popeye to go and get the car while Joe, Hollywood and I waited on the pavement. I hadn't said anything to anyone, but Hollywood must have sensed something because she kept asking me not to cause any trouble. The two bikers came out of the club laughing together and not suspecting anything. I stepped in their way. 'Who you fucking laughing at?' I demanded. They looked confused. 'Leave it out, mate,' said one. 'We don't want no trouble.' But mere words weren't going to stop me now; I had a parcel of hurt to distribute. I swung the jacket, overhand, from my shoulder and I had judged the distance between us just right. The weight of the pint glass in the sleeve went through an arc and smashed straight onto the head of the nearest biker. For a second nothing happened, and then blood began to flow down his face and he bent forward at the waist clutching his head. Hollywood screamed and tried to grab my arm, but I had my razor out and was stepping up to the second biker. I slashed at his face but he managed to dodge the blade and was off down the road like a rabbit.

It all happened so quickly and Joe didn't know what was going on, but another group of bikers had witnessed the whole thing and were now jumping in. The second lot of bikers didn't know the first two, but saw me taking a liberty and tried to help out. One of them grabbed me around the neck from behind and tried to drag me to the ground. Joe stepped up and gave him a couple of nice digs in the ribs and then he was grabbed by another have-a-go hero. Joe didn't even know what the fight was over and struck out instinctively.

There must have been 50 people standing in front of the club but only a handful, all bikers, stepped in. I had got loose from the one who had grabbed me and spun around and lashed out with the razor. Fortunately for the biker, he already had his crash helmet on and my blade scarred his visor instead of his face. There were now five bikers against me and Joe and it looked as though we might end up taking a kicking. Joe was throwing punches and I was circling a biker who had produced a bike chain and I was trying to keep the others at bay with wild lunges of my razor hand when Popeye screeched up onto the pavement, nearly running me over, and came out of the car roaring at the top of his voice and swinging a sawn-off pick handle. The bikers backed off and we all piled into the car as quickly as we could. Popeye burned rubber getting out of there, but one of the bikers threw an iron bar, which smashed the back windscreen and showered us with glass. It was only when we were well on our way back home that I realised that Hollywood was sobbing in the back seat. Popeye, his eyes flitting up every few seconds to the rear-view mirror to make sure there were no motorcycles coming up behind us, asked what the fight had been all about. I shrugged. 'They were giving me evil looks all night,' I said. Nobody said anything about that, as in our world that was a perfectly reasonable excuse to cave someone's head in. I felt better now that I had managed to lay off some of my rage. But Hollywood was absolutely terrified and didn't stop sobbing until we dropped her outside her house in Balham. I kissed her goodnight. And that was really the end of our relationship. However, the repercussions following her infidelity while I had been away were not over yet. After convincing myself that any suspicion I'd had about Joe and Hollywood was completely unfounded, it was something of a double blow when I found out that they actually had been fucking around while I'd been inside. I was at the Chick-A-Boom a couple of weeks after the incident at The Greyhound, talking to a girl from Catford, when the subject of Hollywood came up. I assured the girl that Hollywood and I had split up and she laughed. 'I'm not surprised,' she said. 'I was at a party with her when she got off with Joe K.' I went cold. 'Are you sure?' I asked her. She told me that she was definitely sure as she was in the same room as them when it happened. I looked out at the dance floor and saw Joe jiving away with two girls at once, his party piece, and rage took over. I marched out onto the dance floor, knocking jivers out of the way, and planted a right hook on Joe's jaw. He hit the floor in a heap and looked up at me confused. I remember that the record playing at the time was Louis Jordan's 'Saturday Night Fish Fry' and I've only got to hear it now to get a frisson of the rage I was feeling on that night. 'Outside!' I shouted at Joe, and marched off the floor and out of the club. The car park quickly began to fill with spectators. It must have been great for them, witnessing two of the big dogs fighting each other in public. I knew the smart money would be on Joe, as he was an excellent boxer and I was more a tool merchant. But I was no stranger to fist fighting either and I had rage and righteousness on my side, which can count for a lot in a tear-up. I took my jacket off and draped it over the bonnet of a parked car. Joe came out of the club rubbing his jaw and stripped to the waist. He looked at me. 'What's this about?' he asked. 'Alison,' I spat, and he nodded. 'Okay, do you want to box or fight?' I rolled my shoulders. 'Fight,' I spat, which meant everything except weapons. And I flew into him and head butted him in the face.

Joe K could dance like Fred Astaire and box like Rocky Marciano, although his enemies would probably say it was the other way around, and this made him a very skilful fighter. I felt every punch right through to my bones. It was the hardest fistfight I've ever been involved in and seemed to go on forever, although in actuality it lasted less than 15 minutes. We fought until we were too tired to lift our fists and then we clung to each other, biting and gouging and rolling around on the ground. People who have never had a fight in their lives may not realise just how much adrenalin you use up in a fight situation. Your heart is working overtime to pump blood and adrenalin through your system and, believe me, 15 minutes of this kind of effort can seem like a lifetime. That's why even super-fit and highly trained professional boxers only fight three-minute rounds with a rest in between. I was lucky in that I had broken Joe's nose with my first head butt and that made it harder for him to breathe, which tired him out quicker. Plus, to Joe it was just another punch-up, but I had a lot of reasons to drive me on – rage, jealousy, humiliation. I needed to win this fight in order to prove something to myself and others – that no one could take me for a mug. We eventually fought ourselves to a standstill. My rage had long since dissipated and had been replaced with physical pain and exhaustion. I had literally punched everything out of me. So I was relieved when Barney the bouncer jumped in and split us up, declaring the fight a draw. I knew I must have looked a sight, but I took comfort from the fact that Joe looked worse. His nose was flattened and there was blood all over him. I was wearing a white T-shirt and that too looked as though it had been used to clean the floor of an abattoir, although most of the blood was Joe's.

We stood there facing each other, both breathing heavily, and Joe stuck out his hand. In that moment I felt peace. I shook hands and we all went inside for a drink. Joe and I acted as though we were still mates, but I think we both knew that things between us would never be the same again. I had lost my best pal over a bird and I vowed that I would never trust anyone again as long as I lived. It was a childish response I know now, but I have to admit that I wasn't the most mature person in the world, nor even the most mature person on my street. From now on there would be even more swift and merciless retribution for anyone who tried to cross me. The gloves were off.

Double Trouble

My first Wednesday night up at the Chick-A-Boom club after my release was supposed to be just a bit of a celebration for me, a chance
to show my face again and let people know that I was back on the
scene after the fight with Joe K. But things didn't turn out quite as I'd
planned. For a start, most of the gang couldn't make it. Popeye had
started going out with a blonde bird from Pimlico, named Lorraine,
and though she hadn't yet managed to mellow him he was spending
most week nights with her. Other members of the gang had various
other commitments, so I arranged to meet Joe K and Tooting Roy
at the club and I travelled there by car with our newest recruit, a kid
named Shane.

Shane was a Balham boy and lived on a side road off Bedford
Hill. He was short and stocky and not much of a fighter, but he
could sing and play the guitar like a star. We had met him when he
turned up at The Bedford one night and asked The Rocking Devils
if he could sing one number with them. He got on the circular stage
and sang 'Shake, Rattle And Roll' with the band backing him up,
and he was so good that the crowd wouldn't let him leave until he'd
performed three more songs. It was the band who kicked him off
the stage in the end, as they were getting the hump at all the attention he was getting. Shane's big influences were Elvis, Billy Fury
and James Dean. He could sing like both Elvis and Billy Fury and
he was always hunching his shoulders and pulling James Dean-type
faces and all the girls seemed to like him. Shane had never been
to the Chick-A-Boom club and was eager to go, so I said he could
come with me. Popeye and I had gone halves on a 1957 Ford Consul
Hi Line, although the car was more Popeye's thing than mine as he
had put in many hours of work to get it running and looking sweet.
I loved driving the car and always with the driver's window open
and my elbow on the sill, come rain, shine or snow. I had learned

to drive by stealing other people's cars, and once drove an Austin 1100 from Clapham to Sutton before realising that the reason the car was so sluggish and smelt of burning was because I had forgotten to release the handbrake. So Popeye was never fond of me driving the Consul, but as he was having a night in with his sort there was little he could do about it.

It was a warm evening and still light as I pulled into the club car park and parked amongst the other classic vehicles. There were groups of rockers and rockabillies standing around drinking and chatting and enjoying the early summer weather as I exited the car. I was dressed to impress in Harry's light grey box suit with a half-velvet collar and a pair of black brogues. Harry had reluctantly allowed me to borrow his favourite suit so long as I promised to return it in pristine condition. Though the suit had been handmade for Harry, it fitted me perfectly and I topped it off with a white cotton shirt and burgundy tie. I was walking across the car park towards the entrance to the club, telling Shane what to expect, when I became aware of two geezers blocking my way. I stopped and looked at them. They were both short and pugnacious looking, dressed in identical leathers and jeans, and they both had Mac Curtis hair-cuts and a broken nose each. 'You Razor?' one asked. I nodded. 'I'm Shamus, and this is my brother, Lenny,' he said, pointing at said brother. 'We're Crawley Cats and we're here to do you.'

My first inclination was to laugh out loud. They looked like a couple of munchkins and I couldn't believe that these were the boys who had been causing all the aggro lately. I smiled and looked around the car park. I could see that a lot of people were watching from near the club entrance. 'What? Where's the rest of your gang then?' I asked. Shamus and Lenny grinned. 'Inside,' said Shamus. 'We don't need them for you.' I decided to have a bit of fun and impress Shane and everyone else who was watching. I started to take off my jacket and loosen my tie. 'Tell you what,' I said. 'We'll have a straightener, eh?' Shamus nodded. 'Which one of us do you want to fight?' he asked. I handed my jacket and tie to Shane and rolled my shoulders. 'Both of you,' I said. My offer was obviously acceptable to the Bobbsey twins, because the next thing I remembered was a series of explosions around the area of my face and trying to lift myself off the warm asphalt. Shane told me later that they had both steamed in and hit me with several punches each before I hit the ground, but I don't remember anything about it other than the pain. My legs were like rubber and when I tried putting my weight on them I fell over again. Shane had to help me up. Shamus and Lenny hadn't even broken into a sweat and were both standing in front of me as though they hadn't moved. Shamus spoke. 'The Crawley Cats are the guvnor's here now.'

Then they both walked off into the club. It took me a good few minutes to come to my senses and I had a terrible pain in my jaw where I had obviously taken a good right-hander. My first inclination was to pull my cut-throat and go and put a few stripes across the faces of the dynamic duo, but that would make me look more muggy than I already did. I had called on the straightener and offered the pair of them out and had got a beating, and that was the way it went in the world we had created. Asking for a straightener with someone meant that no weapons could be used and the result of the fight would have to be swallowed by the loser. To then go back on your word and attack your opponent again, but this time with a tool, would mean a serious loss of face, and our fantasy world was all about face and reputation. It had been a big mistake on my part. Shamus and Lenny were well known as fist fighters and were both promising amateur boxers, but I had been arrogant and had paid the price for it. The situation wasn't irretrievable for me, as there was little shame in losing a straightener, particularly against two good fighters. All I had to do was walk into the club and show that, although I might have lost the fight, my bottle was still intact.

I put my jacket and tie back on and felt my face for bruises. As well as the pain in my jaw I had the beginnings of a prize black eye. Shane was a bit shaken over the fight, probably more than I was, but I assured him that everything was okay. I walked into the club as though nothing had happened. There were a couple of tables near the entrance where you could buy records and as I entered I noticed the unmistakable figure of Joe K, with his back to me, sorting through one of the record boxes. I tapped him on the shoulder and when he turned round I saw he had a split lip and blood on his T-shirt and looked even worse than he had after our own clash. 'Shamus and Lenny?' I asked. Joe smiled and shrugged. 'Nah,' he said ruefully. 'Just Lenny. Those boys can fucking ruck.' I was starting secretly to admire the brothers. They had obviously planned to pick us off one by one and had the confidence to put that plan into action. I guessed that Popeye had also been on their list, but I'm not too sure he would have accepted a straightener had he turned up that night.

The Crawley Cats were in full force inside the club, but though we exchanged a few dirty looks during the evening there was no more trouble between us that night. The war was not over and I was determined that the next time we clashed I would be calling the shots. Since finding out about her and Joe, I had seen very little of Hollywood, which suited us both. After coming out of jail it had really only been the sex that had kept us together. So, when I bumped into Denise and Mel again at the Chick-A-Boom that night, I tried to be my charming best. I caught a few looks from Denise, enough to make me think that she might be a little bit interested, but I guessed she would never make a move when her best friend was also making it obvious that she fancied me. There was not a lot I could do about Mel other than to try to make it plain that she wasn't my type and hope she got the message. By this time Joe K was pursuing the lovely Debbie Adams like a hungry dog chasing a bone, but Debbie was still playing hard to get around him. I could easily see how Joe was smitten, as Debbie filled her clothes like she'd been poured into them and when she hit the dance floor she was hotter than a £10 shotgun. Debbie was also one of those girls who could drink her weight in spirits and then fight half-a-dozen rocker chicks at once, a dream package for any violent young man of our persuasion. But at this time she wouldn't give Joe the time of day, so it was a pretty frustrating night for both of us.

After the club had closed we came out into the car park to find that the car had a flat tire and there was no spare. I was fucking fuming. There was no way I could drive it all the way back to Balham on the rim and it was just one more thing to add to my bad mood. Luckily a late, late bus happened to pull up at the circle and about 30 of us piled onto it, as at least it would take us as far as Morden station. On the bus was me, Joe K, Mick (who had turned up at the club late), Shane and Mitch, Snapper of the Streatham Teds and Tooting Roy. There was also a bruiser known as Putney Bill or Skinhead Bill. Skinhead Bill wasn't a genuine skinhead, he was rockin' just like us and it was rumoured that he was as hard as nails. I had to admit that he had plenty of bottle, he would show up at all the rockin' clubs, mostly on his own but sometimes with the Putney or Catford Mob, who were all rockabillies. I think Bill just genuinely loved the music and atmosphere of the rockin' scene but liked being a bit of a skinhead as well, so he got the best of both worlds.

I think I should mention here that although we were at war with all other teen subcultures there were some rules of engagement. If a lone skinhead, punk or mod turned up at one of our clubs they would not be attacked just for being there. So long as they didn't start anything they would be left in peace and, in addition to Skinhead Bill, we often got the odd punk turning up at the Chick-A-Boom and other clubs without incident. It was only when they were mob-handed or out on the street that we would steam in.

On the late bus I was brooding over the evening's events. I'd been bashed up by a pair of midgets, I'd failed to pull a bird I fancied and I'd had to leave my car in the car park, which meant a journey back to change the tire and pick it up the next morning. There was also the worry that the locals might take this opportunity to damage the car, so I wasn't in the best of moods when Skinhead Bill and one of the Streatham boys got into an argument over Gene Vincent. Snapper was wearing a leather with the words 'Gene Vincent Is God' painted on the shoulder panel, and Skinhead Bill, being fairly drunk, said something about it. The next thing I knew, the two were roaring at each other. Skinhead Bill was about 6 foot 2 and 16 stone of muscle and Snapper was 5 foot and a fag paper but had plenty of bottle, so the argument got very heated very quickly. I decided that here was an opportunity to vent some of my anger and maybe redeem my pride after losing the fight with Shamus and Lenny earlier on. So I jumped in. I told Skinhead Bill to shut his fucking mouth or I'd shut it for him. With hindsight, I could easily see how calling on a straightener with a geezer as hard as Skinhead Bill when my bruises from an earlier beating were still not even fully formed could be a bit of a mistake, but youth and arrogance are hard taskmasters. No sooner had I opened my mouth than Skinhead Bill was out of his seat and ringing the bell to stop the bus.

We all piled off the bus and formed a circle on the pavement. Skinhead Bill took off his sheepskin and I stripped to my shirt-sleeves as the onlookers began taking bets on who would win. I had learned some sort of lesson earlier and I was determined not to get caught by surprise this time. We circled each other warily, both looking for an opening. I could see from the way he held his fists that Bill was a street fighter rather than a boxer, and that made me even more cautious. Boxers tend to stick to a set of learned moves but street fighters are all-in and know that anything goes. After a long minute feinting at each other, I made my move and caught him on the cheek with a hard jab that knocked his head back. Bill countered by grabbing me by the shirt and trying to butt me in the face. Once it started, the fight was messy and there was a lot of mauling. I got another punch into his face and then managed to get him in a headlock, but he punched me again in the stomach and grabbed me by the hair and pulled my head back. We split apart again and he caught me a painful blow in the shin with his boot. I grabbed him and we toppled to the ground and, luckily for me, I landed on top of him and trapped his arms under me. I hooked my thumbs into each side of his mouth and banged his head off the pavement a few times to knock the fight out of him. And it worked. 'All right,' he gasped. 'Enough. You win.' I was elated. I had beaten Skinhead Bill in a straightener and that made up for the rest of the night. The crowd had been pretty noisy as the fight was going on, although when you're actually in the thick of it the noise of the crowd seems muted, and now I clearly heard Mick say, 'You should have smashed his fucking baldy head in.' Unfortunately Skinhead Bill heard him say it as well. As we got up off the ground and shook hands a few people patted me on the back, including Snapper. Skinhead Bill brushed himself down and then pointed at Mick. 'You're next, big mouth,' he said. I knew that Mick could have a tear-up as well, but he was fairly drunk and natural brotherly concern took over. 'Leave it out, Bill,' I said. 'That's enough for tonight.' But Bill wasn't wearing that. I have to say, he was as game as a brace of pit bulls and probably would have fought everyone in the crowd one after the other, win, lose or draw. Mick started to remove his jacket, but I jumped in again. 'Turn it in,' I said to Bill, and I put my hand on his arm, only to have it shrugged off again. 'Fuck off,' Bill said. 'You got lucky a minute ago. Don't push it.' That was enough for me and I launched a swift right-hander into Bill's face and the fight was on again.

By now I was completely knackered from rolling around on the pavement with Bill and he started to get the upper hand. I got one good knee into his bollocks, which slowed him down a bit, but when he caught me twice in quick succession with digs to my already tender and blackened eye I had to admit that I'd had enough. The second time I got off the ground it was as a loser. The win seemed to be enough to calm Bill's need to fight on and he was willing to shake hands once more and this time call it a night with his pride restored. The pats on the back I got this time were sympathetic rather than congratulatory. Mick shook his head. 'You should have left him to me,' he said. I could only nod and put my jacket back on. I looked down at the trousers of Harry's best suit and saw that one of the knees had been ripped out as I had rolled around on the pavement with Bill. It had been a bad night all around. We had a long walk ahead of us and it had started to rain. Fucking perfect! I thought to myself. But someone's going to end up suffering for this evening. And God help them.

Part Four

The Hillbillies and Psychobillies

Hillbilly (. Am.) – rustic of the hill country; any unsophisticated person; country-and-western music.

Psycho, si-ko (colloq.) n. – a psychopath.

Hillbilly Heaven

When Elvis Presley first burst onto the scene in 1954 with a new musical sound that had elements of both hillbilly and blues music, a lot of people who heard his records assumed that he was black. That was quite a problem in the still segregated Deep South of America, and in order to let the listeners know that Elvis was indeed a white man he was given the nickname 'The Hillbilly Cat' by a local Memphis DJ. Hillbilly was definitely white music, just as blues was definitely black music, and it wasn't until much later in the 1950s that the lines began to blur. And, as a lover of the blues, Elvis made a large contribution to the new musical integration.

In 1980, in South London, hillbilly music was about to make a comeback, without Elvis. Ever since the rebel Ted movement had mutated from the original Teddy boys, things had not really stopped evolving on the rockin' scene. Just as the rebel Teds and then the rockabilly rebels and cats had sought out new musical strings for the rock'n'roll bow by going back a little bit further into musical history, some of the newer recruits to the scene started looking even further back. If you take it in chronological order, bluegrass music begat hillbilly, hillbilly begat country, country begat rock'n'roll and then mutated into Rockabilly at a very early stage, and rock'n'roll became the commercial success. But, decades later, we reversed it all in a search for something that, although it could in no way be described as 'new', was new to us.

By the summer of 1980, records with a distinct hillbilly flavour began to be played by the more innovative DJs on the rockin' scene. And, not surprisingly, a new subculture began to emerge – the hillbilly rebel. I'm not quite certain where it all started, but some people say it began in West London and quickly spread throughout the clubs. Records like 'Wore To A Frazzle' by The Lamie Brothers, 'The Blues Keep Knockin' by Buck Trail, 'You Oughta See Grandma

Rock' by Hank Cochran, and 'Wild Dogs Of Kentucky' by Nervous Norvus were finding a new audience of boppers. The look of the hillbilly rebel consisted almost uniformly of a straw cowboy hat, patched dungarees, checked shirt, neckerchief and a pair of wellington boots with the tops cut off and then rolled over so there was a white cuff showing at the ankle, navvy style. Some of the hardcore hillbillies even had an unlit corncob pipe hanging from their mouths. They also had their own style of dancing, which incorporated digging movements and strange gurning faces. I must admit that I was attracted to the hillbilly thing. I liked the music and I had a hankering to try something different. So, one afternoon, I went out and got decked out as a hillbilly rebel, one of the few on the South London scene. I suppose it was all part of my need to stand out from the crowd and show off, and also to provoke people into any sort of confrontation. Most of the gang took it in good heart and humour and accepted my change. By this time others were starting to push the fashion boundaries as well. Peter Mayne, always a bit of an oddball, had started his own fashion revolution, although so far only he was in it. Sorting through the clothes in a charity shop, he had come across a pair of loud checked plus fours, and matched them with a diamond pattern V-necked jumper, a tweed jacket and a pair of red and white golf shoes with the studs removed from the soles. He called himself a golfbilly and even had a dance he would do in which he mimed swinging a golf club, then shading his eyes to see how far down the dance floor his imaginary ball had gone. I remember the first time he wore this outfit to the Chick-A-Boom club and everyone started shouting 'Fore!' when he got out on the floor. Joe K had also given some people a moment of despair when he had turned up at The Bedford one night in a mohair suit, desert boots and a pork-pie hat. The word quickly spread that Joe had 'turned mod' and the way it was being said it was as though he had died. There was a real feeling of sadness and betrayal. Joe K going over to the enemy was not the sort of news to inspire anyone on the rockin' scene. Not even his enemies, of whom there were many, would wish that on him. But it turned out that Joe was just jesting to see the reaction. The next day he was back in his leather and jeans.

So people on the rockin' scene were beginning to flex and stretch their fashion muscles, but so were some of the other teenage sub-cultures. Punk rockers seemed to be a dying breed on the streets of South London, and in their place was a small group of strangely dressed and coiffured teens who called themselves Blitz Kids, after a club they attended called The Blitz Club in Covent Garden. These newcomers, a lot of them ex-punks, would later come to be known as the New Romantics and spawn a fashion for frilly shirts, pirate trousers and crap electronic music. Like the original Teds, the New Romantics were very elitist, but unlike the Teds they were to have little longevity and by 1984 the movement was just a memory to most street kids.

The skinheads, too, were evolving from the original boots and braces firm through the Two-Tone revolution, tonic suits and skinny ties, to what was now being called 'Oi'. Oi is a pretty hard movement to define, but from my own perspective they were a mix of ex-punks, skinheads, football casuals and kids who just liked to drink, dance and fight. Oi was what punk rock had pretended to be but wasn't. There was a far-right element among them and this was what the media seized on to define them. According to the papers, Oi were all racist skinheads, but I don't think that was the full story. The sort of bands they were into were loud and aggressive, like Cock Sparrer, the UK Subs and Slaughter And The Dogs. And there was a definite football hooligan flavour to the whole Oi thing.

There were also a few early practitioners of what would become known as psychobilly, a mix of punk rock and rockabilly. The first recorded mention of the word 'psychobilly' can be heard on a 1976 hit by Johnny Cash and The Tennessee Two called 'One Piece At A

Time'. The song is about a man who starts working in a Cadillac factory and steals a car 'one piece at a time' over the next 26 years, so when he puts it all together he ends up with a monster he calls 'the psychobilly Cadillac'. Psychobilly fashions included dyed hair, usually a blond quiff, and a mix of punk and rockabilly clothes such as a leather jacket, bondage trousers and boots. Some psychobillies wore brightly coloured zoot suits that were sold off the peg at Kensington Market. The bands that psychobillies favoured were the likes of The Cramps, The Meteors, Guana Batz, The Sharks and even King Kurt. These bands had elaborate stage shows with smoke, fire and plenty of props, in some cases showering their audience with buckets of animal blood and raw meat, and most of them had a voodoo or horror film theme to their music. The only ones who really touched the real rockin' scene were The Meteors, who had a minor hit in the clubs with a record called 'My Daddy Was A Vampire'.

I saw my first psychobillies at a gig when Screaming Lord Sutch played at the Chick-A-Boom in June 1980. Lord Sutch was a big favourite with the biker gangs and was always guaranteed to pull a crowd at his infrequent appearances because he certainly knew how to put on a show. Sutch was another one who used stage props in his act, such as burning braziers and a coffin, from which he would emerge dressed in a top hat and cloak. The rockers had been requesting Screaming Lord Sutch records at the clubs since the 1960s when he had minor hits with such songs as 'Jack The Ripper' and 'I'm A Hog For You'. Sutch was following in the footsteps of original '50s American artist Screamin' Jay Hawkins, who had the voodoo/ghoul thing off to a tee and always carried a cane with a skull on it. Screamin' Jay's best known song was 'I Put A Spell On You' (1956), and even though he never had a hit with it, others did, most notably Nina Simone (1965) and The Alan Price Set (1966). But it was at the Lord Sutch gig that I first noticed a couple of strange geezers with dyed hair and zoot suits. They were the only ones on the dance floor and were doing this strange, violent dance that involved a lot of bumping into each other and slapping each other's faces before rolling around on the floor like mad things. I almost pissed myself laughing at their antics and a lot of people were amused by the spectacle. At the end of the night I had to go and ask them what it had all been about. That was when they explained that they were psychobillies and that their dance was called 'slam dancing' and that it was all the rage in the Beat Route club up West. I told them that it was a good job they had been slapping each other, because it probably saved them from getting a good slapping from anyone else. I didn't think that this psychobilly thing would ever catch on. But I had been known to be wrong about such things.

Many years later I became friends with Micky White, bass player with The Meteors, who is a lovely fella despite the band's reputation for mayhem and horror. I'm also mates with Alan Wilson of The Sharks, who now runs The Western Star Recording Company, out of Bristol. Psychobilly was a shock to the system for the rockin' crowd but the music is still popular today so, unlike hillbillies, new romantics and disco freaks, the music was to have some longevity.

My own hillbilly phase lasted for about four weeks, until I saw a band called Dexy's Midnight Runners on Top of the Pops wearing dungarees and neckerchiefs and decided the look was deadsville. Once it started becoming commercial it was time to ditch it. Besides, it was costing me a fortune in straw cowboy hats, as every time I got drunk or got into a fight I would lose my hat. By now the Balham Wildkatz and the north Battersea were strong allies, as we had a mutual enemy in the form of the Crawley Cats, and we had a night out together at the old Fountain in Tooting where Moses was now the DJ. By chance there was an amateur Australian rugby team in The Fountain that night celebrating a win. God knows how they found themselves in such a pub, but they were loud and drunk and spoiling for a fight. I was in my hillbilly gear and got a few sniggers from the

Ozzies when I went up to the bar. I was ordering a round when one of the Ozzies snatched my straw cowboy hat from my head, put it on his own head and began to dance, to the amusement of his pals. I've always had a problem with public humiliation – it leads to rage and then violence in me – so with the sniggering and then snatching my hat off I was ready to rumble. I was carrying my cut-throat razor in the chest pocket of my dungarees and I took it out and flicked it open. I didn't say a word. The Ozzies were all laughing at the capering of their pal and he didn't see the razor until it was snapping towards his face. I opened his cheek in one swift movement, and as he bent forward to cup his wound I lifted my hat off his head and put it back on mine. 'Cheers, mug!' I said. The Ozzies were silenced for a moment when their pal lifted his head and they saw the blood, but then there was the sound of breaking glass and howls of outrage as they prepared to steam in. They never really stood a chance against both us and the north Battersea, and in seconds there was a major bar-room brawl going on. There were women screaming, bottles flying and stools being used as weapons. They put up a great fight, but we ended up battering them by sheer weight of numbers. At one point I found myself helping Psycho Joe to lay into the biggest Ozzie, who was battling with a bottle in each hand, and I threw my hat in the man's face to distract him and allow Joe to cosh him. After the fight was over and we were having a drink together, I was moaning about how I had lost another hat as someone had nicked it in the confusion, and it was then that I decided to knock being a hillbilly on the head and go back to the rockabilly style.

As a result of the fight with the Australian rugby players in The Fountain, Moses lost his dee-jaying gig and all the rockin' crowd were barred from the pub. We were told that the police had ordered this and that if the pub manager did not comply then he could lose his licence. Five of the Ozzies had been seriously injured in the fight and required hospital treatment, including the one I striped across the face. The Fountain was the first South London venue that had been lost to the rockin' scene directly due to our violence, but we just took it as a good laugh. Our violence was starting to escalate and we would soon find that The Fountain was not the only place where we were no longer welcome.

Murder at The Balham Hotel

The Bedford pub had become our headquarters and you could find at least a handful of the Balham Wildkatz in there on most afternoons. The only other pub within a couple of miles was a dive called The Balham Hotel, which was up past the station and on the other side of the High Street. The Balham Hotel was known as a 'black' pub because most of its clientele were Afro-Caribbean. They had a small stage in there and local bands would play, including Desmond Dekker, who had a number 1 hit in 1969 with 'Israelites'. Desmond would sing with an Irish band called The Mary Edwards Band, and introduced himself as 'the browned-off paddy' ('browned off' is an Irish expression meaning to be upset or depressed). I had been in The Balham Hotel a few times, but never for long as it was a proper dirty gaff and there would be even dirtier looks from the crowds of domino and card players who frequented the place. Though not exactly a no-go area for us, The Balham Hotel wasn't on the top of our list for a good night out.

One evening there was a crowd of us in The Bedford, knocking back the drink and generally being raucous, as was our wont, when my cousin Ronnie staggered in with blood running down his face. He told us that he had been at a meet with someone at The Balham Hotel when he got into an altercation with a barman and ended up getting jumped and beaten by the barman and some customers. Incensed by what we saw as a dire liberty having been taken with one of our own, and forgetting that we had all done much worse ourselves, we decided to march on The Balham Hotel and teach anyone inside a stiff lesson. A good 40 of us set off on the six-minute walk, with rage and mischief in our hearts. Among the mob were the usual suspects: me, Popeye, Joe K, Mick, Ronnie and Eddie, and Tall Paul. There were also a few people who just fancied a fight and joined in on the spur of the moment, including a smoothie called Glen who happened to be going out with a rockin' bird named Sharon.

At this stage of the game we were mostly veterans of this kind of thing, organised-disorganised violence in groups, so it was just another incident to most of us. There was no reason to assume that there would be anything different about this attack, although I did notice that there were a few people on the march that I didn't recognise. We got to the pub and immediately announced our presence by launching a couple of crates full of milk bottles through the windows as a precursor to charging through every door of the place and steaming into anyone who moved and plenty who didn't. The pub ended up wrecked: the tills and the fruit machines were broken open and robbed, and every fixture and fitting was smashed. Customers were bashed and battered, and when the last of the mob had left there was a dead barman lying on the floor.

On the way back to The Bedford various members of the mob began ditching and hiding their weapons. The drains around Balham must have been half clogged by the amount of knives, coshes and bike chains that were dropped into them. At this time we didn't know that anyone had been killed in the attack, but we didn't particularly care either. We knew that there was going to be a bit of police activity, and before getting to The Bedford a good few people went their separate ways. Me and the core of the gang went into The Bedford and carried on where we had left off, and later that evening this was where several of us were arrested for causing an affray and on suspicion of murder. Being arrested for murder should have been a pretty sobering thing, and in some ways it was, particularly after seeing the grey-faced lifers in the chapel in Wormwood Scrubs prison while on remand. But it was also a bit of a buzz for some of us; a validation of how dangerous we could be. The police questioned me, Ronnie, Eddie, Mario, Tall Paul and Marathon for hours but got nothing out of us. We all knew the drill: keep your mouth shut except to ask for a brief. It turned out that the dead man had been stabbed in the chest and the wound had pierced his heart. I knew I hadn't done it, but I had no idea who had. The police were nicking anyone who might have been at The Balham Hotel and we were being held in police stations all over South London. Then we heard that Glen the smoothie had handed himself in and admitted to the stabbing. He claimed that the barman had come at him with a baseball bat during the battle and that he had struck out blindly, forgetting that the knife was in his hand. Glen was charged with murder and the rest of us were released pending other charges.

After we all got together later that week we all agreed that there was something not quite right about Glen's confession. They did not have the murder weapon, there were no witnesses willing to testify or even identify anyone involved in the fight, let alone the murder, and there was a strong rumour that someone else in the mob had committed the murder. It was felt that Glen had only stuck his hands up to it in order to get a bit of kudos. If so, it was a bit of a silly way to get a reputation. I heard that the real killer had left the country before Glen had even handed himself in. Sharon made a statement claiming that she and her mate had met Glen down in Balham tube station straight after the fight and that he had handed her a knife to hide, and she had thrown the knife down one of the tunnels. When the police recovered the knife, it turned out not to fit the wound in the barman's chest, but the police had a dead body and a live body with a confession and that was more than enough.

Some months later Glen appeared at the Old Bailey and pleaded not guilty to murder but guilty to manslaughter. The Crown accepted his plea and he was jailed for five years. In a strange stroke of irony, when Glen was released after serving his sentence he got a job as a barman in The Balham Hotel, which by then was under new management. By that time a few of the gang had started using The Balham Hotel, as The Bedford was undergoing refurbishment, and every closing time when Glen got a bit lippy about us finishing our drinks and moving on he would often be treated to someone saying: 'Be careful, son, you know what happened to the last barman here.'

Although none of the gang ended up being convicted of the murder, the news that we had been involved in the whole fight soon made the rounds and our reputation as a gang went up another notch. By now we were quite full of ourselves and thought we could get away with anything. We strutted around in our fantasy world, plotting our next move and decided that it was to be on the Crawley Cats. They had to be dealt with once and for all – no straighteners, just an all-out gang rumble. And it was to be a joint operation.

We put the word about in the rockin' clubs that the Crawley Cats were going to get theirs and anyone who wanted to be in on it was welcome. We were to meet, once again, at the breaker's yard on Saturday evening and then make our way to the Chick-A-Boom. To be honest, the Crawley Cats were quite a formidable gang and I was not too sure if the Wildkatz could handle them, and that's why I put out an open invitation to other gangs, although I would never have admitted this at the time. Fortunately, the Crawley Cats had upset so many people on the scene that there was no shortage of people wanting to be in on it.

All through that Saturday afternoon I was amazed to see members of so many different gangs turning up at the yard. There was Psycho Joe and his boys from the north Battersea, Tommy Hogan Jnr, Rockabilly Steve, Little Bopper and Tin-Tin of the south Battersea Katz, Jimmy Harris and a couple of his boys from Bermondsey, two Greek rocker brothers called Kif and Kos, Nutty Noel from the Lambeth Lords, and even one member of Pimlico's Cool Daddio Club. I realised that the Crawley Cats were in for a proper beating when I saw this mob all together.

By now I had worked through my rage over Hollywood and Rockabilly Steve and had dumped Hollywood and confronted Steve about it. I had gone to The Clarence one night with just Popeye and Harry because I'd heard that Steve would be there. I offered him a straightener, which he refused, and that was enough to satisfy my honour. I think Steve had been spared my full wrath because I had taken it all out on Joe K in our epic straightener in the Chick-A-Boom's car park. So, although Steve and I were never going to be best pals, I was on nodding terms with him. Standing on the steps of Popeye's caravan, with the sun sinking low in the sky over the piles of wrecked cars, I surveyed my troops and felt a surge of pride in my chest. This was what it was all about. I breathed deep the smell of motor oil, Brylcreem and Brut aftershave, and listened to the hum of conversation, the creak of leather and the jangle of chains and buckles. The Greek rockers were showing Psycho Joe their home-made knuckledusters and offering to make him one for next time. Popeye and Harry were making final adjustments to the engine of our Ford Zephyr 6 battle wagon, and the south Battersea boys were puffing on joints and doing a good a cappella rendition of Jessie Belvin's 'Goodnight My Love', which was big on the slow dance section at most of the clubs. As I stood there watching and listening, I suddenly had a moment of depressing clarity and it was like a chill breeze across the back of my neck. This is it, I thought. As good as it gets. Pretty soon we'll all grow up and we'll never be able to do this again. For just a second I was able to see beyond the fantasy and I had a feeling of loss, like I'd had as a kid when I had woken up and found all the beautiful white snow had melted overnight, leaving just grey slushy puddles. Peter stepped past me down the steps of our caravan in his golfbilly gear, carrying a metal golf club, and the moment evaporated. I shivered and then put it out of my mind. 'Let's mount up,' I shouted. And I didn't feel silly at all.

Most of the lads had arrived in their own vehicles, but we still had to find room for a few people in the convoy. Everyone squeezed in, but Little Bopper had to get into the boot of Psycho Joe's PA Cresta. We all knew that he could have fitted into any of the cars and vans, but it was funnier to make him travel in the boot. He refused to have the boot lid closed fully, so all the way down to Carshalton we could see him mouthing curses at our windscreen and it helped to lighten the mood.

When we pulled into the car park of the Chick-A-Boom club and emerged from our vehicles, the locals who had been drinking outside the front bar in order to throw a few insults at the arriving boppers, which was their usual amusement, kept their mouths shut and looked as though they wished they were somewhere else. Forty-odd leather-jacketed, hard-faced geezers moving as a group are a pretty formidable and intimidating sight. The rockin' crowd knew what was going on. The rumours about an alliance against the Crawley Cats had made the rounds and now they were witnessing the reality of it. Outside the club we were joined by Mitch, Snapper and Tooting Roy, who had made their own way there. At that moment I almost felt sorry for the Crawley Cats – almost.

Inside the club you could have cut the atmosphere with a spoon. The Crawley Cats had never missed a Saturday night at the Chick-A-Boom, but tonight there was no sign of them. I noticed that Joe K was there, sitting with Debbie, and I went over to have a quick word. Ever since our fight Joe and I had been a bit strained in each other's company. Debbie still had not succumbed to Joe's charms, even though she had split up with her boyfriend Derek, but Joe was relentless in his pursuit. I asked him if he was going to have a bit of the Crawley when they showed up and he said he was game and ready. I looked around the club. A group called Vernon And The GIs were setting up on the stage but I didn't fancy their chances of getting anyone on the dance floor. You could spot the people who had come for the fight by how tense they were, standing around in small groups drinking and letting their eyes flit regularly to the entrance. We had a couple of spotters out in the car park to warn us when the enemy arrived. I saw Denise and Mel sitting at a table over by the decks and went over to say hello. Denise was looking particularly fine in a pink mohair V-necked jumper, tight jeans and Indian moccasins. I got a nice smile out of her and wondered if I would ever get to see her without Mel in tow.

By 10.30 there was still no sign of the Crawley Cats and, as people were getting drunk and edgy, cracks were beginning to show in what was, after all, a fragile alliance between the various gangs. They had all split into their various factions and had taken up their own space around the club. Then one of the spotters told me that there was trouble in the car park, so I went out to see what was happening. Psycho Joe, obviously tired of waiting for someone's head to bash in, had started an argument with a group of rockers. The rockers were clearly independents rather than affiliated with any motorcycle club, as they had no patch or gang name on their leathers, but that didn't make them any less dangerous. Psycho Joe had picked out the biggest of the rockers, a 6 foot 2 and 17 stone fella known as Baby Blue, and was offering him a straightener when I arrived. But Baby Blue obviously knew of Psycho Joe's reputation and was wary. 'Yeah, I'll have a straightener with you anytime, but you're a fucking tool merchant. How do I know you won't stick a knife in me?' Psycho Joe grinned and held his leather open disarmingly. 'I'm not carrying a knife,' he said. 'You can search me if you want.' Baby Blue was cautious. By now around 20 of us had gathered around him and his pals. 'It won't be a fair fight,' he said. 'If I beat you then the rest of your gang will steam in.' Psycho Joe shook his head. 'Just me and you,' he said. 'We'll go around the back of the club on our own.' He turned to the rest of us. 'You lot stay here,' he ordered. 'It's just me and the mug.' With that settled, and with his mates egging him on, Baby Blue agreed to fight Psycho Joe and off they went around to the small patch of grass behind the club.

Not for one minute was I expecting Psycho Joe to have a fair fight with Baby Blue. For a start, it was like the biggest mismatch since David and Goliath and there was no doubt that Baby Blue could probably take Joe's head off with one punch. And Psycho Joe had been just too confident. I would have laid good money on the fact that Psycho Joe had more than a slingshot up his sleeve, and I was right. Within a couple of minutes Baby Blue was staggering back to us holding his broken face and leaking blood everywhere. Psycho Joe had followed jauntily, not a mark on him, with a lead cosh in his hand. As Baby Blue had been taking off his jacket in preparation for fisticuffs, Psycho Joe had slipped the length of pipe from the sleeve of his own jacket and let rip. Baby Blue and his pals were bleating about it not being a fair fight, but Psycho Joe justified his actions. 'Look at the fucking size of him!' he pointed out. 'As if that would have been fucking fair! Besides, everyone knows I'm a fucking fruitcake. I don't play by the rules!' I had to laugh at Joe's audacity, and so did the rest of us – except Baby Blue and his pals. Just then there was a commotion near the front bar and someone shouted that we were having it with the smoothies. We all legged it round to the front of the club and were greeted by the sight of a battle zone. There were people fighting and chasing each other all over the small car park at the front of the pub. I spotted GiGi, a dark-skinned rockabilly who was reputed to be a bit of a kung fu expert, throwing punches at three smoothies and so I joined him.

Trouble between us and the locals had been simmering for a long time and it had finally come to a head when they had beaten up a young Teddy boy who had accidentally wandered into the front bar. Word had quickly spread through the club and, with tension so high anyway, a mob had flown round to the front bar and steamed in. We found out later that our arrival in convoy at the start of the evening had spooked the locals and, thinking that we were coming to do them, they had called in reinforcements. They had been waiting all night for us to attack and when the lone Ted had entered they had got a bit carried away and had broken his jaw.

The tear-up with the locals was terrific. It was one of those fights that spread out all over the place and consisted of loads of running skirmishes. Within minutes of it starting, there were people fighting out in the middle of the road, all over the car park and as far down as the Green about 300 yards from the club. Both sides had been ready for a kick-off and were tooled up, so it was a pretty fair fight to begin with, but as more people joined in we began to have the advantage of numbers. Fair play to the locals, who put up a good showing, and if the police hadn't turned up they might have been able to turn the tide. The police were never far away from The St Helier Arms on most nights and particularly so at weekends. The occupants of the lone panda car parked on the circle knew better than to try to sort out a battle like this on their own, so they had radioed for the riot squad. I was helping Peter to batter a geezer with a dodgy perm when I heard the sirens. I immediately dropped my cosh, and Peter dropped his golf club, and we began to walk away. The last thing we wanted was to be nicked with tools on us.

As the police cars and vans began screeching up with sirens wailing and blue lights flashing, the fighting broke off and people began streaming back into the bars. The few combatants that either ignored or didn't hear the arrival of the police because they were lost in the moment soon found themselves buried under a blue serge mountain as the Old Bill piled right in. Me and a few others ended up on the opposite side of The Circle and watched as the fight was brought to an end and several people were arrested and thrown into police vans. But the adrenalin was still coursing through us and we couldn't contain ourselves, so we began shouting insults at the police and the few locals who were left in the car park. Several coppers ran over to where we were standing and tried to move us on, but we weren't having it. I was slagging off the geezer with the dodgy perm, who was still in the car park wiping blood from his face, when a copper pushed me and told me to move on. I faced the copper. 'Fuck you!' I shouted into his face, and the next thing I knew I was being bundled into the back of a police van. Joe K, Peter, Harry and Tooting Roy were also nicked. We ended up spending the night in Wallington police station and we were charged with obstruction and breach of the peace. I spent a restless night banged up in the same cell as Joe K and was surprised to find that he talked in his sleep, mainly about Debbie. If that was love he certainly had a bad case of it.

We were released the next morning on police bail and boy did we look a sight on our way back to South London. We sat quietly on the tube, worn out and hungover by the previous night's events, hair all over the place and stinking of stale alcohol and police blankets. It was a big contrast to the way we had started out the previous evening. Then we had been an invading army; now we looked more like refugees from a battle zone. It was a couple of days before we found out why the Crawley Cats had not turned up that night. They had been involved in a gang fight on their own turf with a load of soul boys. Things had got out of hand and Shamus had driven a car into a crowd of soul boys, badly injuring two of them. Shamus had been arrested for attempted murder and the rest of the gang were lying low. The Crawley Cats never made a comeback after this and eventually disbanded and went their separate ways. But the war with the locals from the front bar was only just beginning.

True Love Ways

On 1 July 1980 I finally managed to catch Denise without Mel in tow, and so began a relationship that would last, in one form or another, for the next 25 years. It was Denise's birthday, her eighteenth, and she was celebrating at the Chick-A-Boom club, which was really her local as she only lived a few streets away. Mel had woken up one day with an interest in classic British motorcycles and a craving to buy one, so she had started saving every penny in order to be in the position to fulfil her dream. Mel's sudden motorcycle madness meant that she had to drop the club nights out for a couple of months, leaving Denise to her own devices, which suited me just fine. I noticed Denise without Mel as soon as I walked into the club and so made a beeline for her. I hadn't been able to stop thinking about Denise for months. At odd moments in the day her face, framed by that magnificent chestnut hair, would pop into my thoughts and I would find myself smiling. This was very disconcerting and I felt it was a weakness that I could do without. I had thought I was in love with Hollywood and that had turned out so badly that I had vowed never to get too deep with a girl again. I thought of myself as a love-'em-and-leave-'em kind of bloke and there had been many one-night stands since Hollywood, so I told myself that Denise would be just another notch on the bedpost. But I couldn't get her out of my head.

I chatted to Denise in the club for over an hour before I had to go and sort out an argument that was developing between Popeye and one of the Road Rats MC prospects. During the rest of the evening I kept my eye on Denise and winked every time I saw her looking at me and she would smile back. When the band came on, I went out into the car park to watch a straightener between a couple of rockers. I was shadowing Popeye, as he was bulling over the earlier argument and I didn't want him doing anything silly. It was all very well

229

getting into a war with other rockabilly gangs and no-patch bikers, but the Road Rats MC were a different gravy. They had a charter from the original Hell's Angels and you didn't get that by pussy-footing around when it came to trouble. We were violent and reckless young hooligans, but the Road Rats MC were stone killers and in a completely different league. I remember reading in the *South London Press* about some geezer who'd had a run-in with them in The Fountain and they had followed him home and half killed him and wrecked his house. Popeye's gripe against the Road Rat prospect was the usual who-you-looking-at-did-you-spill-my-pint turnout. I knew the prospect was looking for any excuse to show his 'class' and Popeye was looking for any excuse to put the blade to someone and didn't give a fuck who. Popeye was no respecter of reputations. There were three full-patch members of the Road Rats MC in the club watching their prospect, but I knew that there was little point in appealing to them so I stepped in and smoothed things over. I took Popeye aside and warned him not to start again, but from his mood I knew that someone was going to cop an unfortunate one that evening.

While I was watching the straightener with Popeye, Shane came from inside the club and stood with us. He was smiling. 'What do you think of that Denise?' he asked. I squinted at him. 'She's all right,' I said, wondering if I had been so obvious that even Shane had noticed that I fancied her. He nodded. 'Yeah, sounds like she fancies you.' I felt my heart quicken but I played it cool. I took a butt out and lit it with my Zippo, blowing a cloud of smoke into the night air before I said anything. 'How do you know?' I asked. Shane was watching the two rockers hammering the shit out of each other. 'How do I know what?' he asked. I got impatient and threw cool to the breeze. 'How the fuck do you know that she fancies me?' I demanded sharply. Shane looked up, surprised by the tone of my voice. 'I heard her say it,' he said. I waited for him to elaborate and when he didn't I flicked my butt on the ground and gave him a light slap on the top of his head. 'Fucking give,' I ordered. 'Don't make me drag every fucking word out of you, you little fuck.' Shane rubbed his head and looked aggrieved. 'I heard her say it to that Jeanette bird.' I gave him the look. 'And?' I said. He shrugged. 'She just said she thought you were a hunk, and her and Jeanette started whispering and giggling to each other, and that's all I heard. You've fucked my hair up.' He pulled his comb and started doing repair work. I smiled. This was the best news I'd heard in ages. Denise fancied me! I pulled out another butt and sparked it up, but inside I was cheering and singing.

Once back inside the club, I was on my way to see Denise again when I was accosted by Tooting Roy. He was a nice fella when he was sober, but a proper string vest after he'd had a couple of sherbets. He was an independent but allied with the Wildkatz when it came to trouble. He was game and loved a good tear-up and a laugh. I liked Tooting Roy. Now he had a couple of geezers with him who he introduced as his cousin and his cousin's mate, and he said that they were staying with him for a week, on holiday from the sticks. His cousin was a big lump wearing sunglasses, in a club at midnight, a headband around his head and a buckskin jacket. Roy introduced him as Apache and I got a bad vibe off him straight away. He was arrogant and I couldn't see his eyes, a bad combination in anyone. His mate wasn't much cop either – a bucktoothed soul boy with ferrety eyes. I shook hands with them and made a few of the right noises before I managed to get away. I could see that Roy was a bit uncomfortable around these two herberts and knew he would be knocking back the pints as soon as he reached the bar. Knowing what a monster Roy could become when he was drunk, I laid odds that he would be punching one, or both, before the night was over.

I found Denise at her table with her mates and noticed that her eyes lit up when I appeared. I sat down and joined in the conversation. It felt good to take time off from the job of walking around looking tough and exuding an air of menace, all the stuff that went along with the image I had built for myself. Being near Denise made me feel a bit more human and the image didn't seem so important somehow. As it came near the time for the slow dances, I went up to the decks to see what Martin had lined up as the first record. It was perfect: Gene Vincent's echoey version of the Al Hibbler song 'Unchained Melody'. As I reached the table it started and I looked down at Denise and put my hand out. For a split second I thought she was going to refuse to dance with me and an edge of panic started to creep up on me.

There's nothing worse than asking a girl to dance and her saying no. That would have been utterly devastating. But she smiled and took my hand. We stayed out on the dance floor for the duration of the slow dance records and, though the floor was crowded with dancers, it was as if we were the only two there. After dancing we sat talking until the lights came on and the club began to empty. Outside a crowd of people had gathered and I saw Popeye with Tooting Roy and his cousin. I told Denise I'd walk her home and nipped over to see what Popeye was doing. Tooting Roy was lagging drunk and so were his cousin and his pal. Popeye looked happier than he had earlier in the evening and said they were going to walk back to Roy's gaff for sausage sandwiches. Roy lived on the border of Mitcham and Tooting Broadway, about a three-mile walk from the club and on our route back to Balham. So I told Popeye I would join them somewhere along the route home as I was walking Denise to her house. I left Popeye just as Shane, Little Andy and a couple of Tooting boys joined the party. I set off down Green Wrythe Lane with my arm around Denise, leaving the rest of them finishing off their drinks and talking in the car park. I knew they wouldn't leave for a while yet as there were a few birds waiting for cabs. Denise lived in a nice semi-detached house with a lovely big front garden in a quiet residential area. The houses reminded me of the posh gaffs that surrounded Sinclair Estate and I was impressed. I was used to council estates with lifts that constantly stank of piss or squats, so this all seemed very middle class to me. It was a beautiful night, warm but with a nice breeze, and we stopped outside her house. Not many of the house lights were on in the street but the hall light was on in Denise's. We were silent for a while, and then I asked her what she wanted for her birthday. She looked at me shyly. 'A kiss,' she said. So I kissed her. I can still recall the thrill of that first kiss, the feel of her in my arms and the taste of her lips. Little did I know of the trouble and heartache we would share over the next quarter of a century, but even if I had it wouldn't have changed that moment. After our kiss I got the formality out of the way and asked her if she wanted to go out with me. She said yes and that was that. Denise Ann Young was now officially my girl.

I was flying as I walked away after seeing her go into her house. In fact I got halfway down the street and then just felt the urge to run as fast as I could. I legged it down Seddon Road, whooping at the top of my voice and probably waking all the nice middle-class people in their beds. For the first time since I could remember, I was truly happy. I caught up with Popeye and the gang on the outskirts of Mitcham and wasn't that surprised to find an argument going on. Apache had said something to Popeye about his hair. Popeye was a massive Gene Vincent fan and had got the front of his quiff permed so that it hung over his eyes just like Gene, but he was sensitive about it and given the mood he was already in that evening he found Apache's comment cause for violence. As I reached the group Popeye was being held back by several people and Apache was being spoken to by Roy. Feeling as grand as I did, I just wanted to smooth things over and calm everything down. It was too nice a night for someone to get stabbed over a trivial comment. I pushed my way through the group holding Popeye, grabbed his face between my hands and looked into his eyes. 'Calm down,' I said. 'Leave it out. The geezer's a mug. Right?' Popeye was raging but his eyes slowly came back into focus. He eventually stopped struggling, but I could tell that the slightest thing would start him off again. 'Wait here,' I told him. 'I'll have a word with the other fella.' Tooting Roy was waving his finger in his cousin's face and giving him plenty of earache about starting trouble and showing him up, which was a bit rich coming from a geezer who regularly got sick over people's shoes and then punched their lights out when they complained. 'Everything all right?' I asked, and with that Apache puffed up his chest and told Roy, 'You can tell this cunt to fuck off out of my face. It's got fuck all to do with him.' I couldn't believe it and neither could Roy. He was facing me and I saw his face screw up. In one swift move he turned and smashed his fist straight into his cousin's face. Apache went over backwards like a felled tree, arms still down by his sides and with nothing to break his fall except the pavement. Apache lay spark out on the ground with his mouth open but his shades still intact. Roy turned back to me. 'Sorry about that, Raze,' he said and shrugged. 'Families, eh?' I shook my head and turned round to face Popeye, who was no longer being held. 'Happy now?' I asked. Popeye nodded and straightened his jacket. 'Come on,' shouted Tooting Roy. 'Only another couple of miles and its sausage sarnies all round!' And off we marched, leaving Apache stretched out on the pavement.

The relationship I started with Denise that night was to endure for nearly three decades. Denise was different in many ways to the girls I had been involved with before her. For a start, she didn't fall straight into bed with me. I was used to having sex with girls around an hour after I had winked at them and bought them half a lager. Denise was definitely a step up in class for me. Within a year she would be pregnant with our first child and we would be living together. The responsibilities of my new family would do much to slow my casual violence and turn me away from the gang. Unfortunately I turned towards more serious acquisitive crime. But that's another story, and anyway, in 1980 things were about to become a bit more hectic.

Attack of the Killer Smoothies

The war with the front bar smoothies of The St Helier Arms was not over. The battle we had fought on the night that the Crawley Cats failed to appear had been indecisive, as it had been broken up by the police, and an uneasy kind of truce had settled over that small corner of Carshalton ever since. The smoothies in the front bar were no mugs and had some tough boys in their firm who didn't shy away from a tear-up. Looking back, I can see how pissed off they must have been with us. They had this local pub that was in the heart of their estate and where any stranger could be spotted straight away, they had a reputation as a hard firm, and then, out of nowhere, their turf was getting invaded by hundreds of strutting greasers every Wednesday and Saturday night. We're giving it the big 'un, screwing them out as we pass and making it plain that they're not welcome in part of their own local. I should think I would be a bit peeved myself had I been in their shoes, and not only because their shoes were by and large horrible-looking disco-boppers.

One night we came out of the Chick-A-Boom and piled into a couple of motors for the journey home. Mick was driving a midnight blue Zephyr 6, a beautiful car that he had recently purchased. In the Zephyr with Mick were Big Chris, Tank, Alan, Dennis and Olly the Cat. I was a passenger in Harry's jacked-up Vauxhall Cresta, along with Harry, Popeye, who was driving that night, Joe K and Tooting Roy. We were halfway down Green Wrythe Lane when our headlights picked out a couple of rockabillies getting a beating from some smoothies. Both our cars screeched up onto the pavement and we all jumped out to lend a hand. The two kids who had been getting a kicking were Little Derek, one of the new lot who called themselves the 'junior Wildkatz', and a girl called Beverley, who was the best mate of my sister Samantha. I'll give the smoothie firm the benefit of the doubt in one respect and say that they might not have known they were attacking a girl as, at that time, it was the fashion among rockabilly chicks to have a short haircut in the same style as the boys – I think Debbie Adams made that fashionable – and wear jeans and donkey jackets. Also the street lights on Green Wrythe Lane were not that good, so a mistake could have been made, but where my benefit of the doubt stops is the fact that Derek and Beverley were both young kids, and looked it.

We were incensed that a gang of blokes, armed with sticks and baseball bats, could launch such a cowardly attack. We were out of the cars and after them over a large patch of green and into the darkness. Popeye, Harry and I were the front runners and the first into the waiting ambush. Fuck knows how long it took them to plan it or whether they sat around a scale model of the area with little Matchbox cars and figured it all out, but it worked a treat. As we pounded over a small hillock we were hit with high-beam headlights from several vehicles and the sound of engines roaring into life. It was the revenge of the front bar smoothies and we were bang in it. They were in a couple of souped-up smoothie-wagons, Ford Cortinas or Escorts with mag wheels and extra headlamps, and a van of some description, probably a Transit. And they were also on foot. It seemed as though about 60 of them were charging out of the darkness and waving weapons at us. I only had my razor and when I saw them my arsehole went. 'Leg it!' I shouted, as though anyone needed to be told – but apparently Popeye did: he stood there with a knife in each hand and steamed into the first of the mob who reached him. I only saw this in silhouette over my shoulder as I legged it back to our cars. I was aware of the noise of engines behind me and the bloodthirsty roars of the smoothies as I ran flat out to get away. I could see the poorly lit road up ahead and our cars sitting there with the doors open, and all my concentration was on reaching the safety of the cars. Then my panic abated for a second and I thought of Popeye. He was my pal, my blood brother, and I was leaving him to face the mob alone. I started to slow down, not because I wanted to, believe me – I was still shitting myself, but my sense of shame somehow outweighed my fear. I was still clutching my razor but wished I had a length of lead pipe instead. A razor is great for close contact fighting but not much cop against a club-wielding mob. I forced myself to turn around and run back towards the trouble, all the while wishing that I was at home safe in bed.

The sight that greeted me was like a scene from a horror film. There were headlights blazing, engines gunning and moving over the grass in my direction and a howling mob of tooled-up smoothies spread out over the green and heading towards me. I tried to psyche myself up for the coming beating. 'COME ON THEN, YOU MUGGY CUNTS!' I shouted at the top of my voice, and I saw the first dark shape come towards me. I lashed out with my razor and felt it bite into something, probably cloth, and then my head lit up with bright blue sparks as something crashed into it, a baseball bat I would wager if I had to. I staggered forward and got another whack, this time across my back, and I was aware of dropping my razor onto the dark grassy ground. Now I was defenceless and at the mercy of the mob. I dropped to the ground and covered my head with my hands and felt another whack across my legs. I could hear shouting and running feet all around me and I thought I was going to be beaten to death right there on the green. Then I heard Popeye's familiar voice – 'Have some of that, you prick!' – and I dared to look up. Popeye was standing over me, holding four or five smoothies at bay with his knives. In the light from the headlamps I could see blood all over his face, like a black mask, and I quickly got to my feet. He had already stabbed three of the smoothies, two of them quite badly, and they were wary of getting too close. 'Back to the car!' I shouted, and we both ran in that direction.

Though a small crowd of the smoothies had been held up laying into me and Popeye, the main bulk of them had chased the rest of our gang back to the cars. Getting into the cars had been a tactical mistake and the smoothies were all over them, smashing windows in and puncturing tires; one even had a complete pickaxe and was caning the bodywork of the cars with the pointed end, leaving holes through the metal. When we had originally pulled up, our Vauxhall had been the lead car and Mick had pulled his Zephyr up to our bumper, so when we had jumped out of the Vauxhall Popeye had switched off the engine and taken the keys with him. When the rest of the gang reached what they thought was the safety of the cars and got inside for a quick getaway, Harry found no keys in his ignition and Mick had no time to manoeuvre around the Cresta before the mob were on them. A few of the lads tried to get out of the cars and fight but it was no use, they were trapped. And Popeye and I saw this as we ran back but there was nowhere else to go. The street was wide with a green on both sides, the perfect spot for an ambush like this, and I knew we could never outrun the mob. It was do-or-die time and I made a beeline for a big fucker in a Minder leather who was banging a sawn off pick handle on the bonnet of the Cresta. He had his back to me and I just crashed bodily into him and knocked him off his feet. He dropped the pick handle and I snatched it up. I ran to the back passenger door of the Cresta and stood there with the weapon raised to fend off anyone who might fancy a piece. Harry was in the driver's seat of the Cresta, bloody-faced and sparkling in the street lights from the bits of car windscreen glass that were buried in his face. 'THE KEYS, THE KEYS!' he shouted at Popeye desperately.

Popeye had a crowd around him but he was keeping them at

arm's length with one knife, having lost his second blade somewhere along the way. I ran forward and swung my pick handle at the mob around Popeye and this gave him the space to push the keys in Harry's direction. Once Harry had the keys I backed up to the rear passenger door and jumped into the car and Popeye launched himself across the bonnet and straight through the empty space where the windscreen had been.

I think that if we'd had any sort of luck that night we might have got away, but as Harry went to put the keys in the ignition the mob surrounded the car and began to rock it from side to side. The keys slipped through his fingers and into the darkened footwell among the piles of broken glass, and that was that. The smoothies went to work on us and the cars. I caught an iron bar in the face, which split my right eyebrow and knocked me out for a while. When I came to, the ambush was over. There was the sound of groans and the occasional tinkle of more glass falling out of battered window frames. I tried to push my door open, but it had been smashed so hard that the metal was warped and bent and it wouldn't move more than a couple of inches. In the end I crawled out over the parcel shelf and through the back windscreen. The street was empty except for two cars, which looked as though they had been in a particularly rough demolition derby.

Nobody had escaped the beating and we were all injured to some degree. I thought I was blind in my right eye, but it turned out that there was a piece of windscreen glass in the skin below it and the blood from the cut above it had congealed slightly. Popeye had been dragged from the Cresta and they had broken the fingers on his knife hand with a crowbar, although he was more interested in how many of them he had managed to plunge. He also had a cut to his scalp that had bled profusely. Most of us had head injuries, but Olly had been caught by two of the smoothies as he reached the Zephyr and had been beaten around the legs before he finally managed to get into the car, so he was limping like a raspberry. The Cresta had taken the worst of the damage and the pickaxe had pierced the radiator, so it was going nowhere, but the Zephyr turned over like a good 'un and the engine seemed undamaged. We put the worst of the wounded into the Zephyr and Mick set off to take them to St Helier Hospital, which, luckily, was not too far away, as he was driving on three bare rims because the smoothies had slashed his tyres.

Once I realised that I wasn't blind I didn't feel too bad for a geezer who'd just survived being beaten half to death by the cast of *Night Of The Living Dead*. I had a cut and a swollen eye, a lump the size of a ping-pong ball on my head and various aches and pains all over my body, but I was alive and still walking. The smoothies had caught us lovely and there was no point whining about it. It was all part of the game and no worse than what gangs of football hooligans were doing to each other every Saturday afternoon. We would make our comeback on them in time, once we had recovered from our injuries. No one was dead and no one had been nicked, and in itself that was a result. This wouldn't damage our reputation, as there's no shame in losing to overwhelming odds, and it would probably win us a lot of recruits when we decided to take our revenge.

Those of us who didn't fancy hanging around in a hospital casualty department until dawn made the long walk back to Balham. Harry had to leave his car by the side of the road as it was un-driveable, and he said he would pick it up the next day. The next morning he got a lift in his cousin's low-loader down to Carshalton, with his bird, Sharon, and found that his motor had been moved up to the car park and placed in front of the smoothies' bar like a trophy. As he and his cousin winched the wrecked Cresta up onto the truck a few of the smoothies came out of the bar and stood there sniggering into their drinks. Once the car was on the truck Harry got under it and drained the sump, catching the oil in a cut-down plastic container. He then climbed into the cab of the truck with it and told his cousin to drive as close as he could get to the smirking smoothies on the way out of the car park, and he launched the oil all over them as the truck passed. I'd love to have seen it. Harry reckons they've still probably got bruises on their toes where their jaws dropped when the oil hit them. It was a small victory, but then, isn't that what life is all about?

The Beat Slows Down

Balham Continental Market was situated on Bedford Hill Road opposite the outdoor market at Hildreth Street and was a large single-storey hangar-type building that had 30 small shop fronts inside, including a cafe that was owned by my Auntie Marie. No one knew why it was called a 'Continental' market, as the only shops that were even vaguely Continental were a second-hand furniture shop called 'Luigi's Second Hand Furniture' and a greengrocers that sold yams. And that was about as exotic as it got. The indoor market at Balham became our HQ throughout the winter months of 1980/81 as my brother, Mick, had a shop in there and so did Moses. Mick had a record shop that specialised in oldies and he called it The Living End, which was a joke from the end titles of the 1950s rock'n'roll film *The Girl Can't Help It*, and I think he gave away more records than he ever sold, especially to the girls.

To Mick the shop was more a place to hang out and chat up girls than a business, which, I suppose, is why he had to close down in the spring of '81. Moses, the Teddy boy DJ from The Fountain, had a shop in the market that sold 1950s clothing and accoutrements such as belts, badges and hats, and he rather imaginatively called it '50s Clobber'. Had Moses situated his shop anywhere but Balham Market, I fancy he may have made a go of it, but with us lot on his doorstep every working day he didn't stand much of a chance. Whenever we were going out for the night we would use Moses' stock like our own personal dressing-up box. At first we did it under the guise of being interested in purchasing the clothes and wanting to try them out first, but soon we didn't even bother with this excuse. Moses was in his thirties, a good bit older than us, which is why we nicknamed him Moses, and though not exactly scared of us he had kind of a nervous disposition. I couldn't really blame him for being cautious around us; after all, he had seen us in action during the fight with the Australian rugby team and he was a nervous wreck that night. So Moses would give us stern warnings about having to pay for dry-cleaning bills and any damage to the clothes and we completely ignored him. It was a situation that would see Moses going out of business around the same time as Mick.

We would all hang out in the Market when The Bedford was shut. These were the days when pubs opened at 11 in the morning, shut again at 3 in the afternoon and then reopened at 5.30, and most days there would be cats and kits from all over coming to see what was going on. Mick had a set of speakers outside his shop, so often there would be people bopping and jiving in the aisles. Ronnie and Eddie and the old Wanderers gang would be at their mum's cafe, and Gerry of the now disbanded Pharos had a key-cutting stall at the front of the market. By now we were the only real force left in Balham and even the Flash Pakis had moved further down the Northern Line to Tooting Bec. The Balham Baldies/Boot Boys were no more, though Junior was still a punk rocker and we would see him occasionally walking by. We still had the squat on Ferndale Road, but Jenny was now going out with Olly the Cat and had moved in with him, so no one lived in the squat permanently. We would usually end up in the squat at night after the pubs and clubs closed. Now that the nights were colder it was somewhere to go and it had working gas fires. For some of us, myself included, it was a drifter's lifestyle: we would sleep in a different place every night and eat whenever we got the chance. Clubbing, drinking and fighting were more important than eating and having a permanent roof over our heads. We were totally free; we worked when we felt like it and thieved and conned when we didn't. Our whole focus when we woke up in the morning was to get enough money together to go out and get drunk that evening.

Popeye lived in a caravan in the breaker's yard, Harry lived out of his car, Mick was living back at home in our parent's flat on the Sinclair Estate, and I usually just slept wherever I dropped. Peter had met a Teddy Girl, called Angela, at The Fountain one night and they had moved into a bed and breakfast gaff off Bedford Hill together. He was still going through his golfbilly stage and could be seen walking around in plus fours, long socks and two-tone golf shoes. He had even added a moody-looking tam-o'-shanter to his outfit and got some very strange looks from nearly everybody who clapped eyes on him. Peter had always been a bit strange and there were plenty of people who dismissed him as stone cold mad. He could be very violent if he got frustrated with anyone or if he thought someone was taking the piss. I remember one time we were on our way to a fight with the Brixton soul boys over some mis-demeanour and we were all tooled up. Peter had an iron bar inside his coat. Suddenly Peter stopped and clutched his chest. He stood for a minute with a look of pain on his face, breathing heavily, and then he straightened up and his face cleared. 'What's up?' I asked. Peter shrugged casually. 'I think I just had a heart attack,' he said. We all started laughing loudly at this, as you would, and Peter whipped out his iron bar and smashed it straight across his brother Harry's head. Harry dropped to his knees from the force of the blow and began to bleed profusely from his scalp. We all jumped back from Peter. 'What the fuck did you do that for?' I shouted at him. Peter frowned. 'I don't like people laughing at me,' he replied, and then he walked off. So his dressing in some 1930s-looking golfing outfit was always going to get someone a clump sooner or later.

One day Peter and Angela were in Woolworths in Streatham doing a bit of browsing in the music section when a couple of smoothies started sniggering at Peter's golf outfit. Never backwards at coming forwards, Peter asked them what they found so funny, and they told him. Angela told me that Pete knocked the first one out cold with a right hook and threw the second one over the pick 'n' mix counter before a uniformed security guard arrived and tried to intervene. Pete drop-kicked the security guard and then beat him around the head with a revolving display of Max Bygraves and Des O'Connor tapes. The police finally arrived and dragged Pete off to the station still kicking and screaming. After eight hours in a cell he finally calmed down. The two geezers refused to press charges, fair play to them, but the security guard was not so forgiving. Pete was charged with GBH and criminal damage and was given bail. After this incident I talked him into giving up his golf gear. Pete always listened to me for some reason and I was the only one who could get away with telling him off. So he traded in his plus fours and tam-o'-shanter and his next metamorphosis was into a biker. This I could live with.

A lot of things changed in the winter of 1980. Denise told me she was pregnant with our first child for a start. I found out in the visiting room of Lewes prison where I was on remand for drunk and disorderly, obstruction and possession of an offensive weapon. The charges stemmed from the night that a few of us had been nicked outside the Chick-A-Boom. It took place after our first big fight with the front bar smoothies when they had ambushed us on Green Wrythe Lane and wrecked our cars. I was outside the Chick-A-Boom talking to Tooting Roy and a couple of Dutch Teddy Girls who had come to London for the weekend when a mob of drunken smoothies started giving it the big 'un. One of the smoothies, a big lump with a shaggy perm that made him look like an irate poodle, was particularly vocal so I offered him a straightener. I handed my razor to Tooting Roy and told him to feel free to cut any of the other firm that wanted to get involved. After a few digs had been exchanged I got the big fella down on the pavement and was in the process of giving him a sound thrashing when a few of the rockin' crowd piled out of the club and started kicking the shit out of him and his pals. I was annoyed because I hadn't asked anyone to join in and I'd got the situation under control. Barney and the bouncers came out and stopped the fighting and then old poodle-perm, sitting on the ground and holding his broken nose, started shouting about how I'd needed help to beat him. I had a pair of steel toecap commando boots on and I took a run-up and booted him straight in the face. It was a terrible, sickening blow that shattered both his jaw and cheekbone and, as he went backwards, spark out by this time, he cracked his head on the pavement. The police told me later that the hospital staff thought he had been in a car crash.

Now, I'm not proud of that kick, but at the time it was just one more violent act in a series of increasingly reckless and violent behaviour. I got my razor back from Tooting Roy and made myself scarce, but the police were now all over any report of violence from the Chick-A-Boom. They were compiling the evidence that they would need to object to the renewal of the club's licence and close it down. So I was quickly picked up by the police half a mile away from the incident and arrested for GBH with intent and possession of the razor. On processing my details they also came up with the warrant for the previous case and I found myself on the bus to Lewes prison on a three-week remand.

One day I was called down for a visit and found Denise and her mate Julie waiting for me. I'll never forget the look of fear and trepidation on Denise's face when she told me she was pregnant. It was as if she were expecting me to fly into a rage and start wrecking the visiting room and chinning people – maybe even her as well! I acted pretty cool about it but inside I had a warm glow. I was going to be a daddy! I had never even thought about having a kid. It was a big step for anyone, but particularly for me as I had never really settled down anywhere and a kid would change all that. I think my exact words to Denise were: 'Pregnant eh? Whose is it?' I only said it to lighten the moment and realised almost straight away that it was the wrong thing to say. Her face dropped and I thought she was going to cry, and Julie gave me the kind of look she must have reserved for things she had to scrape off the bottom of her shoes. 'Just joking, just joking!' I said hurriedly. And that was my first wake-up call.

While I was on remand the police got to question poodle-perm for the first time and he said that he had no idea who had attacked him, if at all anyone had, and that he was very drunk and may have fallen over. I admire that kind of attitude – if you call on a fight and then get your head kicked in you should be man enough to accept the consequences. Unfortunately I was later to come across some people who did not have that kind of honour and who would run crying to the police in similar circumstances. Once poodle-perm made it clear that he had no intention of pressing charges, the GBH with intent was dropped from my sheet. I appeared at Wallington magistrates court in early December 1980 and pleaded guilty to drunk and disorderly and obstruction, but not guilty to possession of the offensive weapon. Pleading not guilty in a magistrates court in those days was a complete waste of time, as the 'trial', if you could call it that, came down to whether the magistrate believed those lovely police officers who he saw every day in his court, or the toe rag with the leather jacket and tattoos. The only reason I opted for a trial was because my brief told me that if I pleaded guilty to the razor I would cop six months. As usual, it was a case of a solicitor offering a worst-case scenario so that the client would think he was mustard when the magistrate handed down anything less than six months. My defence was that I had found the razor on the pavement and had picked it up in order to hand it in at the police station as lost property and just forgot it was in my pocket before the police searched me. Pretty feeble, I know, but it didn't matter as I was found guilty in less time than it took to read the charge. The magistrate gave me a £5 fine for drunk and disorderly, a £10 fine for obstruction and one month's imprisonment for the razor, but as I had already been on remand for 21 days I was able to walk out of the court.

Mick had driven my mum and Denise down to Wallington for my court appearance. My mum now knew that Denise was pregnant with her first grandchild and she and my dad were offering to put us up in their flat until we found somewhere to live. Denise's parents had reacted badly to the news of her pregnancy and ordered her out of their house. This confirmed my belief that middle-class people were strange and unforgiving. Denise and I spent a couple of nights at my mum and dad's place and then went down to Brixton and declared ourselves homeless. We were given a one-room place in a reception centre at the top of Cedars Road, overlooking Clapham Common. The building was an old seaman's mission and a grade II listed building, so it was ancient and filthy. We lived on the fourth floor and shared a kitchen, bathroom and toilet with 16 other tenants. Denise hated it, but to me it was the first settled address I'd had since I officially left home four years earlier. Part of me wanted the stability of a family and a place of my own and I was really looking forward to a life of domestic bliss. Moses gave us an old black and white telly and I carried it on my shoulder from Balham Market to Clapham Common North Side and set it up as a surprise for Denise. We were really kids and had little idea of what we were getting into. I remember that the first meal Denise cooked was pork chops and it set off the smoke alarms, leading to the whole building having to be evacuated. We were struggling financially. Denise was still working at The Prudential and I was still doing the odd day on building sites and the odd bit of thieving. The gang and all the fighting we were doing took up a lot of my time, and I'd now reached the point when I needed to have a serious think about it all. It had been fun at the start but now it was getting out of hand, and with a kid on the way I figured that this might be a good time to start slowing down. But, as I was about to find out, you can't always get what you want.

Lean Times

The year of 1981 opened with a new mutation on the rockabilly scene and this one was started by my old mate Joe K. Around this time the BBC were showing an adaptation of James Joyce's book about Dublin in the early twentieth century, *Strumpet City*, and Joe watched it one night when he didn't have the money to go out. He liked the dress style of the working-class Dubliners – big flat caps, long overcoats, tweed trousers held up with skinny braces over white cotton shirts with granddad collars, and boots – so he decided to adopt the look and take it onto the rockin' scene. A new club had opened up near Tooting Broadway in the function room of a pub called The Castle and this was where Joe K debuted his new look.

The disco at The Castle was run by that 1970s stalwart '50s Flash and had become the in-place amongst the South London rockin' crowd. With all the violence and rivalry between the different gangs on the scene, it was no longer safe to travel too far out of your own area, so the scene was becoming fragmented and marginalised. We all complained about it, but it was us who had caused it. In the '70s we could travel to clubs all over London and the only trouble would be with different subcultures on our way to and from the venues, but now rockabilly gangs would fight each other at the drop of a hat and if you wanted to travel outside your manor you had better be mob-handed and flying colours. The Castle was one of the new breed of rockin' clubs in that the manager, Big Alvyn, a retired gangster from Wales according to the rumours, had his own team of bouncers working the door. In the past, the bouncers at places like the Chick-A-Boom, The Squire and The Greyhound were just guys who were really into the scene and friendly with most of us, even when they had to jump in and stop a ruck. But the bouncers at The Castle were all professional fighters in their thirties and cracked heads for a living. Obviously some of us saw this mob as a challenge to our manhood and reputations and trouble would follow, particularly when they implemented a rub-down search policy on the door to stop weapons getting in. At this stage the kind of gang members using The Castle were the hard core who were veterans of violence on the scene and saw the bouncers as lairy bastards who seemed a bit too flash for their station. But before that happened there was a quiet couple of weeks when the place first opened.

One night in early January Joe K turned up in what he called his Strumpet City Rebel gear and caused a bit of a sensation among the sartorially aware. The look was cheap – you could pick up everything at jumble sales and in charity shops for a couple of quid, it was practical with the freezing weather that was upon us, and it was stylish. The haircut that went perfectly with the look was called the GI and was based on the American Forces haircut, number one shaved sides, high and wide, and a bit of a quiff. Andy's of Water Lane was inundated with requests for the GI and within two weeks every charity shop in South London had sold out of overcoats, flat caps and old man's trousers. Even I got into the look and had a lovely three-quarter-length grey overcoat and a cashmere muffler that I found in an Oxfam shop in Brixton. Of course not everyone took to this style. Psycho Joe of the north Battersea was one who rarely changed, and Jimmy Harris of Bermondsey was another. You could see this pair in their leather jackets all year round and they were amused by the sudden influx of Strumpet City Rebels onto the scene, just as they had been equally amused by the short-lived hill-billy craze.

By now I was on friendly terms with Psycho Joe and Jimmy H.

We'd had our differences in the past, and some said, though never to our faces until years later, that our fight at The George in the summer of 1979 had led to a lot of the trouble there had been on the scene, as it was the first of the internecine battles that would eventually destroy all that we had. It was funny that we could never see the damage we were doing at the time and actually thought that when people showed us a bit of respect it was because we were well liked and not because our very presence in a club made people edgy and scared. I certainly thought of myself as a nice guy and thought that people bought me drinks because I was very witty; after all, everyone seemed to laugh at my jokes. The only time I really got any inkling of the way I was viewed on that scene was one night at The Castle when Harry and I got talking to a group of girls from Wandsworth. We were outside the club having a crafty nip from a gin bottle – bar prices were always high in the rockin' clubs – when one of the girls, who were sheltering in the doorway of a furniture shop next to the pub, asked us for a light. It turned out that it was their first night at The Castle and they were leaving early and waiting for a cab. I started teasing them about having to be in bed before they turned into pumpkins and we were all having a laugh when one of them explained why they were heading off so early. Wide-eyed, she told me that there was a rumour going around the club that Razor Smith was in there and that he was going to be starting trouble later on. Harry thought it was the funniest thing he'd ever heard, but I wanted to hear more. 'Who is he, then, this Razor Smith?' I asked. 'He's mad!' said one of the girls. 'He always carries two solid gold razors, and he starts on people for no reason. My mate was at the Bobbysox club last year when he slashed some girl across the face cos she wouldn't dance with him!' I was horrified at this. I had never razored anyone who wasn't in the game and I had certainly never slashed a female.

By now Harry was doubled over with laughter but I didn't find it amusing. 'Listen, girls,' I said. 'You don't want to believe every-thing you hear. People just make shit up. Razor Smith is a lovely fella.' But just then their cab pulled up and they hurried out of the doorway and into the warmth of the car. I wanted to follow them and plead my case some more but it was too late. I looked at Harry. 'Do you believe that shit?' I asked. Harry chuckled and shrugged. 'What do you expect, mate?' he said. 'You've cut your share. If you want someone to love you then get a dog! Anyway, any chance of you flogging one of your gold razors so we can get inside out of the cold and get a few pints in?' I should have realised how bad things were getting by the number of people who were leaving the gang and the scene. Alan and Dennis, Johnny Boy, Ahmet and Gordon had all drifted away and rarely came to the clubs. Perry was wanted for bottling a skinhead and had gone to live in Ireland and Olly the Cat had become a part-timer since he'd started going out with Jenny. Now the Wildkatz was made up of hard-core violent vet-erans like me, Popeye, Mick, Peter and Harry, and youngsters like Shane, Ricky the Fly, Tank and Big Chris who just wanted to prove their manhood by clumping someone.

Tank looked the part at 6 foot 4 and 18 stone, but he was barely 17 and couldn't fight to save his life. Big Chris was also a size but his heart wasn't really into the heavy violence; he was too good natured. Ricky the Fly came from a good fighting pedigree – his two brothers, Gerry and Gary, had both been in the old Pharos gang – but he was untested and only 16. As for Shane, he was a good kid but he couldn't hold his drink and would be legless after a couple of pints and unable to hold his hands up. Big Nose Eamon had also settled down with his childhood sweetheart and was working as a van driver, so he rarely had time for clubbing. Joe K was still at it but we had grown distant since our fight over Hollywood and he had finally managed to pin down the lovely Debbie Adams and they were going out with each other. Joe and Debbie went together like explosives and detonators and their relationship always seemed to be bordering on furious. There was never a dull moment when they were around.

The scene was thinning out and where once it had been standing room only at the clubs you could now see the gaps left by those who had drifted away. A few of the old crowd like Chinese Chris, Glen, GiGi, Lloyd, Pink Pegs Terry and Roger the Dodger were still about, and most of the south Battersea crew like Tommy Jnr, Tin-Tin, Rockabilly Steve, Little Bopper and Steve the Spiv, but there was a feeling of gloom about that couldn't just be put down to the cold weather. GiGi, who had always been a flash cunt, had become even more outrageous. He had a load of badges printed up with his own photo on them and would give them out to girls to wear. I never liked him, mainly because he was flash and had a reputation as a kung-fu expert, which I found slightly threatening, but he was always an independent and had never allied himself with any of the gangs. His brother, Lloyd, had been one of the mob I had chased out of the flat at Poynders with a carving knife, so I was always expecting a pull about it from GiGi. A few people told me that the brothers weren't that close. Little did I know, however, that GiGi was just biding his time.

One of our newer members in the gang was Colin, Olly the Cat's brother, who was a good driver even though he couldn't fight for shit, and he would often drive whatever motor we had on hand at the time. Colin may not have been able to fight but he was game and would never run out and leave you in the lurch. However, on some occasions we really did have to leg it. One afternoon Colin and I met up with Tommy Jnr and Tin-Tin down in Balham Market. The Battersea lads were out doing a bit of thieving and we decided to join them. We cobbled together a plan to nick a few car stereos. At that time Blaupunkt sets were all the rage and we could get £50 a go for them. Tommy and Tin-Tin were experts at this game and

Colin and I were only along to learn about it. The first thing we had to do was nick a car that we could use to get about in, and in this respect Tommy and Tin-Tin were also the experts.

Both Tommy and his brother, Bopper, were infamous for their driving skills and were rarely seen without a purloined motor around them, so I watched with interest as Tommy quickly opened an Austin 1300 with the blade of a pair of household scissors and then started the ignition in less time than it would take to use the key. I was impressed and we all jumped into the motor and off we went. Further down the road we spotted Little Dave, who was one of the newer members of the Wildkatz, and pulled up to ask him if he wanted to join us. Just as Little Dave climbed into the back seat with me and Colin a police Sherpa van pulled up behind us with its lights flashing. Tommy, never being one to stick his hands up and surrender meekly, slammed the car into gear and shot off, leaving about an inch of burned rubber on the road and a van-load of frustrated coppers. The chase lasted about ten minutes, up and down the backstreets of Balham, and in that ten minutes there were many moments when I thought we were going to die, but Tommy handled that motor like a pro racing driver. After a couple of minutes the police Sherpa was joined by two panda cars and we led this convoy, blue lights flashing and sirens wailing, a merry dance. At this time Tommy was living with his pregnant girlfriend, Vanessa, in a halfway house on Nightingale Lane, and as this was not too far away Tommy shouted that we should bail there. Bailing out of a stolen car during a police chase is a pretty dangerous act and usually involves jumping out of the car while it's still moving. I looked through the rear window as we turned onto Nightingale Square and saw that the police vehicles were close behind. Colin, who had never been in a police chase, clutched my arm. 'What do I do?' he asked desperately. I shrugged him off and gripped the door handle. 'Just follow me,' I shouted.

Tommy and Tin-Tin jumped out of the front doors at the same moment, leaving the car whilst it was still travelling at quite a speed. Now that there was no driver, the car started going to the left and heading straight for a garden wall. I took a deep breath, pushed my door wide open and jumped onto the road. I came down running, almost stumbled and managed to right myself, and didn't stop. I looked back once and glimpsed our stolen car crunching into the wall and what seemed like hundreds of coppers alighting from their vehicles and chasing us. Colin was right on my shoulder and we both ran like the wind. We bolted through the grounds of the halfway house and then through the dense gardens at the back of it. I could hear Colin panting at my shoulder and the shouts of the coppers further back and I was determined not to be caught. I jigged and zigzagged through the undergrowth until I came to a 20-foot fence at the boundary of the property. I knew I couldn't climb it without being seen by the coppers, so I headed off through the bushes parallel to it. I found a particularly dense clump of undergrowth and threw myself into it. A second later Colin came hurtling in after me. 'What are you doing, you cunt?' I whispered. 'You'll get us nicked!' But Colin wasn't moving, he was staying right there. We could hear the coppers thrashing about in the bushes nearby, but they never got too close to where we were. Eventually it all went quiet, but just to be sure we waited until it was getting dark before we came out.

We made our way through the grounds and into the halfway house where we found Tommy's door and knocked. Both Tommy and Tin-Tin were in there. Tommy had run up the fire escape and hidden on the roof during the chase and Tin-Tin had hidden in a bath on one of the upper floors. The only thing that tempered our joy at escaping the police was the fact that Tommy had witnessed Little Dave being nicked from his vantage point on the roof. Tommy told us that the coppers had given Little Dave a proper kicking when they had found him hiding in the back seat of the stolen car. Once we were safe in Tommy's gaff I turned to Colin. 'How come you didn't find your own hiding place?' I asked. Colin shrugged. 'You told me to follow you,' he said, simply, and I had to laugh. But that's what Colin was like when you gave him an order, single-minded. I filed that away for later.

After the car chase incident I had another serious think. I had a kid on the way and I couldn't afford to be getting myself nicked now and leaving Denise pregnant and on her own. I made up my mind to cut out the silliness in future. But I was never that good at keeping promises – especially to myself.

Storming The Castle

With so many hard-core gang fighters using The Castle as a winter meeting place, it was inevitable that there was going to be trouble with the bouncers. The bouncing team consisted of six pug-uglies, way over the top for such a small venue, and they had an attitude about them. It was obvious that they had been specifically hired because of the trouble in other rockin' clubs and they made it clear that if anyone stepped out of line there would be trouble. To people like me, Popeye and Psycho Joe, the bouncers were a ham sandwich at a bar mitzvah: offensive and not to be tolerated for too long. So the honeymoon period at The Castle was brief. The first sign of what was to come was when my Denise, of all people, started a fight with one of the Catford girls. Denise was five months pregnant at the time and I had seriously underestimated the extent to which her hormones were affecting her moods. We were at The Castle for a rare night out together and I had left her sitting at our table while I went up to get the drinks. There was a girl at the bar who I had once met at The Squire in Catford and had a couple of slow dances with, and she started talking to me as I waited for my drinks. I didn't realise that Denise was watching, but when the girl leant into me so that I could hear what she was saying above the noise of the music it all kicked off. Denise came flying up to the bar and punched the girl square in the face. It was a good punch and took everyone by surprise, especially me and the girl. The girl bounced off the bar and Denise grabbed her by the hair and started laying into her. I managed to get in between them and copped a punch in the ear for my trouble, and a couple of the lads held them apart. It was all over bar the shouting, but the bouncers came rushing across, pushing people out of the way and wanting to get involved. I had hold of Denise and when one of the bouncers reached out to grab her arm I pushed him back and stood in front of her. The bouncer, a big fucker with scary eyes, shaped up to me. 'Come on then, you cunt,' I said, and I put up my fists. But the other bouncers pulled him away. One of them seemed half sensible and started trying to calm everything down and eventually we all dispersed.

For the rest of that evening I kept my eye on the bouncer who had shaped up to me and saw that he was also watching me. I told Denise that I was going to get a cab and send her home, but she wasn't having any of it. She probably thought that I wanted to cop off with another bird, but I wanted her out of the way to kick off with the bouncer. In the end Denise and I left together at the end of the night, and when she went into the toilets I walked up to the bouncer. 'I'll see you again,' I told him. He smiled. 'Any time,' he replied. I was bulling all the way home. I hated bouncers anyway and I particularly didn't like this one. I always classed bouncers as bullies, giving it the big 'un and pushing people around, and I couldn't even see the irony in my hatred of them. Some years later I became a bouncer myself and realised what a difficult job it really is. I always tried to be polite, but when you are dealing with lairy drunks and young tearaways, like myself, who want nothing more than a fight, it can be hard to keep the smile on your face for long.

The next week I was back at The Castle, this time armed with a lead cosh and spoiling for a fight. I got Bopper Hogan's sister, Tina, to smuggle my cosh in under her jacket, as the bouncers couldn't search girls. But the one I was looking for wasn't on that night. I told myself that old scary eyes had bottled out, as surely he must have known I'd be back the very next week. If I had been him, I would have made it a point of honour to be ready and waiting and it was a terrible loss of face for him as far as I was concerned. Anyway, I relaxed a bit when the fella wasn't there and decided to enjoy myself. I got talking to a rockabilly chick called Maggie, who was from Battersea and was married to the lead guitarist of the best young band on the scene in those days, called Cat Talk. Maggie was a lovely girl, really enthusiastic about the scene and the music, and she told me that she was going to write a book about the scene and fill it with photographs of all the characters. I thought it was a great idea and agreed to pose for a photo. I liked Maggie. She was a young kid and as she knew Denise was pregnant she began telling me what her own baby was up to. After a while she heard one of her favourite songs just starting and went off to have a bop. In those days the bop was a male preserve on the dance floor; girls were expected to jive or stroll but not bop. In fact the only girls I ever remember bopping were Maggie and Debbie Adams, but they could both pull it off. I ambled over to Psycho Joe's table.

Although I always got on with Psycho Joe, I knew his younger brother, Steve, didn't like me very much. I didn't really care; he could give me sour looks for as long as he liked and I wouldn't bite. I knew he was a good kid and that he was looking to prove himself and step away from the shadow of his brother's reputation, so I never took it personally – which was unusual for me. Anyway, Psycho Joe, Steve, Jimmy H, Toothless Terry and a few others were in the club that night and were fuming over the bouncers. Apparently Steve had refused the rub-down search on the door and Joe had let him in through the fire door at the back of the club. We were all sitting down in the darkest corner of the club next to the stage on which '50s Flash was spinning the records, and there was a lot of drinking going on and a lot of talk about teaching the bouncers a lesson. Steve went up to the bar to get a round in and one of the bouncers spotted him and followed him back to our table. 'Get out,' the bouncer told Steve. Knowing what was coming, I slipped over to Tina Hogan and retrieved my cosh. I wedged it in my waistband, and by the time I got back to the table Steve had nutted the bouncer and he was staggering back to the door and his pals. It was on.

For some reason one of the things that sticks in my mind about that fight with the bouncers is the record that was playing. It was a big jiver in all the clubs at the time and was called 'Bim Bam' by Sam Buttera and The Witnesses. '50s Flash was an old-style DJ who, when trouble started, turned the music up rather than down, so the record was blaring as we faced the bouncers on the dance floor. The bouncers had a cupboard by the entrance where they kept their tools, mostly lengths of heavy rubber hose, and they raided the cupboard before coming for us. We saw them come out on the dance floor, pushing jivers out of their way and clearing the floor in a minute. Psycho Joe turned his table over and ripped one of the wooden legs from it. I pulled out my cosh and Steve took out an iron bar from his jacket. The rest of the lads picked up bottles. The fight out in the middle of the dance floor was short but brutal. The bouncers could certainly have a tear-up, which is why they were hired in the first place, and they were as game as fuck. I grabbed hold of the smallest one, and started laying into him with my cosh, but he pulled some kind of fancy Steven Segal move, grabbed my lapels and threw me over his hip. Once I was on the deck he started smashing me all over with the rubber hose and it fucking hurt. Someone from our side gave my attacker a dig in the jaw and I got off the floor and steamed at him again with my cosh, this time making sure to keep him at arm's length. The music was blaring and I realised that I was swinging my cosh in time to the beat!

There was a break in the fighting, something that is common in these kinds of situations, and we all caught our breath, tools ready, staring each other out before round two commenced. There were a few bloody heads, although not on our side as the rubber hoses the bouncers were using would bruise but rarely cut. I remember seeing the bulk of the club goers bunched up around the bar, keeping well away from the violence. One of the bar staff held a telephone receiver above the heads of the crowd and shouted, 'The police are on their way!' The record had just come to an end and we heard the words in the relative silence before the next record started. I later played 'Bim Bam' on my record player at home and timed the duration of the record as 2 minutes 27 seconds, although when we were fighting it seemed more like 10 minutes.

None of us could afford to get nicked, so after a few verbals to the bouncers we backed away and piled out of the fire door and into the car park. The front of The Castle was on Tooting High Street and we had to go past the side windows of the club to get there. There were a few garden tables and chairs in the alley from the summer and, as we passed, Joe picked up one of the chairs and threw it through one of the plate-glass windows. The rest of us followed suit and we heard the screams from inside the club as the windows went through. As we got out onto the high street we could hear sirens coming down Tooting Broadway, the police station only being a five-minute drive from the club, so we all split up and legged it. Toothless Terry and I ended up down in the tube station, but we all got away. It wasn't over for me. My stubbornness and pride urged me to return to The Castle at a later date and duke it out with scary eyes. There was something in me that wouldn't leave it alone, like your tongue forever seeking out an aching tooth despite the fact that you know it's going to be painful. I think I was like this because the bouncer had tried to grab Denise and I couldn't tolerate that kind of thing when it came to the mother of my unborn child. I know that might sound a bit melodramatic, but that's how I felt.

I waited a couple of weeks for the heat to die down and then, one Saturday afternoon, I was having a piss-up with my dad and my brother Mick in their local pub in Brixton and started on the gin. By 6 in the evening I was staggering drunk and decided, on the spur of the moment, that the best thing to do was to get into my old Zephyr 6 and drive down to The Castle for a straightener with the bouncer. In my drunken state it seemed like a good plan, so off I went. How I managed to drive without getting pulled or crashing into some poor innocent motorist I'll never know. Luckily, the car ran out of petrol just as I was passing Clapham Common and I left it there, half up on the pavement. But I was determined to get to The Castle and take care of business, so I hopped on a bus. By the time I reached The Castle I was still fairly lagging. The club at the back was closed, so I walked into the front bar and ordered a drink. The bouncers were nowhere to be seen, but the owner, Alvyn, was sitting up at the bar with a crowd of people. Alvyn was about 20 stone with a face like a battered potato and it was rumoured that he had been a very naughty villain at one stage. I didn't care about his reputation and focused on him as my new enemy. I slid along the bar to where he was sitting and poked him in the shoulder. 'Oi you, fat boy,' I growled. Alvyn stopped what he had been saying and turned to me. He looked me up and down and then smiled. Had I been sober I would have recognised that smile for what it was – a precursor to violence – but my body fluids were nine-tenths pure gin and my mind was three sheets to the wind. 'Yeah, you,' I said. 'Where's your fucking bouncers?' I poked him again. One of the girls at the bar giggled nervously. Alvyn put a huge hand up on my shoulder and, swift as lightning, brought his other fist around and smashed me straight in the jaw.

When I came to, it was dark and I was lying in an oily puddle in the car park outside the pub. My head was pounding and I had a lump the size of an egg on the side of my jaw. I felt terrible and when I finally managed to get to my feet I vomited all over my boots. I staggered away from the pub and down into the tube station. I made it home but I don't remember how. Thirteen years after being knocked out by Alvyn, I met and became good friends with one of the ex-bouncers from The Castle while we were both serving long sentences in Highdown prison. Alex, the ex-bouncer, told me that he had heard all the details about my confrontation with Alvyn and we spoke about it. 'He had some fucking punch on him!' I commented, and Alex started laughing. 'I'm not surprised you say that,' he responded. 'He hit you with a fucking knuckleduster! A pound of brass knuckles! That was his trademark!' I shook my head. 'Fucking fat liberty-taking cunt!' I said. But that was all part of the game.

You Can't Win 'Em All

The Norwood gang were based around three hard-case brothers and their pals and had been on the rockin' scene since the early Teddy boy days. I had personally never had much contact with them, as they came to prominence when I was in jail. There was no doubt that they were a formidable team of fighters and I had heard a few rumours about them, but our paths had never crossed in a bad way. Now and again they would turn up mob-handed at the Chick-A-Boom club in a couple of flash motors. Alan, the oldest brother, had lost his hair and always sported a shaved head, which was unusual on a scene where hair was such a big part of the identity, but that was all I knew about them – until the autumn of 1980. How I came to fall out with the Norwood gang was indirectly due to Joe K and his own appetite for violence. Joe and I were never as close after our falling out over Hollywood, but we were still friends and I could never stand by and watch anyone try to take a liberty with him. Sometimes I think I had too much loyalty to my friends, and it has often got me into trouble over the years. But that was a big part of gang mentality – loyalty and staunchness in the face of long odds – and what kept the gangs going; that, and the feeling of belonging to something. So when I saw Joe K about to have his head caved in from a sneak attack I had to jump in and stop it. And this was eventually to lead to my own downfall.

It was a chilly and damp Wednesday night in September 1980 and I had no intention of going out at all until Popeye showed up and talked me into it. I was living in my cousin's house in Carmina Road at the time and had just started going out with Denise, but she was still living at her parents' house in Morden, and because I had kept her out all night on the previous Saturday they had put their foot down and kept her in. She was over 18 but it was a case of while she was living in their house she had to abide by their rules. It might sound pretty quaint in these days of ASBOs and hoodies, but back in the day it was standard to obey your parents, particularly for middle-class girls! So I was just settling down to a quiet evening watching Minder on the telly when Popeye screeched up outside the gaff in our '57 Consul. It turned out he'd had an argument with his bird and fancied going rockin' and relieving a bit of tension.

The Chick-A-Boom club was still doing a Wednesday evening session, so I let him talk me into getting suited and booted and heading up to Carshalton for a night out. I remember getting into a brown Italian pinstripe box suit that I had been saving for a special occasion. I had paid a fiver for it in Brixton market and I thought I'd give it an airing. Wednesday nights at the Chick-A-Boom were usually jeans and leathers affairs, but I wasn't expecting to be rolling around on the ground – I wasn't going mob-handed or flying colours. As I got ready, Popeye went and got a litre bottle of cheap gin from the motor and we mixed it with a bottle of undiluted orange squash before slugging it back.

Once in the car and on our way, Popeye mentioned that he might have a bit of agg with a couple of the Catford boys and that they might be at the club that evening. He dropped it into the conversation casually, but I knew him and knew that he was looking for a ruck that night. I told him that I had left my razor in the house and that I fancied a quiet night. He laughed and told me to reach under the car seat. I pulled out a sawn-off pick handle and noticed that he had another one next to his seat. Popeye grinned maniacally and I just sighed. I knew that come hell or high water there was going to be trouble that night. I finished off the gin and squash and felt a buzz. Fuck it, I would go with the flow.

We reached the club around 8.30 and as we pulled into the back car park a sizeable crowd had already gathered at the far end. On a normal Wednesday evening there would be a maximum of 150 people at the club, but on this night, for some unknown reason, there seemed to be more like 250, the sorts of numbers that would be usual for an early Saturday evening. Both Popeye and I took our pick handles from the car after parking up. Popeye put his in the waistband of his jeans, but I didn't want to ruin the cut of my suit so I slipped it up my sleeve. We made our way across the car park towards the entrance of the club and bumped into Mitcham Roy and Little Andy as they were coming out of the club with drinks in their hands. 'What's going on?' I asked. Roy grinned. 'It's all fucking kicking off tonight! Two different rocker gangs have turned up and a couple of them are having a straightener over there.' He nodded towards the cheering crowd in the corner. Popeye shrugged and spat. 'Any of the Catford mob in?' he asked. Roy shook his head. 'Ain't seen none,' he said. 'But the Norwood gang are here in force.' I nodded, although I wasn't really that interested. 'The word is that they're after Joe Kennedy for something.' This interested me more.

'Is Joe in?' I asked. Andy smiled. 'Yeah, and he's in a proper fighting mood!'

The club was packed inside and Popeye and I pushed our way through to the bar to get a couple of pints. I surveyed the hall and noticed Joe K off in one corner. I could tell he was pissed, as he had his leather off and was showing off his muscles to a couple of giggling Teddy Girls. 'He's split up with Debbie again,' Popeye told me with a raised eyebrow. Joe always tended to go a bit off-key when he and Debbie were at odds. That was one relationship that could truly be described as destructive. I noticed a lot of familiar faces around the club and nodded to a few of them as I made my way over to our corner. For about 30 minutes I just sat there, enjoying the music and watching the jivers on the big dance floor. Popeye had mooched off and was chatting up a biker bird on the far side of the club. I'd lost sight of Joe, but when a commotion broke out near the entrance I had a feeling he was involved. I drained my pint and headed over to see what was going on.

By the time I'd reached the entrance, Joe and his opponent, one of the Norwood gang, had already dispensed with the verbal formalities and were on their way out into the car park to duke it out, followed by a large crowd. I tagged along. The word was that it was to be a straightener – no weapons and one on one – so I relaxed and got ready to enjoy the show. Joe went into his usual routine of stripping to the waist and flexing his muscles. He was sporting a new tattoo on his upper arm – 'Johnny Burnette', who was Joe's favourite rockabilly artist and responsible for such dance floor classics as 'Tear It Up', 'Lonesome Train' and 'Rockabilly Boogie' – and the whisper was that, tough as he was, Joe had nearly fainted when Barry Louvane had started the needlework! Some people get that way around needles, a phobia I suppose, but I knew that Joe was bulling over it and had already threatened to do anyone he heard repeating the rumour, so maybe the reason he was spoiling for a fight that evening was to wipe out the embarrassment of that episode and show that he was still on top of his game. But, then again, Joe K never really needed a reason for a ruck – he was one of 'The Fighting Irish' through and through. The crowd formed a large circle and Joe and his opponent went at it. The fella Joe was fighting was no sissy and for the first five minutes he made a good fist of it. But Joe's boxing skills came to the fore and pretty soon he was throwing combinations with amazing speed and it was all over bar the fella hitting the ground. While I was standing in the crowd I noticed a couple of the Norwood gang getting ready to wreak some swift and merciless retribution for their now beaten champion. One of them was holding a heavy pint mug, the kind with a handle and diamond patterned glass, and he reached down and smacked it on the kerb, leaving a wicked-looking tool when the glass broke. I can only assume that the plan was to rescue some sort of face for their gang by jumping into the fight and catching Joe unawares. Of course, I couldn't have that. I slipped the pick handle down my sleeve and into my hand and stepped forward, swinging it like I was going for a six. The thick end of the pick handle crashed into the head of the fella with the pint mug and I felt the vibrations of wood on bone right up to my shoulder. He went down like the Titanic, only faster and with a lot less screaming. I steamed into the other fella and the crowd opened up and scattered in fear and panic at the violence in their midst. Those who just wanted to spectate quickly vacated the immediate area and left the hard-core gang fighters to battle it out. Tools were coming out of all sorts of hiding places, slipping down sleeves, jerking out of waistbands and pockets, and it was on. In seconds there was a full-blooded gang fight going on. I saw Popeye leap into the fray and Joe, now finished with his straightener, throwing digs at anyone who came close. I chased a fella across the car park and swung my pick handle at him, but he dodged and I ended up hitting the bonnet of an immaculate Rover 3500 S that was parked there. The bonnet on this particular model was made of aluminum and my blow left a large dent. I didn't think about it at the time, but that dent was to cost me plenty further down the line.

As quickly as it had started, the violence stopped after a few frantic minutes and left two breathless, wounded and divided factions staring at each other over a no-man's land of damp asphalt. A few insults and threats were shouted from both sides and for a long moment it looked as though the fighting might start up again, but everyone decided they'd had enough. The Norwood gang piled into their motors, but not before issuing dire threats about a comeback. It seemed that the Rover that I had dented was theirs and they were fuming about the damage. That's how skewed our priorities were in those days: you could be stabbed, coshed or hacked at and have no complaint, it was part of the game, but damage someone's car and you'd better watch your back. As they pulled out of the car park in a slow convoy we wankered them off and called insults and threats of our own. Then it was back into the club to show off our wounds, get lagging drunk and bop to Gene Vincent and Mac Curtis. Just another night out on the rockin' scene. But already our days were numbered, although we didn't yet know it. The violence was becoming too commonplace and too severe for most of the normal, decent people who just wanted to come to the clubs for a drink and a dance or to meet up with their mates.

Over the next few months I began to hear whispers that the Norwood gang were going to do me, but these sorts of rumours were always floating in the ether of the rockin' scene. Someone was always going to do someone else – it was standard – so I didn't take a lot of notice. I realise now that I was way too cocky for my own good. I had taken a few beatings but had never really been taken to the edge. Violence for me was normal and I was not frightened to inflict it on other people or have it inflicted on me, but I was naturally cautious and always aware that there were people who would do me if they were given half a chance. You can't cause the amount of damage to people that I had done and not be expecting a comeback. So I started checking places out before I entered them, finding out who exactly was going to be there and never leaving the house without a tool. But my caution didn't stop me going to the pubs and clubs, it just heightened my awareness.

One of the clubs I started going to on a regular basis was the Charlie Chaplin in the Elephant & Castle. Moses, with his Transistor Twister Roadshow, was the DJ there and he had even started playing a bit of rockabilly along with the Dodie Stevens and Chubby Checker records. The Charlie Chaplin was a fairly small gaff and had a minuscule dance floor, but it took place on the same night as Tommy Hogan's Edwardian Dreams at The Duke of Clarence, which was only a five-minute walk away, so when the Chaplin got too packed we would take our drinks and walk up to the Clarence. One night at the Chaplin I ran into Lloyd, the half-caste rockabilly I had once chased out of Poynders Gardens with a butcher's knife over Elaine. He told me that my days were numbered and that there was a firm out to do me in. I laughed it off and ended up giving him a slap. I then took a walk up to the Clarence, and Toothless Terry told me that he had also heard that the Norwood gang had a list with both mine and Joe K's names at the top. Once again I shrugged it off, but over the next few weeks I was to hear the same thing again and again. Maybe I should have taken it more seriously.

The Night of the Long Knives

The fallout from the fight with the Norwood gang was finally to catch up with me on a damp night in November 1981 back at the Chick-A-Boom club where it had all started. I was on my own, not flying colours and, for some reason, completely unarmed. I was having a drink with Mitcham Roy and Snapper when I was approached by GiGi, half-caste Lloyd's kung-fu merchant brother. We had never been great pals, more nodding acquaintances, so I was a bit suspicious when he started acting all friendly. He told me that the Norwood gang were in the club and that they were after me. I told him I already knew that, and if any of them wanted a straightener to sort it out then I was more than willing. GiGi scurried off back to the gang, who were gathered at the end bar and looking daggers in my direction. I waited for a reply but GiGi never returned, so I figured that tonight was obviously not the night. I can't honestly say I was completely cool about being in a club where a gang of hard cases were after my blood, but that was the life I was leading at the time. It would have been more painful for my pride to suffer the shame and humiliation of simply walking away. I could have slipped out of the back door and avoided trouble, but my ego would not let me. So I stayed where I was and kept my eyes open for any sudden moves.

Around 10 I got word that Popeye wanted to see me in the car park. At this time Popeye was at war with a lot of people on the scene, including Joe K, so he had a habit of turning up at clubs and checking who was there before entering, something most of us had to do at one stage or another. Popeye and Joe had fallen out over who else but Debbie Adams. A whole crowd of people had gone to a party in Balham at a rocker bird's flat and Joe and Debbie had ended up arguing, as usual. Debbie had then started playing up to Popeye and they were slow dancing together when Joe went berserk and steamed into them. He gave Debbie a right slap and then knocked Popeye all over the gaff. Although Popeye was a very violent man he wasn't a fist fighter, so Joe bashed the shit out of him and left the flat. Popeye, his pride in tatters, vowed revenge on Joe, and so began a protracted period of rumours and tit-for-tat violence. Popeye went everywhere with a 16-gauge shotgun for a while and stated that his intention was to shoot Joe dead. There is a story that Popeye caught up with Joe one night on Queenstown Road in Battersea and made him kneel on the pavement and apologise before putting the barrel of the gun in Joe's mouth and making him beg for his life – though how true that is only Joe and Popeye know. Anyway, when I heard that Popeye was outside the club and asking for me I had no suspicions at all. I left the club and, sure enough, in the darkened car park there was Popeye sitting at the wheel of an old Morris Oxford. I leant through the driver's window and was having a chat, telling him who was in the club and that Joe wasn't inside, when I became aware of a crowd of people coming out of the club behind me. I heard someone shout 'Hi Razor!' and I turned around to find myself confronted by several members of the Norwood gang, including GiGi. Before I could say anything I was hit in the face with a cosh and then they all steamed in. I don't remember going down, but I did, and the only thing that saved my life that night was the fact that so many of them were trying to hit me at once. One of them had a camper's axe and I was partially scalped by a blow from it. My wrist was broken and I've still got the clearly visible scars from that beating today. Luckily I was knocked out for most of it, but I came to as they were throwing me in the back seat of Popeye's car. I remember one of the gang telling Popeye to 'Take him to a hospital or a morgue, whichever one he needs.' After all the months of rumours and warnings, the Norwood gang had finally done me.

The beating I suffered that night stayed with me long after the physical wounds had healed. I fell out with Popeye over it for not coming to my aid, but looking back I now know that it wouldn't have made any difference. He would have ended up getting it as well. It was after this that I decided to leave the scene behind and go back to being a professional criminal. For months I didn't leave the house unless I was armed with a gun and at least one knife. And I was more inclined to paranoia when in crowds, my violence becoming more senseless and pre-emptive. I stopped going to rockin' clubs, unable to face the humiliation of everyone knowing I'd been done, and also afraid I might bump into old enemies who might now feel brave enough to take advantage. As far as the rockin' scene went, I was a spent force who pretty soon would become forgotten in the natural progression of things. My day had come and gone.

But the Norwood Gang were not finished with me yet. When they found out I was still alive I began to hear rumours of how they were planning on doing me again, properly this time. One night Denise was at the Chick-A-Boom club for a night out with her friends when she was confronted by several of the Norwood Gang or their hangers-on. They issued dire threats about what they were going to do to me next time and even began to threaten Denise with violence. Luckily Denise was standing with one of my sister's friends, Caroline Bateman, who was from a well-known rockin' family in Carshalton. Her dad was a Ted, her sister, Jo-Ann, was well known on the scene and had even become a punk rocker for a while. Caroline's mum, Jean, used sometimes to pick up all of us stragglers from the Arms in an old van and deliver us back home after the last buses had gone, or cook us sausage sandwiches and let us kip at the house if we were cold, hungry and desperate.

Caroline was going out with a well-known face on the scene called Steve Chadwick, from Eltham, a great dancer and all round good fella. It just so happens that Caroline was standing close-by when the gang approached Denise, and she was not the kind of girl to stand idly by and let someone be bullied. Fiery little Caroline fronted the gang and told them to piss off and pick on someone else and the cowardly bastards backed off. When I heard about it I wanted to kill them, but I was also grateful to Caroline and never forgot it.

About a year after my beating at the hands of the Norwood gang, they were to suffer their own humiliation. There had been a war brewing between the Norwood gang and the north Battersea crew for a long time, and me getting done had helped to escalate it. Popeye joined up with the north Battersea and he, Psycho Joe and his brother Steve became the nucleus of one of the most violent gangs on the scene at that time. First there was a skirmish at the Charlie Chaplin pub in the Elephant & Castle in which baseball bats were brandished and used by both sides. Then, in early 1982, the north Battersea crew stormed a rockin' gig at The White Swan public house at Crystal Palace – stronghold and home turf of the Norwood gang. The brutal battle resulted in one of the Norwood brothers coming close to death – his arm was hacked off with a samurai sword, his skull was fractured in two places and he suffered multiple stab wounds. Surgeons, using ground-breaking microsurgery, managed to sew his arm back on during an 11-hour operation. The massacre at The White Swan, as the newspapers were calling it, was the death knell for our era. The Norwood gang were in disarray and it is rumoured that some of them were going to give evidence if it came to a trial. Which is a big no-no in our world.

There were many rumours on the rockin' scene about people making statements to the police about the incident, and the whole scene in South London became fractured and began to fade away. Twelve months after the night of the long knives in Crystal Palace, Popeye, Psycho Joe and Steve stood trial at the Old Bailey for attempted murder, GBH and affray. The prosecutor opened his case by directing the jury to 'Take a look at these men in the dock and then ask yourself if any right-thinking member of the public would not feel a shiver of fear and revulsion just by passing them in the street.' The case got heavy press coverage and the outcome was that Psycho Joe was convicted of GBH with intent, for which he received five years' imprisonment, Popeye was found guilty of affray and was jailed for 18 months, and Steve got six months for assault.

After The White Swan trial the whole rockin' scene was all but dead in South London and what was left of it ended up in North and West London. The Chick-A-Boom club closed down, as did most of the rockin' nights at other pubs and clubs. Within a few short years The St Helier Arms and The Tower would be razed to the ground by developers and replaced by luxury flats. The Bedford became a cabaret pub, including a comedy club night. Charlie

Chaplin's was taken over by a brewery firm and went all brass ornaments and fake log fires. The Edwardian Club catered for the rave and disco crowd. The George at Balham Hill became the favourite haunt of off-duty police officers from the nearby police training college. And a long cold winter dawned on what was left of the rockin' crowd. South London had a reputation for violence and it would be almost a decade before anyone could hope to run a rockin' gig and get a decent crowd south of the river. As Oscar Wilde once said:

> 'And all men kill the thing they love
> By all let this be heard
> Some do it with a bitter look
> Some with a flattering word
> The coward does it with a kiss
> The brave man with a sword.'

We did it with any weapon we had at hand and with rarely a moment's thought. Now we all had to find something else to belong to.

Aftermath

Over the following 25 years I lost touch with various members of the Balham Wildkatz as we all went off and did our own thing. I saw my brother, Rocky Mick, and Harry quite a bit. I worked as a hod carrier for Olly the Cat when he started his first building firm. I became crime partners with Tin-Tin and he stood by my side at Knightsbridge Crown Court and received 13 years' imprisonment for a series of bank robberies we committed together. I also saw a lot of Tommy Hogan Jnr, who ended up married to my sister Samantha, and Tommy Snr and Linda, and their oldest son Bopper – he and I served time together in many jails and fought back to back on some occasions. When I escaped from prison in 1992 and went on another bank-robbing spree, I moved in with Jenny and we started an ill-fated and short-lived affair. I lived as a lodger with Mandy Hogan for a while when I was out of prison on parole in 1997, and had a falling-out with her sister Tina, who I've always liked despite my behaviour towards her. And I had a belated affair with the luscious Debbie Adams after meeting her again at a party at my old flame Hollywood's flat in 1987. I saw Joe Kennedy now and again, as he worked as a ticket collector at Kensington tube station. As for the rest? We just drifted off each other's radar.

The first Brixton riots in 1982 happened while Denise and I were living together at Clapham Common, about a mile from the epicentre. A few of us got involved in the fighting and looting in several ways, although, as I'm not sure of the statute of limitations in terms of these crimes, I cannot say much about them here. However, I will say that Olly the Cat's brother, Colin, was driving us about at that time and one night, at the height of the rioting, Harry, Mick, Colin, Ricky the Fly and I were on our way to a bit of skulduggery when we were pulled by a van-load of Special Patrol Group riot coppers. They got us to pull up on a quiet side street and then gave us plenty of stick – saving their worst for Colin, who they quickly pointed out was 'a fucking nigger'. They also kindly told us that as we were with Colin we were all 'a bunch of nigger lovers', and then proceeded to put the cosh about. A few hours later we got our own back when the police were bombarded with bricks and bottles by a large crowd on the elevated walkways of Stockwell Park Estate.

After the riots it seemed that our teenage years were truly over. I was 22 anyway, and had strung it out for as long as I could. The riots seemed to be a termination point for everything that had been happening since that long hot summer of 1976, like the final volcanic eruption after a long series of mini outbursts and earthquakes. After the riots everything changed. The youth of London seemed sated and unnaturally quiet. Eventually the teen subcultures began to fade away. Now and again you might catch a glimpse of a New Romantic, a skinhead or a colour-flying biker but, on the whole, the party was over.

I settled down with Denise (although 'settled down' doesn't really describe my behaviour), and we ended up with three lovely children. We could have had a great life together but the madness was still strong in me and in the end she had enough. Another regret in my life. But, despite everything, I still loved the music and every now and again, when I was not in prison, I would grease up my hair and drop into one of the new clubs for the night – The Phoenix, Silks, Lipstick – and see a few of the old faces amongst the new crowd. Eventually I became a DJ myself and, in partnership with Eamon and Harry for a while, I got residencies at a few South London pubs – The Clockhouse and The Acre Tavern being the most memorable – and in '86 Tommy Hogan Snr reopened The Edwardian Club, which had been closed down and derelict since 1980. He hired some of the old bands and got a 2 a.m. licence, but the club never really took off again. Nobody wanted to come into the heart of Brixton on a Friday night, as it was still too soon after the riots, and there didn't seem to be enough of a crowd in South London to make the club viable. After a while he handed the club over to me and Tommy Jnr, but soon after that I was arrested for GBH and went back to prison. In 1990 the club became one of the most popular rave clubs in London under the name of The International. But by then I was serving 19 years for bank robbery.

I also did a bit of dee jaying on Tommy's pirate radio station, Radio Southside, 106.8 – 'The music's great, it's on till late, don't hesitate!' – until we got closed down by the DTI. I was still in close contact with Big Beat Kris and when I was paroled in 1997 he offered me a few guest slots at The Castle in Camden Town, where he was a resident. It felt great to see people up dancing to Johnny Burnette, Gene Vincent and Joe Clay after all those years. But the scene was not the same. The elitists were now into Japanese surf music and strange instrumentals, and one night I was accused of playing 'too much white music' – on a rockabilly set!

My own life has not been without its trials and tribulations – actually a lot more trials than tribulations – but I have paid for my criminal indiscretions, and continue paying to this day. I am no longer as disturbed as I was when I was a teenager, and my outbursts of violent rage are few and far between these days. Once I reached the age of 40 I realised the true futility of my life, and a personal tragedy forced me to reassess everything. Am I ashamed of the things I have done? Some of them. Would I do things differently if given the chance? Most certainly. Could I have followed a different scene, been part of another subculture? Never in a million years. For me it was the pure adrenalin-soaked excitement of the music that hooked me in the first place and which kept me coming back for more. The music was everything, and still is. I have now lost my hair, and bopping for more than one verse of 'Lonesome Train' leaves me knackered, but the thrill is still there. Just like I swore at the start of the summer of 1976 – I'm forever rockin' rockin' forever!

And that's about the size of it.

1st Edition Afterword: The Living End

So that was the story of the Balham Wildkatz, a bunch of kids from a small corner of South London who adopted the mantle of an earlier, less complicated era and then smashed it to pieces on the altar of violence and savagery. We were the first generation of young men who had no war in which to prove our manhood, no real enemy to defeat, no foe to subdue or land to liberate – so we turned on each other. On the whole we were just kids – reckless, dangerous kids, but kids nonetheless. Our 'wars' were childish and protracted because we didn't know how to end them, our violence was savagely over the top because we had no awareness of our own or other people's mortality, and behind it all was juvenile angst and the desire to belong to something unique. And, of course, I cannot discount the fact that some of us were plain mad – albeit temporarily in some cases – and our subsequent lives would prove this. But by the early 1980s most of us, the sane ones, had outgrown the fantasy, had become sated and then sickened by the violence, and had drifted away. Many of us settled down and started families. We washed the Brylcreem and Truegel out of our hair, hung our leather jackets in the back of the wardrobe, went to work and no longer attacked people who did not conform to our taste in fashion and music. Some of us would never be seen again inside a pub or club where rockabilly was being played. Others would occasionally grease up the thinning quiff, don the cat clothes and venture out to see how the scene was doing. You could normally spot us – hard-faced originals, usually standing at the bar, foot tapping along to the music as our eyes roamed the bopping and jiving crowds for any sign of an old enemy who might still want to settle a grudge.

In 1987 I was with Big Nose Eamon and Mad Harry in a rockin' club downstairs at The Phoenix, in Cavendish Square. It had been a few years since any of us had been on the scene and we were enjoying our night out, minding our own business and just having a few drinks and listening to the music. A new dee-jay called Tom Ingram was making a splash on the scene. There were a couple of the old faces in the club, but we just nodded to each other and left it at that. At around 2 a.m. I went up to the bar to get a round in. The bar was thronged with people, and as I reached for my money I felt a blow to the side of my face. I looked around to see who had punched me and caught another one in the mouth. I wasn't that hurt, but a bit stunned. I stepped back and reached automatically for my razor, and then remembered that I no longer carried it. The fella who had punched me was a big skinny kid with blond hair, wearing a buckskin jacket, and he was standing there shaping up like an old-time boxer. His face didn't ring any alarm bells in my memory, so I asked him what his problem was. It was then that I noticed he had a few mates with him and they were all looking daggers at me. 'You're Razor Smith,' he said. 'You cut my brother, down The Squire!' I was amazed. The last time I had been to The Squire, in Catford, was in 1982! I didn't remember his brother, nor any reason why I might have cut him, but this fella meant to have his pound of flesh. By this stage of my life I was overweight and unfit, so I considered grabbing a bottle and laying him out, but an old school pal of mine, Lawrence, was the bouncer at the club and he quickly stepped in and asked us to take it outside. By this time Big Nose Eamon and Mad Harry had come over and the kid in the buckskin was calling for a straightener – so I had to agree. The trouble was that the club was at the bottom of a long, steep flight of stairs and by the time I got to the street I was puffing and blowing like an old steam engine. The kid in the buckskin had skipped up the stairs like a gazelle and was waiting for me out on the pavement, jacket off and ready for action. The fight was short and brutal. I threw a right-hander, slipped and caught a haymaker to the mouth, and went down like a sack of spuds. The kid gave me a few kicks to the face before Eamon and Harry jumped in and stopped it. My nose was broken, again, my lip was split and my shirt was soaked with blood. The kid in the buckskin went back down to the club, his mates patting him on the back and laughing. I looked at Harry. 'How'd I do?' I asked. Harry smiled sadly. 'Yeah, you proper showed him,' he said. I had to go home. In the taxi back to South London I thought about what had happened and knew my day in the spotlight was long gone. Even the legend I had spent so long carefully constructing had faded so much that I could get my head kicked in by a kid who was still shitting yellow and crying for his mother's tit when I had been in my prime.

The whole scene had changed, and it was time for me to move on. Of course, not everyone on the rockin' scene in the old days was part of the gang culture. There were many kids who just went out to enjoy themselves in a more peaceful and wholesome way. And those who were not scared away by the violence and mayhem were to inherit the scene after the likes of us had gone. For a few years the scene struggled on, numbers dwindling as many moved on, and there just wasn't the interest from the generation of disaffected youth who were discovering hip-hop, techno, pop, jungle and rave. By the late '80s the original teen subcultures had all but faded away. And in their place was a homogeneous mass of baseball-capped, baggy-trouser-wearing, jafaken-talking generation, some of whom would shoot each other dead with automatic weapons if they felt 'dissed'. The rockin' scene had shrunk and, in the capital at least, seemed to fit into one small corner of Camden Town. If you wanted to see the latest band or bop the night away to the uncommercial sounds of the '50s then you had to head north on the Northern Line. It all became very small.

Then in the '90s, for a while the rockin' scene flourished again, but this time it was driven by a new breed of DJs and entrepreneurs, some of who saw the scene as primarily a business opportunity. They hired their own security, usually steroid-guzzling bikers and ex rockabillies, organized weekenders and annual trips to sea-side resorts and sold advertising space on their fliers and fanzines. Some of the old DJs were still around, but they were mainly rele-gated to small out-of-the-way pubs that catered for what was left of the Teddy boy army. They kept the flag flying throughout the '80s and '90s while the new, younger breed of disc-spinners played the more upmarket venues in the West End to a mainly younger audi-ence of hipsters.

By the start of the millennium the rockin' scene had come full circle from the days of the original Teddy boys. The elitism and snobbishness that we had encountered as young retros in the mid-1970s was back with a vengeance. Nowadays a lot of people on the scene seem peculiarly obsessed with getting the 'right look' – from the cut of your jeans to the heel on your motorcycle boots, every-thing has to be just so if you do not want to be held up to ridicule. Nobody would dare to boast openly about getting their suits for two quid at a jumble sale or their shoes from their granddad. It was the Teds all over again. It would seem that when a subculture that is based on a particular style of music and fashion goes through a fallow period where membership is severely whittled down, those that remain will compensate for their small numbers by becoming ever more 'special' and compiling rules to reinforce this status. The trouble is that when a new generation of kids 'discover' the scene again, as they inevitably will, the originals will lose their special status. The Teds were not strong enough to withstand the last wave, and they suffered the ignominy of seeing their whole scene overrun. I just hope the new breed might prove more flexible.

Due to other commitments, it is over ten years since I was last in a rockin' club, but I have tried to keep a weather eye on what's going on. Quite simply, I am a die-hard rockin' fan – I still love the music and it still has the power and magic it had over me when I was a kid. I listen to the Mark Lamarr show every Thursday night on BBC Radio 2 with the same sense of excitement and wonder I had when, at the age of 15, I tuned in to the Stuart Coleman show in my borstal cell. I hear that others from my day still sometimes show up on the scene and that all the old feuds are now forgotten. For us the war is long over. We are the veterans, the originals, who now see the horror and futility of the battles we waged in our youth, and watch with silent resignation as history continues to repeat itself. Rockabilly music is now becoming popular again, even in America where it has always been the forgotten cousin of rock'n'roll, and as the scene starts to grow there is a young and violent element rising up with it; another wave of wild, wild young men who don't think twice about fighting and wrecking whatever stands in their way. Nothing changes for long.

So, as I sit here in my top-security prison cell, I wonder if I would change anything if I could. Sure I would. I'd have taken more care of my hair and teeth and I probably would have avoided that Flying Squad ambush back in '98. But I don't know if I would have been capable of being more peaceful when I was a teenager. I was troubled and confused and eager to lash out. I had come of age in the brutal gladiator schools of this country's most violent young offenders' institutions and then prison. I needed to stamp my mark on the world or die trying. So now I've got the scars and the memories – but just for a short while I was part of something, became something that no one could lock down, until it burned out like a shooting star. Once … once we were warrior kings.

Noel 'Razor' Smith
August 2007, in prison

2nd Edition Afterword: The Final Chapter

As I said in the preface, this book was written while I was in prison in 2007. At the time I was serving eight life sentences under the two-strike Act for armed robbery and possession of firearms. Happily for me, I was finally released on parole in May 2010, and I have changed my life. Instead of being a violent criminal and professional prisoner I am now the Commissioning Editor for *Inside Time*, the national prisoners' newspaper. I have published several books, acted in many films and become something of a regular on television, and I also give talks to young offenders and criminology students about the futility of crime and violence. But something was missing from my life.

In 2010 South London was still a bit of a wilderness as far as the rockin' scene was concerned. It was all still stuck in Camden Town, and even some DJs who cut their rock'n'roll teeth in South London were pretending that they were North Londoners. There has always been a bit of friendly (and sometimes not so friendly) rivalry between South and North London on the rockin' scene. The first rock'n'roll venue I went to on my release was a little pub in Battersea, opposite the Battersea Dogs Home, called The Pavilion. It was a tiny oasis where those who loved rock'n'roll could still meet south of the river and listen to that fine music. It was known as a Teds pub, as so many of its clientele were the older drape-suit-wearing Teddy boys of old. Every Friday night the crowds would bop, jive and stroll to live bands and DJs. The moment I walked into The Pavilion and soaked up the atmosphere I knew I was home.

With my old mates, Big Beat Kris, Tommy Hogan Jnr and Rockin Os, I went back to dee-jaying. My new DJ name is The Jailhouse Rocker, and I haven't stopped rockin' since. I did a year of Saturday nights at a pub called The Pied Bull, opposite Streatham Common, and some of the old faces began to drift back. From there I moved to a residency at The Hand in Hand in Brixton, and then I moved on to The Pavilion, in Battersea, where I ran a regular rockin' Saturday night, along with Big Beat Kris. We had some great rock n roll/rockabilly bands, such as The Broadway Twisters, Pete Hutton & The Beyonders, and were able to offer the first paying gig to a 13-year-old guitar prodigy and his band, Denvir Jet and The Shockwaves, who are now massive on the scene. One night we even had the legendary Johnny Earl, who had recorded with Elvis Presley's old backing singers, The Jordanaires, and guitar legend Scotty Moore. Johnny was kind enough to jump on the Pavilion stage and give us an impromptu mini-concert, ably backed by Denvir Jet. There were some good times at The Pavilion. Unfortunately, it wasn't to last.

The Pavilion pub was hit with a compulsory purchase order from the company that bought the Battersea Power Station just across the road. No doubt this old historic music pub will end up being razed to the ground in order to make way for luxury apartments for the rich foreign investors who seem intent on buying up large swathes of our capital city. The Pavilion closed its doors for the last time in April 2016 and will be sadly missed by both The Battersea Rockers and other patrons.

We were due to play the last gig at The Pavilion but had to find another venue at short notice. Luckily enough, The Grove, on Battersea Park Road welcomed us. Along with another two great South London dee-jays, The Phantom and Rockhouse Mark, me and Big Beat Kris set about building a reputation as the premiere South London record hop. We hold The Wildcat Shakeout there once a month, playing the music of our youth and dancing the night away with friends new and old.

My aim was to bring the rockin' scene back to South London once again. I had been part of the reason it had died out in the early 80s and I feel it is now my duty, and pleasure, to try to resurrect it.

Many of my old friends and former enemies are back on the scene we had abandoned and this time it is all peaceful. We are older and wiser and we all still love the music and most of us have shaken hands and left our youthful indiscretions in the past. Which is how it should be. On my club nights you'll find a mix of Teds, Rockabillies, rockers, bikers, smoothies and even the occasional punk or skinhead all enjoying the music and atmosphere.

Where Are They Now?

I served approximately 30 years in various prisons for armed robbery, possession of firearms with intent, prison escape and grievous bodily harm. While serving my life sentence under the two-strike act, I gained an A Level in law and an Honours Diploma in journalism from the London School of Journalism – and have had work published in the *Guardian*, the *Independent*, *Loaded* magazine, the *New Statesman*, *Punch*, *The Big Issue*, and many others. My first book, *A Few Kind Words and a Loaded Gun – The Autobiography of a Career Criminal*, released by Penguin in 2004 sold very well worldwide, leading to me writing and publishing several others. I was finally released from prison in May 2010 and have no intention of ever going back. On Valentine's Day 2014 I married Caroline Bateman, the fiery little girl who stood up against the Norwood gang for Denise back in 1981. We are very happy.

- Rocky Mick – settled down and had a posse of kids, worked his way up from a labourer to the high echelons of management of a London Council, and is now the karaoke king of South London at weekends. Still loves the music and still has a magnificent quiff!
- Samantha – married Tommy Hogan Jnr and also has a posse of kids. Fulltime housewife and mother. Still loves the music, though no longer wears bobbysocks or circle skirts.
- Potty Pete – died in a motorcycle accident in 1986, leaving two kids and a heartbroken girlfriend. Rockin' till the end, but had left his golfbilly days behind him. Sadly missed.
- Mad Harry – became an independent biker for a while before a serious crash took him close to death and left him with a permanent limp. Took up building choppers for a while with some success, before moving to Northampton. Still occasionally shows up at the clubs.

- Dave Wall – became the lead singer of new-wave band, Road Runner, in the early '80s and then disappeared from the scene.
- Olly the Cat – became a top-class plasterer and builder, started his own building firm and is still doing well. He forsook rock'n'roll for soul and doesn't really like to be reminded of his Teddy boy days.
- Popeye – the kid for whom severe violence had always been a way of life. Turned smoothie again and carried on cutting people on that scene. At one stage he opened a tattoo parlour on the King's Road. I last saw him in 1997 and he was handing out leaflets for a church meeting. He told me he had become a born-again Christian and had found peace in Jesus. I believed him.
- Dennis and Alan – Alan had a serious illness at one time – it was rumoured that he'd had a stroke, but by then we had all lost touch. I hope they are both doing well and have settled down. I recently got in touch with them via Facebook and they are both doing well.
- Joe Kennedy – Joe eventually turned smoothie and I heard he had broken his neck diving into a swimming pool in Spain. But he recovered and I often saw him in the '80s working as a ticket collector for London Transport at Kensington High St station. We've lost touch. Since I've been out I have tried to trace Joe but with no success. My old mate seems to have disappeared off the face of the earth.
- Psycho Joe – served five years for the Massacre at The White Swan when he was convicted of GBH on one of the Norwood gang. I saw him at The Tennessee Club in Wood Green when I was out of prison in 1997. He recently showed up at The Pavilion with his brother Steve, and it is rumoured he has a life-threatening cancer.
- Debbie Adams – continued to show up at rockin' gigs throughout the '80s and '90s and could still dance up a storm or throw a

right-hander if the situation called for it. Now settled down with one son and a garden to tend.

- Denise – stuck by me until 1992, despite my erratic lifestyle of crime, imprisonment and womanising. Still goes rockin' regularly and lives quietly in Surrey, where she works for the NHS. Still loves the music.
- Adrian Street – moved to Milton Keynes in 1980 and had an interesting career of music producing, playing guitar in many bands, writing and travelling the world. Ade is back in MK and presently appearing as Buddy Holly (his idol) in a stage show, among other things. He still loves the music. He formed a rockabilly band called The Broadway Twisters and I booked him for one of my Saturday night gigs, where they went down a storm.
- Vince Street – 'the best drummer in the music business today!' – has been in many bands and is doing well. He no longer sports a quiff but does occasionally whistle the opening bars to Ray Campi's 'Quit Your Triflin'.
- Tommy Hogan Jnr – married to my sister Samantha and now works for the council. Still has his quiff and leather and still loves the music. He worked as a DJ with me for a while at The Pied Bull and The Hand In Hand, and still occasionally turns up at my gigs.
- Tommy Hogan Snr – lost his wife Linda very suddenly to a heart attack and I wish him well. Tom and Linda kept the rock'n'roll flag flying throughout the lean years of the '60s and early '70s by gigging all over London and making time for the kids who were getting into the scene. True classic originals. Tom Snr was still a Ted and still jiving at 75 years old!
- Bopper Hogan – now in the 30th year of a life sentence for murder. Still loves the music and looks forward to tearing up the dance floor again at some time in the not too distant future. Fingers crossed!

- Big Nose Eamon – became landlord of a pub in Brixton Road for a few years, but since it closed down he has disappeared.
- Tin-Tin – after serving ten years for armed robbery as my co-defendant in 1988, he has settled down and is working as far as I know. Still turns up on the scene occasionally and still loves the music.
- Rockabilly Steve – hasn't changed a jot! He still comes to the clubs.
- Big Beat Kris – has been gigging steadily as a DJ for many years now and also has not changed. He and I are now partnered up and running rockin' club nights. He is still a fully-fledged Teddy boy.
- Alan (of the Norwood gang) – still rockin', became a bodyguard in the mid-1980s and was involved in a love triangle between a gorgeous model and Hollywood actor Sylvester Stallone. Alan ended up with the girl and Stallone had to swallow. It made the centre pages of the *Sun*. I read it while sitting in my cell at Parkhurst serving a 20-year stretch. My comment was 'Lucky bastard!' Still on the scene and no longer an enemy.
- GiGi – saw him early one Sunday morning in 1987 in a Wimpy bar at Clapham Common and he had just come back from India. Debbie Adams and I were coming back from a club called Silks in Shepherds Bush and we all had a cup of coffee and a chat about the old days. GiGi seemed as though he had matured well and had lost all his old flashness.
- Lee and John Carey – moved to West London, where Lee had a car front in the early '80s.
- Kevin 'Kidd' Griffiths – became a Rastafarian and sadly died a couple of years ago.
- Steve the Spiv – disappeared and was rumoured to have gone to Afghanistan to join the Taliban when they were still at war with the USSR. Has not been seen since.

- Moses – married a Teddy Girl and moved to Milton Keynes. I missed his stag night due to being in Wormwood Scrubs, but I heard it was a blinder!
- Hollywood – went through a Boy George/Alison Moyet phase after leaving the rockin' scene, married a smoothie, had a child and settled down. She's now a big U2 fan. I suppose there's no accounting for taste, or lack of it! I became friends with her on FB.
- Perry – went on the run to Ireland at the height of the gang hostilities to escape violence charges. Heard he was working on fishing boats and he's not been seen in over 26 years.
- Gordon – never really took to the gang violence, became a smoothie and settled into the straight life.
- Tooting Andy – became quite a talented amateur boxer and then disappeared off the scene.
- Colin – after a chequered career of near-crime, during which he was very lucky not to go to prison, he settled down.
- Jenny – had a lot of hardship in her life, including a spell living with me. Became a soul girl type trendy, but still had a soft spot for rockin' music and probably still has. Lives quietly with her son and has done some work as an extra on television, most notably in *Bad Girls* and *Peep Show*.
- Marina – got into reggae in a big way and everything that goes with that lifestyle.
- Ahmet the Rockin' Smoothie – probably owns a string of dry-cleaning shops and is married to a nice Turkish girl.
- Johnny Virgo – been on the missing list since about 1984.
  All those not mentioned – you are not forgotten!